CHOOSE LIFE

By the same author:

More than Conquerors: A Call to Radical Discipleship

Dangerously Alive: African Adventures of Faith under Fire

Sacrifice: Costly Grace and Glorious Privilege

Bike for Burundi

CHOOSE LIFE

365 Readings for Radical Disciples

SIMON GUILLEBAUD

MONARCH BOOKS

Oxford, UK, and Grand Rapids, Michigan, USA

Published by Monarch Books
an imprint of
Lion Hudson plc
Wilkinson House, Jordan Hill Road,
Oxford OX2 8DR, England
Email: monarch@lionhudson.com
www.lionhudson.com/monarch
ISBN 978 0 85721 522 2
e-ISBN 978 0 85721 523 9

First edition 2014

A catalogue record for this book is available from the British Library

Printed and bound in the UK, April 2016, LH36

INTRODUCTION

We make dozens of choices every day.

Some are relatively inconsequential, but others are totally life-shaping. Some are made subconsciously, while others are very deliberate. Some are positive and life-giving, while others can be deeply destructive.

In Deuteronomy 30:19, we read: "This day I call heaven and earth as witnesses against you that I have set before you life and death, blessings and curses. Now choose life!"

What you have before you is an invitation to a year of good choices. If you embrace the challenge fully, I have no doubt *it will be the most memorable year of your life!* Notice I didn't use other adjectives like "happy", "fruitful", "enjoyable", or "exciting". I was tempted to, but I don't want to make any false promises. After all, Jesus was explicit in saying to his disciples that "in this world you will have trouble". Authentic discipleship will lead us into trouble, be assured of that. Thankfully, in that same verse Jesus goes on to reassure us: "But take heart, I have overcome the world" (John 16:33).

Let me share briefly with you how this devotional came about. I had been planning to write it for a while, but only started during a week spent preaching in Canada. I had flown from my home in Burundi to Halifax for a conference, and went to bed on my first night with jetlag. That feeling of jetlag, nine months on, is still with me. I preached at the conference and spent the rest of the week either having tests at hospitals or lying in bed.

This strange fatigue could not have hit me at a more unlikely time. I turned forty that week and was the fittest I'd ever been, training for an Ironman, simply in great physical shape. So the last nine months of physical brokenness have been a challenging time, and they have required me to make daily choices – will I indulge myself in self-pity, or make the most of it? Will I waste the day in bed, or use that time constructively in writing and praying? Will I count my blessings or focus on the negatives – ultimately, will I choose life or death?

After about a month of frustration at not recovering, I made one very deliberate choice. Whatever the root cause of my sickness, I would not let Satan get the victory in my life. However long the sickness would last, I would make sure that God would get the glory, and the time would be maximized for him. My most influential book, *More Than Conquerors: A Call to Radical Discipleship*, was written during a similar season of fatigue eight years ago, and I have loved seeing how even that dark time was totally redeemed and how many lives were stirred up through the fruit of my own physical weakness. May that similarly be the case this time! That is my prayer.

So I invite you from a place of triumphant brokenness – which is surely what the cross symbolizes – to join me on this daily journey. As you will read, my context is no doubt very different from yours; but we follow the same Lord Jesus, and hopefully hear the same call towards total surrender. And may we all, wherever we find ourselves, choose to love God and love people with all that we've got, living life to the full as we follow unashamedly in the footsteps of the risen Jesus Christ.

Here's to a memorable year.

Choose life!

Simon Guillebaud (June 2014)

RESOLUTION OR RESIGNATION?

1 Corinthians 2:2

"For I resolved to know nothing while I was with you except Jesus Christ and him crucified."

Happy New Year!

I wonder how the year has started for you. Maybe you've made a few New Year's resolutions, maybe not. I remember one year breaking my major resolution within minutes of the New Year kicking in. It was deeply depressing. I felt useless and discouraged. I gave up and resigned myself to failing in that area.

The naysayers will declare it's the same for you. They will say that you can try to make some resolutions, and you'll probably have given up within a month at best, but can then plan on trying again during Lent a few weeks after that! Aargh! Resolution, or resignation?

Paul went to the Corinthians "in weakness and fear" (verse 3), but his resolution involved knowing "Jesus Christ and him crucified" (verse 2). He knew how weak he was, and that he would mess up, but he also knew how strong Jesus was, and how Jesus took our mess on him.

Jesus wants a relationship with you this year. We all know the following is true, but it's worth hearing again:

> *For a relationship to be healthy and growing, there has to be a commitment to regular two-way communication.*

So don't resign yourself to failing this year. No, *resolve to get to know Jesus better.* Don't set unattainable goals, but know that he is with you from your morning ablutions through work and play to bedtime. Share the highs and lows with him. That's what a real relationship is about. And maybe these short readings can be a part of that journey for you. Go for it!

Lord Jesus, I resolve to get to know you better this year. I won't resign myself to spiritual drudgery, so help me to spend time with you each day. Amen!

FITNESS OR FATNESS?

1 Corinthians 6:20

"You are not your own; you were bought at a price. Therefore honour God with your body."

Ken Cooper said: "We do not stop exercising because we grow old – we grow old because we stop exercising."

I was on a three-hour flight to Chicago and I knew it wasn't going to be fun. I was wedged in next to a man literally three times my girth. He was already snoring when I arrived, and every breath he took was accompanied by thunderous nasal eruptions, which elicited rolled-eyed sympathy from several rows of my fellow passengers. Worse was to come when I felt God telling me I needed to talk to him about it. Please Lord, don't tell me that! He might smother me to death…

When he eventually woke up, I introduced myself, quaking inside. I took the plunge: "I believe God wants to tell you something…" *(Lord, do I have to do this?)* "He loves you very much, but if you don't shape up, you're going to die!" I waited for his supersized fist to munch my face, but it never came. We had a great chat and exchanged details. Oof!

Over half of us are obese. It's a big deal, literally.

Please, there's still time to make a New Year's resolution, even if you're not fat but simply unfit, which is most of us: I'm going to take good care of God's temple, my body!

I want you to have a full, long, healthy life. Everyone's a winner if you do – you, your loved ones, your employer, the government. As I told Mr Big above, surely you want to see your kids and grandchildren grow up? And if you won't find time for exercise, you will be forced to find time for illness. Choose well and you could have several extra productive years for God's glory.

Your choice.

Lord, help me to honour you with my body this year. Amen!

Matthew 25:13

"Therefore keep watch, because you do not know the day or the hour."

READY OR NOT?

I once preached on the parable of the ten virgins near the Burundi/Congo border. It's not a complicated parable. Do take a look at it in Matthew 25. My sermon could be boiled down to three things:

1. *Jesus is coming.*
2. *Nobody knows when.*
3. *Are you ready?*

A number of people responded to the invitation. Plenty of others declined. Two days later I was driving towards their village on my motorbike only to be turned back by a group of soldiers as killing was taking place up ahead in a rebel attack. An undisclosed number of people died, and it struck me as never before just how urgent a message we have been entrusted with. How many of those who died had accepted or declined the invitation just forty-eight hours earlier? God knows. For each of those people unfortunate enough to be caught in the crossfire, their time to meet Jesus had indeed come, they hadn't known when, but the most important issue remained the same: were they ready?

How about you?

If no, what needs changing? If yes, then Smith Wigglesworth lays out the following challenge:

> *Live ready. If you have to get ready when the opportunity comes your way, you'll be too late. Opportunity doesn't wait, not even while you pray. You must not have to get ready, you must live ready at all times. Be filled with the Spirit; that is, be soaked with the Spirit. Be so soaked that every thread in the fabric of your life will have received the requisite rule of the Spirit – then when you are misused and squeezed to the wall, all that will ooze out of you will be the nature of Christ.*

Dear God, please help me today to get ready, live ready, and to help others around me likewise to get and live ready. Amen!

POOL OR MIRAGE?

Isaiah 35:7

"The mirage shall become a pool." (NASB)

4

JANUARY

A platoon of soldiers was marching through the blistering heat of the Egyptian desert during the Second World War in desperate pursuit of water. Their guide was confident of where to find it, but suddenly one of the troops spotted a beautiful desert lake several miles away. It was undeniable. So despite the guide's pleading, they hurried off course towards that beautiful water. Sadly as they approached, the lake grew smaller and smaller until it disappeared in the sand. It had been appearance without reality. They had chased a mirage, and we only know about this because one of the soldiers recorded it in his journal in his dying hours.

Are you caught up pursuing mirages, rather than the pool (God himself)? We're bombarded with adverts promising happiness and fulfilment if only we acquire what they suggest we can't do without. Can you think of any potential mirages in your own life?

Sometimes even perfectly good things can end up being mirages. Phil Vischer, the founder of the children's hit series *Vegetales*, crashed from being a multimillionaire to bankruptcy when one of his distributors sued him. In Phil's words:

> *If God gives a person a dream, breathes life into it and then it dies, then God might want to know what is more important to the person—the dream or God? The impact God has planned for us doesn't occur when we're pursuing impact. It occurs when we're pursuing God. At long last, after a lifetime of striving, God was enough. Not God and impact or God and ministry. Just God.*

So much of that hit me hard. Think about it: the impact God wants you to have for him doesn't come when you pursue impact – *it comes when you pursue God!*

Lord Jesus, please help me see the mirages for what they are, and to pursue the pool! Amen!

BOLD OR ASHAMED?

Romans 1:16

"I am not ashamed of the gospel, because it is the power of God for the salvation of everyone who believes."

A Zimbabwean young man wrote the following before he was martyred:

> *I'm part of the fellowship of the unashamed. I have the Holy Spirit's power. The die has been cast. I have stepped over the line. The decision has been made – I'm a disciple of his. I won't look back, let up, slow down, back away, or be still… I will not flinch in the face of sacrifice, hesitate in the presence of the enemy, pander at the pool of popularity, or meander in the maze of mediocrity… I am a disciple of Jesus. I must go till he comes, give till I drop, preach till all know, and work till he stops me. And, when he comes for his own, he will have no problem recognising me… my banner will be clear!*

I support Ipswich Town FC and I'm not ashamed. I'm a U2 fan and I'm not ashamed. I wear a ridiculous mankini when I go cycling and I'm not ashamed (well, maybe a little!). So why is it that when a friend or a colleague gives me an ideal opening to talk about Jesus, I suddenly get moist palms and my voice goes a little higher?! Seriously, what is our problem? What do we have to be ashamed about?

Jesus has completely transformed my life. My wretched past has been dealt with, I've got purpose in the present, and my future is absolutely guaranteed. I don't need to feel guilty anymore. Instead I feel hopeful, joyful, peaceful (some days more than others, admittedly). I'm a child of the King, for goodness' sake! So let's shout it from the rooftops – or probably, more effectively – live authentically, love wholeheartedly, pray for opportunities, and then seize them boldly when they come.

Lord, may my banner be clear today. Amen!

WORLD CITIZEN OR INSULAR INDIVIDUAL?

Psalm 24:1

"The earth is the Lord's, and everything in it, the world, and all who live in it."

6
JANUARY

Sometimes I'm so overwhelmed by the needs I see around me or those I see on TV from around the world that I just want to blot them all out by switching channels and watching a football match or a film. I'm tempted to retreat, batten down the hatches, and just seek to meet my own needs and those of my family. What can I really do about it anyway? But I simply have to resist that defeatist mindset. Abraham Kuyper wrote a century ago: "There is not one square inch in all of God's creation over which Jesus does not cry out, 'Mine!'" We are called to be world citizens, and have been given a world mandate.

The insular individual, on the other hand, has given way to cynicism. Jim Wallis explains why:

> *Cynicism does protect you in many ways. It protects you from seeming foolish to believe that things could and will change. It protects you from disappointment. It protects you from insecurity because now you are free to pursue your own security instead of sacrificing it for a social engagement that won't work anyway. Ultimately, cynicism protects you from commitment. If things are not really going to change, why try so hard to make a difference? Why take the risks, make the sacrifices, open yourself to the vulnerabilities? And if you have middle-class economic security (as many cynics do), things don't have to change for you to remain secure. That is not intended to sound harsh, just realistic. Cynics are finally free just to look after themselves.*

What will you choose? Every inch you walk today is God's, every person you meet, those you see on TV, all belong to him. So pick a fight – lots of issues need addressing in the realms of injustice, environment, education, politics, in our community, our nation, or the world.

Lord, use me as part of your movement to change the world today. Amen!

2 Timothy 1:7

"For God didn't give us a spirit of fear."

FAITH OR FEAR?

My book *Dangerously Alive* starts as follows:

> *I sped around the bend in the road on my motorbike, but quickly scrambled to a stop, surprised to see a figure in the middle of the road, just ahead of me. He was holding a grenade in his hand, ready to blow me up. I knew this for a fact – he had made his intentions clear two days before when he'd written saying he was going to cut out my eyes. My guard waved at me – a pre-arranged sign not to approach. This was both surreal and yet chillingly real. "God, what on earth shall I do? If it has to be, I'm ready to die. Let's go..."*

Most people don't live in such extreme circumstances. Interestingly, the question I am most commonly asked is: aren't you frightened for your kids' safety in such an unstable country like Burundi? But let me ask you this: don't you realize you're in a war zone too? Ostensibly it's very different, but if you scratch beneath the surface you will find that the grenades of apathy, materialism, and relativism are far more dangerous where you are. And maybe you and your family are casualties of that war. Watch out! Wake up! There's no need to fear, but you do need to live by faith!

If we're completely honest, when we analyse the root motivation behind most of our significant decision-making in life, it's grounded in fear. We choose to do x so that y doesn't happen. We have fears regarding the future, finances, health issues, family breakdown, death. So we take out a second mortgage in the house of fear. Listen: the bottom line is that we are all called to live by faith, not by fear.

Bring God your fears right now. Trust him. He can handle them.

Father God, today with your help I choose to reject fear and live by faith. Amen!

ADVENTURE OR SAFETY?

Philippians 1:21

"For me, to live is Christ, and to die is gain."

Life has become so dull and safe for many of us. Risks, we are warned, should be avoided at all costs. Safety seems to have become the highest goal, and the worship of safety emasculates creativity and life. It seems that we can end up with our highest aspiration being to arrive safely at death! In a scenario of such suffocating dreariness, can we realistically hope for anything better?

Keith Johnson splits us into two groups when he asserts that "there are those who like to say 'yes', and there are those who prefer to say 'no'. Those who say 'yes' are rewarded by the adventures they have; those who say 'no' are rewarded by the safety they attain."

Saying "yes" to God's call on your life doesn't mean selling everything you have and moving to Africa. It doesn't necessarily mean quitting your job, studies, or relationship (though equally it might do). But what it absolutely does involve is a willingness to step out of your comfort zone. By definition, that is uncomfortable. However, we have a need for significance, an inbuilt longing for authenticity, and we know it makes sense to do so rather than embracing the staleness of the status quo.

Andre Gide wrote that "one does not discover new lands without consenting to lose sight of the shore." Why don't you try to spend a few minutes today with God to think about how or where he might be wanting to journey with you? Maybe your current circumstances prohibit radical changes. Maybe God just wants to tweak areas of your life rather than engage in whole-scale transformation. Seek him about it. Whatever the case, at the end of your life, you don't want to have lots of regrets that you played it safe all the way and missed out on the adventures he was calling you to. Agreed?

Lord, help me to say "yes" rather than "no" to your call for my life, wherever that leads. Amen!

RELATIONSHIP OR RULES?

Luke 15:29

(The older brother said to his father): "Look! All these years I've been slaving for you and never disobeyed your orders. Yet you never gave me even a young goat so I could celebrate with my friends."

A poor Burundian woman found herself in a violent marriage. Her overbearing husband would write out a long list of household chores to be done each day before he returned from work. At the end of each day, he would tick off all that she'd done, and beat her mercilessly if anything was outstanding. So she was beaten every night. To her relief, he became sick and died, and within a few years she was blessed to remarry – this time to a kind and loving husband. Gone were the lists. She simply loved serving him. Months into the new marriage, she found a crumpled piece of paper behind one of the cupboards. It was one of the old lists from her previous husband! She read through it nervously, wincing as the old memories came flooding back. But then, to her amazement, she realized that she had completed everything on the old list that very day. What she couldn't accomplish motivated by fear of punishment, she had fulfilled out of energizing love.

In Jesus' famous parable of the lost son, which son was more lost? Ultimately the older one was, because he was exposed as being lost even when at home. He had, as John Wesley spoke of his own pre-conversion experience, "the religion of a servant, not a son". He'd played it by the rules while completely missing out on the relationship. Tragic!

It may sound like a cliché, but there is nothing you can do to make God love you more, and there is nothing you can do to make him love you less. God is a God of relationship. Away with images of a hard taskmaster or a cranky old man, he is the best loving Father, beyond what you could possibly imagine. Enjoy him!

Father, I choose to follow you today, grateful that you want a relationship with me, not my obedience to a long list of rules. Amen!

HOPE OR DESPAIR?

Isaiah 40:31

"Those who hope in the Lord will renew their strength."

10

JANUARY

As Father Raniero Cantalamessa writes, the three virtues of faith, hope, and love...

> *are like three sisters. Two of them are grown and the other is a small child. They go forward together hand in hand with the child hope in the middle. Looking at them it would seem that the bigger ones are pulling the child, but it is the other way around; it is the little girl who is pulling the two bigger ones. It is hope that pulls faith and love. Without hope everything would stop.*

Biblical hope is not like the world's hope – an expression of desire for an uncertain outcome – as in "I hope things work out in the end". No, as followers of Christ, our "faith is being sure of what we hope for and certain of what we do not see" (Hebrews 11:1). Fyodor Dostoevsky seemed to understand this. He said, "To live without hope is to cease to live."

I have been in places devoid of hope: tens of thousands of refugees forced into small areas with no toilets; disease rife and death a regular visitor. Despair seemingly ruled. And yet one old man in his seventies, who'd witnessed his wife and kids hacked to death and his house burned down, was able to declare despite losing everything: "I never realized that Jesus was all I needed until Jesus was all I had!"

This old man was still hanging in there while others were dying of despair. How about you? If you're ever struggling, look to Jesus, our sure and certain hope. And if you're doing fine today, look out for someone else who needs the offer of real hope, and reach out to them.

"May the God of hope fill you with all joy and peace as you trust in him, so that you may overflow with hope by the power of the Holy Spirit" (Romans 15:13). Lord, I choose that hope! Amen!

PROACTIVE OR REACTIVE?

Matthew 25:21

"Well done, good and faithful servant! You have been faithful with a few things; I will put you in charge of many things."

In Jesus' parable, there were two servants: one was proactive; the other was reactive. The latter got an ear-bashing ("You wicked, lazy servant!") before being thrown out. He wasted what had been entrusted to him.

That's what reactive people do – and often I have to admit I am reactive rather than proactive. When we're reactive, we're driven by feelings, circumstances, or conditions. We procrastinate; we wait. But if we wait to be acted upon, we will indeed be acted upon; whereas proactive people are driven by carefully considered and internalized values, so it's as if they carry their own weather with them wherever they go, and make things happen.

Everyone is predisposed to being one or the other. I suspect most of us are more on the reactive end of the spectrum. In the Bible, love is a verb, but reactive people make it a feeling. However, if our feelings control our actions, as Stephen Covey says, "it is because we have abdicated our responsibility and empowered them to do so. Proactive people make love a verb."

Remember, we are responsible (i.e. response-able) for our actions or inactions, for how we use or misuse our God-given talents. Is there something you need to do today that you've been putting off? Is there an initiative that God's been laying on your heart? Is there a relationship issue that needs addressing? Anything else you can think of? Come on, finish reading this, pray, and then go and do it, for Christ's sake!

Lord God Almighty, forgive me for the times, gifts, or opportunities I've wasted. Help me choose to be proactive today. Amen!

FORGIVENESS OR BITTERNESS?

Romans 5:5

"God has poured out his love into our hearts by the Holy Spirit, whom he has given us."

A young lady I know in Burundi watched her mother and father being hacked to death right in front of her. From that day on, and for the next seven years, she simply stopped growing. Then, at the age of twelve, she read Jesus' words above. However painful it was, she chose to forgive the undeserving murderers of her parents. As soon as she did this, an extraordinary thing happened: she started growing again – literally, physically, as well as emotionally and spiritually! *That* is the power of forgiveness.

During the war, my friend Sarah rushed home to find her husband and three children murdered. She fled to the Congo with her remaining three kids but was stopped by a group of militia. She declared boldly, "I'm not afraid to die because I know I'll go straight to be with Jesus." One of them spat back: "God is dead!" She prayed silently: "Lord, I don't want to die if you're dead, so please show me you're alive." The soldier stripped her to rape her but found her money hidden in her bra, so he ran off with the others, and she was able to flee to safety. After the war, she heard that rapist and murderer was in prison. She went to see him and said, "You told me God was dead. I'm here to tell you he's alive, he loves you, and he's told me to do the same, so I love you!"

Forgiveness or bitterness?

They may not deserve forgiveness, but if you hold on to bitterness, you're doubly the victim. "To forgive is to set a prisoner free and discover that the prisoner was you," wrote Lewis Smedes.

Most of us have got either someone we need to forgive, or someone we need to ask for forgiveness of. Let's set some prisoners free!

Our Father, forgive us our sins, as we forgive those who sin against us. Amen!

MATURITY OR IMMATURITY?

Luke 2:52

"And Jesus grew in wisdom and stature, and in favour with God and men."

I was an immature and late developer in every way. I didn't go through puberty until my late teens, and boys at school who were several years younger were bigger and hairier than me, much to my embarrassment. But it wasn't just physical immaturity. Some of the unrepeatable antics I used to get up to beyond school and into university years beggar belief. Even now, I still catch the look of feigned despair that crosses my parents' faces on a regular basis as they "tolerate" my often puerile sense of humour! So is there any hope for me, and can I still strive for maturity?!

Well, let's see what maturity is not: it's not conformity. It's not becoming boring, dull, safe, tame, or respectable. It's not about knowing your Bible. Interestingly, the group who knew the Old Testament Scriptures the best were the very ones who arranged for Jesus' crucifixion. Knowing isn't enough. It leads to pride, which is the antithesis of spiritual maturity. Going to church, reading this each day, hopefully doing some more Bible study besides, praying – these are all good activities, but are they the barometer of spiritual maturity?

It's not how many years you've been a Christian that determines your spiritual maturity. *It's how many days you walk with Christ.* Growing towards maturity is a lifelong ongoing process of becoming more like Jesus, of recognizing the actual while aiming for the ideal. It begins with the acceptance of personal responsibility. It involves learning progressively more effectively to live a life that reflects the truths, values, and principles of the Scriptures. It is to live differently, not just to know or think differently, and is gauged by application, not just contemplation. As James warns: "Do not merely listen to the word, and so deceive yourselves. Do what it says" (1:22), and "Faith without deeds is dead" (2:17).

Lord, help me live, walk, and grow daily more and more like Jesus. Amen!

CONDUIT OR CUL-DE-SAC?

Luke 12:48

"From the one who has been entrusted with much, much more will be asked."

We are blessed to be a blessing.

John Piper writes on the subject of money:

> *The point is: a $70,000 salary does not have to be accompanied by a $70,000 lifestyle. God is calling us to be conduits of His grace, not cul-de-sacs. Our great danger today is thinking that the conduit should be lined with gold. It shouldn't. Copper will do. No matter how grateful we are, gold will not make the world think that our God is good; it will make people think that our god is gold.*

Hmm... Does your life look like your God is good, or your God is gold? Ouch! My pastor's eighteen-year-old brother died in his arms because he couldn't afford £3 for the medicine across the pharmacy counter. It's a sick world, isn't it? Think what a difference you can make by being sacrificially generous. Copper or gold? Conduit or cul-de-sac?

Now you may or may not have spare money with which to bless other people, but gauging our level of blessing by the state of our finances is way too narrow. Living in one of the poorest countries in the world forces me, positively, to count my blessings on a regular basis. I have an education. I eat more than one meal a day. I can afford to go to a doctor when I get sick. I have access to clean water. I am free to tell people about Jesus. These, and many more besides, are incredible blessings. Too often we focus on what we don't have rather than on what we do have.

So beyond your money (or lack of it), please recognize afresh today how you are deeply blessed. Be grateful. Enjoy. And God wants you to pass on that blessing to others.

Lord Jesus, I choose to be a conduit of your blessing, not a cul-de-sac. Show me whom you want me to bless today. Amen!

Romans 8:37

"We are more than conquerors."

FAST OR FAR?

An African proverb says that "if you want to go fast, go alone; if you want to go far, go together".

Confession time: I'm all about speed. I love going fast. And sometimes it's fine, but sometimes it really backfires. I'm always walking ten yards ahead of my Missus into the restaurant, so I get there first, I get there faster, but she's not with me, and the romantic meal's got off to a bad start! We were made to go together.

When I cycled over 3,000 miles across the USA in 34 days, there were seven of us. We were a team. We had different roles – support driver, navigator, food, logistics, cyclist. Wired as I am, for better or worse, I was usually at the front. One time I turned around and I'd lost the others. My going faster proved dangerous. Being in the desert without enough water means you don't go far. I had to swallow my pride, turn around, and rejoin the pack. Then, together, we could go far.

Paul asks, "Who shall separate us from the love of God? Shall trouble, or hardship, or persecution, or famine, or nakedness, or danger, or sword? No, in all these things *we* are more than conquerors..." (Romans 8:35, 37). Why "we"? Because life's challenges will take you out if you insist on doing it on your own. We need each other. That's how we win. If you want to be a lone ranger for Jesus, you're toast!

How fast and how far have you gone? How far do you want to go?

We need each other. Who's on your team, or whose team are you on? It's critical – please think about it today, and make a plan if you're isolated – you don't want to run out of water in the desert...

Thank you Jesus for your promise that in and through the tough times "we are more than conquerors" by your strength. Help me identify the "we" and journey far with them. Amen!

SUCCESS OR SIGNIFICANCE?

Philippians 3:8

"I consider everything a loss compared to the surpassing greatness of knowing Christ Jesus my Lord."

16

JANUARY

Just about everyone wants to be successful, but what is success? Rock band Queen's Freddie Mercury, who died of AIDS, said: "Success has bought me world idolisation and millions of pounds, but has prevented me from having the one thing we all need – a loving ongoing relationship." Was he successful? Success is so often narrowly defined as accruing lots of money, possessions, power, and prestige. But Freddie, along with so many others, discovered that *you can have everything to live with and nothing to live for.* He never made the step from success to significance.

How about you? Are you still striving for success, or do you recognize that significance is of higher worth? Often we learn the hard way, striving in our former years in our quest for worldly success before realigning our priorities on our journey to significance. Success isn't wrong – let's be clear on that – we just need to know what real success is, and recognize that it is easy to confuse our success with God's approval. Maybe we could merge the two words by redefining success as finding the will of God and doing it, no matter what.

Zig Ziglar wrote: "Success is not measured by how you do compared to how somebody else does, but by how you do compared to what you could have done with what God gave you."

So is it time for a change of direction, job, career? Maybe, or maybe not. A journey towards significance doesn't necessitate a change of jobs. It could, more profoundly, involve a change of heart and a change in the way you order your life and view the world.

Take a look at what motivates your choices, your priorities, your objectives. Do you think you're on the right track? It's well worth heading in the right direction…

Lord, I choose to follow your call for my life. Show me the way, that I may walk in it. Amen!

Proverbs 4:23

"Above all else, guard your heart, for it is the wellspring of life."

WELLSPRING OR CESSPIT?

In biblical language, the heart is the centre of the human spirit, from which spring motivations, thoughts, emotions, courage, and action. If we don't guard our heart, we're going to be in trouble.

When Leonardo da Vinci was painting his masterpiece *The Last Supper*, he needed a model for his Christ. He tracked down a chorister called Pietro Bandinelli in one of the churches of Rome, who was boyishly attractive and fresh-faced. The painting took years to complete – in fact da Vinci turned his hand to other works until eventually he determined to finish it. He'd painted all the disciples except Judas, so now he was looking for a face which was hardened and distorted by sin. He came across a beggar who welcomed an easy way of making some money by just sitting there in front of da Vinci. Once they were finished, da Vinci said: "I have not yet found out your name." "I am Pietro Bandinelli," he replied, "I also sat for you as your model of Christ."

Whether that story is true or not, it's a tragedy when innocence is corrupted, when beauty is distorted. Maybe I have a heightened sensitivity to this because I always come back from Africa into Western culture in a very abrupt way (within a few hours on a plane). I am amazed about how many followers of Christ don't guard their hearts. We will watch anything on TV and read the most trashy magazines without discerning that their impact is to turn our wellspring into a cesspit. How can we possibly hope to stay spiritually sharp and sensitive if we constantly allow filth to blunt our cutting edge?

Please, *please*, guard your heart. It *is* the wellspring of life. What goes in comes out. If you feed it trash, that will come out. "What is this doing to my heart?" is a great question to ask in any given situation.

Lord, I choose to guard my heart today. Amen!

ORDINARY OR EXTRAORDINARY?

Philippians 2:6, 7

"[Jesus] did not consider equality with God something to be grasped, but made himself nothing."

On one occasion, Mother Teresa of Calcutta was asked: "How do you measure the success of your work?" She looked puzzled for a moment and then replied, "I don't remember that the Lord ever spoke of success. He spoke only of faithfulness in love. This is the only success that really counts." She was the living embodiment of what Oswald Chambers meant when he wrote: "It is inbred in us that we have to do exceptional things for God; but we have not. We have to be exceptional in the ordinary things, to be holy in mean streets, among mean people, and this is not learned in five minutes."

My granny prayed for me every day of my life – that faithfulness is my kind of extraordinary. A friend of mine read the Bible weekly with a Sikh for twenty-two years before the latter came to faith – that's my kind of extraordinary. Can you accept that definition? Being "exceptional in the ordinary things"? "Holy in mean streets"? This is not learned in five minutes…

All the more nowadays in our twisted celebrity culture, which offers some people at least fifteen minutes of fame, we can wrongly aspire to pseudo-greatness and recognition. Jesus calls us to another way. To be truly extraordinary is the preserve of the smallest minority, by definition. So in all likelihood you, like me, are relatively ordinary. And yet we ordinary beings serve an extraordinary God, and so are capable of extraordinary things in his name for his glory. But let him be the arbiter. Some exploits are obviously extraordinary, while others go unseen, beneath everyone's radar except the radar of the Most Important One of All.

Dear truly Extraordinary God, help me to choose to be exceptional in the ordinary, for the approval and satisfaction of the Audience of One. Amen!

Genesis 12:1

"Leave your country, your people, and your father's household, and go to the land I will show you."

CLARITY OR TRUST?

A brilliant, spiritually-searching physicist, John Kavanaugh, spent an extended season at Mother Teresa's "House of the Dying" in his quest for direction in life. As was her habit, she asked him on their first morning together, "What can I do for you?"

"Prayer."

"What kind of prayer?"

Immediately, sensing he was getting nearer to the Holy Grail for which he'd travelled thousands of miles, he said, "Please pray that I get clarity for the future."

"No!" she retorted emphatically, "I will not do that. Clarity is the last thing you are clinging to and must let go of."

"But you always seem to have clarity," Kavanaugh pleaded, somewhat discouraged.

Mother Teresa laughed and through her winsome smile said, "I have never had clarity; what I have always had is trust. So I will pray you trust God."

It is human instinct to want to cover all our bases, to have all our ducks lined up, to be in control of our circumstances. So we end up living by sight, not by faith. Instead God beckons us forward in our journey of faith, stretching us out of our comfort zones. Notice how Abra(ha)m was called to go "to the land *I will show you"*. He didn't know where on earth he was going, but had to step out in trust, with very little clarity, just clinging to the promise that God would unfold his plan.

Whatever you're going through today, God's got big hands. He is trustworthy. Only through trials and testing do we develop stronger faith muscles. Be comforted by Oswald Chambers's words: "Future plans are uncertain, but we all know that there is first God's plan to be lived, and we can safely leave everything to Him, '*carefully careless*' of it all."

God Almighty, I choose to trust you today, whether things are crystal clear or not. Amen!

REMEMBER OR FORGET?

Proverbs 16:3, 9

"Commit to the Lord whatever you do, and your plans will succeed. In his heart a man plans his course, but the Lord determines his steps."

20
JANUARY

Three sturdy trees were on a mountain top dreaming about what they wanted to be. The first said it wanted to contain treasure. The second said it wanted to be a strong sailing ship, and carry powerful kings. The third wanted to grow tall, and make people think of God. Years passed. Three woodcutters came by and chopped them down. The first wasn't fashioned into a treasure chest but rather a simple feed box for animals. The second was made into small fishing boat rather than a mighty sailing vessel – and then it was lowered into in a lake and daily filled with smelly fish. The third was confused at being cut into beams and left. Years passed and all three nearly forgot their dreams.

Never forget your dreams.

Then a lady laid her baby in the feeding tray, and the first tree knew it held the best treasure in the world. The second tree was in a storm with a stranger, who calmed the waves and brought peace. Then it knew it was carrying the king of all the earth. And one Friday morning the third tree's beams were yanked from a forgotten wood pile, but Sunday morning, when the sun rose and the earth trembled with joy below, the third tree knew God's love had changed everything. For all three their dreams were better than being the tallest tree.

What are your plans? What are your dreams? The above verses from Proverbs became very real to me at a time when things in my life were totally out of my control and unclear, and I was questioning the plans and dreams I believed were God-given but didn't look like happening. I memorized them and held on to the promises contained in them. May you do the same.

Lord, I choose to entrust all my plans and dreams to you, to remember them and not give up. Amen!

Colossians 1:17

"He is before all things, and in him all things hold together."

SUPERHERO OR NORMAL?

Do you remember Ursa, the Kryptonite villainess in *Superman 2*? She wreaked havoc on planet Earth in pursuit of Superman's destruction. Sarah Douglas, who played the role, spoke in an interview of an incident during the filming. In one scene, she picked up and threw a bus on Forty-Second Street. Of course in reality she was in the studio, but she had to keep her arm raised for hours on end during the multiple takes with the bus held above her by a crane. At one stage the bus slipped down six inches on the chain, and, she thought: "It's slipping!" Instinctively she tried to push it back up, picking up a back injury in the process. She spoke of how if you spend the whole day dressed up like a superhero or villain, you start believing you are them. Reflecting on the incident, she said: "For that split second, I knew that I really was Ursa from Krypton, and it was my job to hold the bus up!"

This is often very much like us as believers – because by the grace of God he allows us to stand there on Forty-Second Street lifting up a bus in the air. Not literally of course, but he allows us to be involved in his work, and then we end up believing that it all depends on us; and then when the bus slips, we think: "That's my job, I have to hold it up!" But God says: "It was never your job! I am the one holding the bus up. I love having you work with me. But remember that it is never you who is ultimately holding it all together, it is always me."

Some of us really need to hear that. I know I do. Sometimes I put myself under ridiculous strain and pressure thinking the future of Burundi depends on me (how arrogant as well!). Any lesson there for you?

Lord, help me to trust you to keep the show on the road. Amen!

PERFORMING OR PRODUCING?

John 15:5

"I am the vine; you are the branches. If a man remains in me and I in him, he will bear much fruit; apart from me you can do nothing."

22

JANUARY

God has chosen and appointed you to "go and bear fruit". He is the vine and we are the branches that produce fruit – fruit that will last (John 15:16). The branch doesn't strive or strain to produce fruit because it is connected to the vine.

However, so many lives and ministries are driven by the need to perform, to achieve, and to be successful. Sadly, this results in a lot of fruitless activity, burnout, and wasted resources. Our need for acceptance, affirmation, and significance drives us to perform. We become disconnected from the vine and become reliant upon our own gifts, strengths, and resources to "make things happen".

Here are four key principles to produce fruit that will last:

1. *Submit to the pruning process. The Lord cuts back and prunes the branches that have both good and bad fruit. We find pruning so difficult because we attach so much of our identity to the activities that we are involved in.*
2. *Establish rest in your life. People who perform cannot rest. They think that if they just work harder they will become more productive. In fact it is the exact opposite, as in order to produce fruit in the kingdom, he makes us lie down in green pastures.*
3. *"Apart from me you can do nothing." Let go of fruitless striving and return to the vine. Producing fruit begins in that secret, intimate place with Jesus. Our activity is founded upon what we see the Father doing and is made possible and sustained through the Holy Spirit.*
4. *This is to my Father's glory. Producing lasting fruit is for the Father's glory, not ours. We need to ask ourselves whether what we are doing is really "for God" or whether it remains about us.*

Lord, I choose to resist being a performer. Help me to be someone who produces lasting fruit. Amen!

EVERYTHING OR NOTHING?

John 3:16

"God so loved the world that he gave his one and only Son, that whoever believes in him shall not perish but have eternal life."

The story is told of a rich man who enjoyed collecting rare works of art with his son, including some Picassos. His son then died in Vietnam as he sought to save another soldier's life. Months later, there was a knock at the door, and the man whose life was rescued presented the grieving father with a painting he'd done: "Your son was my friend, I loved him too. He spoke so highly of you as his father. It's not great art, but I painted him one day in the jungle. It's for you." The father loved and treasured the painting of his son.

A few years later he died, and all his works of art went to auction. The auction began with the picture of the son. The connoisseurs complained that it didn't constitute real art. The auctioneer asked for bids, but nobody responded. He insisted: "The son! The son! Who'll take the son?" Eventually a frail gentleman – the deceased man's long-term gardener – offered $10. It was all he could afford. Nobody raised the bid, so it was his. With that, the auctioneer laid down his gavel and declared: "I'm sorry, the auction is over." There was confusion and outrage: "What about the real paintings?" "I'm sorry. The will stipulated that whoever bought that painting would inherit the entire estate, including the other paintings. The man who took the son gets everything!"

Jesus plus nothing equals everything; everything minus Jesus equals nothing. Just like the auctioneer, God is asking everyone today, "The son, the son, who'll take the son?" Because whoever takes the Son gets everything." Ephesians 1:3 says that God "has blessed us in the heavenly realms with every spiritual blessing in Christ."

Recognize today who you are and what you have in the Son.

Thank you Jesus that in you I have everything. I choose to live that truth today. Amen!

RANDOM THOUGHT OR GOD'S PROMPTING?

Ephesians 6:18

"Pray in the Spirit on all occasions with all kinds of prayers and requests… be alert and always keep on praying for all the saints."

A missionary was back in America on furlough and speaking at his home church. He told of how one of his jobs was to go to the nearest town to collect the rural health clinic's staff salaries at the end of each month. One particular end of month, he saw a fight taking place, so he intervened, nursed the injured man, told him about Jesus, and then went on his way to the bank and then home to dispense the money. The following month, the man he'd nursed stopped him and told him how his gang had followed him into the bush to kill him and steal the money, but they couldn't because when they approached him they suddenly saw he had twenty-six security guards. The missionary laughed and insisted he was alone, but the young man was adamant that all five of them had seen the guards.

At that point in the story, a man in the congregation jumped up excitedly and insisted on knowing the date that had taken place. When the missionary gave him the date, the animated man told how that very morning he was about to play golf when he felt the urge to pray for his missionary friend in Central Africa. The Lord's prompting was so strong he'd left the golf and called others to join him at church and pray. He asked those he'd involved to stand up. Twenty-six men rose to their feet in that sanctuary. A hush descended as the realization dawned on those gathered of what had taken place.

Have you ever felt a prompt to pray for someone? I think it happens all the time but often we ignore or miss it. Prayer works. It's powerful. There's a spiritual battle going on. Red alert!

Lord, today I choose to be alert and pray for people you bring to my mind. Amen!

1 Corinthians 13:12

"Now we see but a poor reflection as in a mirror; then we shall see face to face. Now I know in part; then I shall know fully, even as I am fully known."

CLEAR OR FOGGY?

Everything happens for a reason. When God closes a door he opens a window. God will never let you go through more than you can handle. It'll all work itself out in the end. Really?

Most of us have experienced times of confusion, uncertainty, and doubt in our faith journey. We want to do the right thing. We pray about it. We seek advice. But things don't pan out as we'd hoped. Maybe that's you now, or you at least know what I'm talking about. Or maybe it's coming your way. Nobody loves those times, but they're an integral part of the faith journey.

A few years back we had visa issues as a family, and were stuck in England for almost a year. There were seven of us, including a newborn baby, in my gracious in-laws' two-bedroom apartment for six months. I railed at God as doors didn't open on my timeline. I questioned whether we'd got it all wrong. Retrospectively, it was the best year of our marriage as we had quality time with family outside of the cauldron of Burundi. However, in the thick of it, it wasn't fun. Many times, and sometimes with tears, I prayed this beautiful prayer by Thomas Merton. Maybe it'll hit the spot for you as it did for me:

My Lord God, I have no idea where I am going. I do not see the road ahead of me. I cannot know for certain where it will end. Nor do I really know myself, and the fact that I think I am following your will does not mean that I am actually doing so. But I believe that the desire to please you does in fact please you. Amen!

FINISHED OR UNFINISHED?

John 19:30

Jesus said: "It is finished!"

When Jesus died on the cross, his last words included the emphatic "*Tetelestai!*", or "It is finished!" What did that phrase convey? Several things:

"*Tetelestai*" was used on a receipt to indicate the bill had been *fully paid.* Jesus actually bought us when he died on the cross. In 1 Corinthians 6:20 it says, "You were bought at great cost, therefore honour God with your body."

In the first century, guards would commonly nail the charge-sheet to the prisoner's door, listing all crimes committed. Having served the sentence, the prisoner would receive the charge-sheet back with "Tetelestai" stamped on it, i.e. sentence served. "He forgave all your sins, and blotted out the charges proved against you, the list of his commandments which you had not obeyed. He took this list of sins and destroyed it by nailing it to Christ's cross" (Colossians 2:14 LB).

Upon returning from a victorious military campaign, a general would parade his captives of war through the streets of Rome and shout "*Tetelestai! Tetelestai!*" i.e. *mission accomplished.* Colossians 2:15 says, "Having disarmed the principalities and powers, he made a public spectacle of them, triumphing over them on the cross."

So the bill has been fully paid, the sentence has been served, and the mission has been accomplished – that's great news, and that's the finished part. The unfinished part is that although the ultimate victory has been won, the battle is still ongoing for us. All historians recognize that D-Day was the costly moment when Allied victory was won, yet there were many more casualties until VE-Day was declared with the full German defeat eleven months later.

The Devil is still very much in business. He wants to take you down with him. He'll use whatever it takes, so stay alert, on your toes, guard your heart, watch out for others, prioritize what matters, and fight for the King of Kings!

Lord Jesus, thank you that ultimately victory is assured. Help me to fight the good fight of faith today. Amen!

Ephesians 2:6

"God raised us up with Christ and seated us with him in the heavenly realms in Christ Jesus."

ABOVE OR BELOW?

"Under the circumstances" is a common enough phrase, but if Jesus is over and above all circumstances – and as our verse says we too are seated with him "in the heavenly realms" – then maybe it's not one we should use as his followers. We never have to be "under" the circumstances.

When it rains, most birds head for shelter, yet the eagle is the one bird which, in order to avoid the rain, will fly above the cloud. Maybe we who hope in the Lord should, like we read in Isaiah 40:31, "soar on wings like eagles, run and not grow weary, walk and not faint".

We are seated "in the heavenly realms *in* Christ". Many years ago, Tony Bennett sang, "I left my heart *in* San Francisco". What did he mean? Well, he meant that San Francisco was his passion, his love, his true home – even though he had temporarily moved to Chicago. Similarly for us and heaven – there lies our passion, our love, and our true home. We're exiles and aliens on earth. The world has no claim on us. We're in Christ, and heaven is always pulling us upwards and holding our affections.

Colossians 3:3 says, "For you died, and your life is now hidden with Christ in God." Whatever you are going through today, remember where you are hidden, remember you are not under the circumstances, remember where you are seated, all *in* Christ! Paul wrote from jail in Philippians 4:13, "I can do all things through Christ who gives me strength." In jail, yet not "under the circumstances". Paradoxical maybe, but still "able to do all things through Christ".

Please help me live today with the right perspective on everything I come up against. In Christ. Amen!

DIPLOMATS OR PROPHETS?

2 Timothy 4:2

"Preach the Word; be prepared in season and out of season; correct, rebuke and encourage – with great patience and careful instruction."

Today's choice comes from A.W. Tozer's quote: "We are not diplomats but prophets, and our message is not a compromise but an ultimatum." Really? It doesn't sound much fun! However, if we see prophecy as simply faithfully relaying God's Word into any given situation, then I agree with him. Prophets begin in judgment, in social critique of the status quo, but end in hope – that those realities can be changed. G.K. Chesterton wrote of our need nowadays for a new kind of prophet, not like the prophets of old who reminded people that they were going to die, but more positively someone who would remind them they were not dead yet.

Here's a challenging question: If we were arrested today for being followers of Christ, would there be enough evidence to convict us?

American apologist Francis Schaeffer was a modern-day prophet in many ways. He founded a community called L'Abri and wrote,

> *In about the first three years of L'Abri all our wedding presents were wiped out. Our sheets were torn. Holes were burned in our rugs… Drugs came into our place. People vomited on our rugs… How many times have you had a drug-taker come into your home? Sure it is a danger to your family, and you must be careful. But have you ever risked it?… If you have never done any of these things or things of this nature, if you have been married for years and years and had a home (or even a room) and none of this has ever occurred, if you have been quiet especially as our culture is crumbling about us, if this is true – do you really believe that people are going to hell?*

Lord, I choose today to speak up uncompromisingly, in love, and also not just with words but by getting my hands dirty. Amen!

Colossians 3:23

"Whatever you do, work at it with all your heart, as for the Lord, not for men."

EXCELLENCE OR MEDIOCRITY?

Why is it that often Christians are known for doing things shoddily? In Burundi, we've attempted to build the best conference centre in the country to generate funds for God's work, and people come up to me and say: "Don't think this is yours, it's ours!" They're proud of it because it's one of the best, and they can see it brings glory to God. We aspired to excellence rather than mediocrity.

In Russia in the eighteenth century, hundreds of builders were involved in a big construction project. Three of them who were mixing cement were asked what they were doing. The first replied, "I'm mixing cement." The second replied, "I'm putting up a wall." The third replied, "I'm building a magnificent cathedral to the glory of God!" They were all doing the same task, but you can guess which one was likely to be the most energetic and committed.

In the series *The Office*, Ricky Gervais says: "Put the key of despair into the lock of apathy. Turn the knob of mediocrity slowly and open the gates of despondency – welcome to a day in the average office." How tragic! And yet maybe that is where we currently find ourselves. It can change. We don't need to remain harnessed to the treadmill of the trivial.

Pete Greig writes, "The eyes of the Lord are still searching out those willing to live their lives above the gunnels of mediocrity and beyond the realms of inevitability. In our cynical age, God is looking for those naïve enough to believe that the world can still be changed, those simple fools whose vision is to live and die for Christ alone."

Excellence honours God and inspires people. Will you commit yourself to that today?

Forgive me, Father, when I've settled for mediocrity rather than aspiring to excellence for your glory. Help me to change, starting today. Amen!

SPEAK OR LISTEN?

James 1:19

"My dear brothers, take note of this: everyone should be quick to listen, slow to speak..."

30

JANUARY

My name, Simon, means "Listener". My wife finds that ironic. She says I never listen to her... at least that's what I think she said! Most of us are better (or quicker) at speaking than at listening. The above verse's context is between people, but no doubt we're the same with God – we're quick to speak and slow to listen, rather than vice versa.

Dietrich Bonhoeffer wrote:

> *Silence is the simple stillness of the individual under the word of God... But everybody knows that this is something that needs to be practised and learned in these days when talkativeness prevails. Real silence, real stillness, really holding one's tongue, comes only as the sober consequence of spiritual stillness... The silence of the Christian is listening silence, humble stillness... Silence before the Word leads to right hearing and thus to right speaking of the Word of God at the right time... Many people are looking for an ear that will listen. They do not find it among Christians, because Christians are talking when they should be listening. He who no longer listens to his brother will soon no longer be listening to God either.*

Are you listening to God? How? There's no way we will hear him unless we take serious measures to make time to listen. From the moment I get up in the morning and know there are several dozen emails (voices) waiting for me to deal with, to driving to work and being blasted by adverts on the radio and on billboards, to competing demands from colleagues, friends and family, there are a lot of other voices drowning out the most important one. This devotional might be a help on your journey, but is no substitute for quality stillness before the Lord. What will we do about it?

Lord, I choose to set aside some time to be really still and listen to you today. Amen!

FACTUAL OR PERSONAL?

Philippians 3:10

"I want to know Christ."

Why would the apostle Paul pray such a basic prayer? Surely he knew Christ already? He certainly knew him far better than we do. But he recognized how far he still had to go. And he knew there was a clear difference between knowing about someone, and truly knowing them.

Let me share how I first fell in love (or maybe it was lust!): this beautiful blonde bombshell called Gini sauntered through the playground and I was mesmerized. I started stalking her. I knew where she lived, who her friends were, what she liked, and more. I wanted her to love me in return, but there were two massive obstacles to that happening. First, she was already going out with Randy, the school hunk. How I hated him! And second – and maybe more insurmountable still – was the fact that Gini was thirteen, and I… I was five!

I never spoke to Gini. I knew lots about her, but I didn't know her at all.

Most people have a basic grasp of French. In French, there are two words for the English verb "to know": "savoir" is used for facts and "connaître" for people. In John 8:32, Jesus says: "You will know the truth, and the truth will set you free." You would expect him to use "savoir" in that context, as the truth is surely factual – but no, the truth is a person, Jesus himself, and so he's talking along the lines of "connaître" – personal intimate relational knowledge.

That is what God wants for us. The Pharisees had plenty of knowledge about Jesus, but they didn't *know* him. Let's not make the same mistake.

The depth of any relationship is contingent on the quality of time invested. If we give God our crumbs, no wonder we're struggling. How are you getting on in this area?

Lord, I choose today to seek quality time with you, because I want to go way deeper in my relationship with you. Amen!

LAUGH OR CRY?

Ecclesiastes 3:4

"There is a time for everything... a time to weep and a time to laugh."

It was probably malaria. Before dawn, after umpteen hot and cold sweats, and regular dashes to the lavatory, I got ready to go to the doctor. Not only was there no electricity, but the water had been cut off temporarily. I fumbled around barefoot in the dark and didn't see a glass bottle left on the ground the night before. So I accidentally kicked it, and it shattered, spraying glass shards across the bathroom floor. In my feeble, dazed state, I prepared a stool sample. But to my horror I discovered I hadn't taken the lid off the container, and faeces were everywhere, including all over my hands. So there in the dark I swayed, disorientated and feeble, barefoot amidst the broken glass, hands covered in mess, and no water to wash it off with!

Laugh or cry? I think I did both that time!

One thing I've learned living in a war zone is that having a sense of humour is a life-saver. There are plenty of times to weep in life, so make sure you have some laughs as well. Jesus wept, and I have no doubt he laughed a lot too. Maybe one of the unstated reasons he liked children so much was because they laugh, according to statistics, six times as much as adults. We're far too serious far too much of the time...

Why did I ask Lizzie Corfe to marry me back in 2003? Not just because she's a holy honey, but because she makes me laugh. And vice versa. When we first met, I cracked a joke and she laughed through her nose and snotted across the table at me – that's when I knew she was the one!

Do you laugh much? Can you laugh at your own expense? If you want to laugh at mine, as thousands have done so already, go on YouTube and type in "dstrausspics hilarious bike crash"!

Lord, thanks for the gift of laughter. Amen!

PITY OR COMPASSION?

Matthew 9:36

"When he saw the crowds, he had compassion on them, because they were harassed and helpless."

2
FEBRUARY

I was on a short-term mission trip in Sao Paulo, Brazil. We were trying to "minister" to street children. But these weren't cute little kids. They were tough, hardened, aggressive, and dangerous. We were approached by a ten-year-old in broad daylight and he exploded in hateful invective. He said to our 6ft 4in leader: "You may be big and you may be strong, but there's only one of you." Then his gang attacked us, pelting us with glass bottles as we fled to seek police protection. It was the most frightening experience of my life. That night, as a team, we processed the experience. I simply wept for those kids' brokenness. But then the team leader said something that has been etched deep in my soul ever since that day:

"Pity cries, and then goes away. Compassion stays."

Pity often assumes a place of superiority and looks down. Compassion comes alongside, shoulder to shoulder – from the Latin "com pati", "to suffer with".

My world was rocked, and I didn't want to just walk away. I had to leave, but I carried on being involved, raising funds by selling my CD collection. I'm not saying that to impress you. I just had to do something. I left, but in another sense I stayed.

We get bombarded by images of scrawny, dying kids on TV, by pleas for our money, by endless needs in our broken world. It's easy to harden our hearts and just switch TV channels.

My advice is: ask God what he wants you to get involved in. You can't respond to every need. But you can definitely pick one person, one place, one issue – in your area or across the oceans – and let it get under your skin, break your heart, make you weep, and decide to stay.

Lord, I choose to stay. Move me to tears, and beyond that, to compassionate action. Amen!

Psalm 19:7

"The Law of the Lord is perfect, reviving the soul."

LAW OR GRACE? (PART 1)

Many of us don't really understand the role of God's Law – particularly the Ten Commandments – so we immediately jump to his grace. This shift broadly happened from the beginning of the twentieth century. So John 3:16 became our favourite text: "For God so loved the world that he gave (Jesus) for us..." But the sinner needs to be told that he *needs* saving as a Law-breaker before he's told *how* to be saved; his conscience needs wounding (Law) or he will see no need for his wounds to be bandaged (grace).

Jesus always preached the Law to the proud and arrogant and grace to the meek and the humble (Luke 10:25, 26; 18:18–20; John 3:1–17). He never gave good news to proud Pharisees. They needed humbling. In a similar vein, Wesley said that people need 90 per cent Law followed by 10 per cent grace. Why? Because the Law breaks hardened hearts while the gospel of grace heals broken hearts. You need to plough the land before you sow in order to reap after that same sowing.

D.L. Moody said:

> *It is a great mistake to give a man who has not been convicted of sin certain passages that were never meant for him. The Law is what he needs... Do not offer the consolation of the gospel until he sees and knows he is guilty before God. We must give enough of the Law to take away all self-righteousness. I pity the man who preaches only one side of the truth – always the gospel and never the Law.*

I look back to my own conversion and question whether the gospel I heard struck the right balance. The consequences of misunderstanding are significant. We potentially end up with a diminished view of sin and its effects, and of our need for a Saviour.

It's food for thought. We'll explore further tomorrow!

Lord, thank you for both your Law and your grace. Help me grow in understanding and living out your beautiful gospel. Amen!

LAW OR GRACE?
(PART 2)

Romans 7:24, 25

"What a wretched man I am! Who will rescue me from this body of death? Thanks be to God – through Jesus Christ our Lord."

4

FEBRUARY

A caricature of modern Western evangelistic preaching is this: Come to Jesus and he will bless you. He will satisfy your needs. He's got a wonderful plan for your life. He'll take away your problems. He'll give you life to the full.

There's some truth in that, but is it a timeless message across cultures and contexts? Does it ring true to our brothers and sisters in the persecuted church? Are they blessed, satisfied, enjoying life to the full? Hmm…

What is the gospel? Is it that God has a wonderful plan for your life, or that we sinners can be made righteous in Christ and escape the just punishment for our sins, which is God's wrath and eternal separation from him, hell? I fear we have opted for a different gospel, which reflects our self-centred, soft-sell consumer culture. Yet what makes it great news is dealing first with the bad news.

Spurgeon wrote:

> *Ho, ho sir surgeon, you are too delicate to tell the man that he is ill! You hope to heal the sick without their knowing it. You therefore flatter them and what happens? They laugh at you; they dance upon their own graves. At last they die! Your delicacy is cruelty; your flatteries are poisons; you are a murderer. Shall we keep men in a fool's paradise? Shall we lull them into soft slumbers from which they will awake in hell? Are we to become helpers of their damnation by our smooth speeches? In the name of God we will not!*

What is the relationship between Law and grace? I'd strongly recommend Ray Comfort's *The Way of the Master* if you want to delve deeper. It's worth wrestling with. The stakes are high.

Thank you, Jesus, that although the wages of sin are death, the gift of God is eternal life in you. Amen!

Colossians 3:17

"Whatever you do, whether in word or deed, do it all in the name of the Lord Jesus Christ."

CALLING OR CAREER? (PART 1)

John Ortberg wrote:

> *Western society does not talk much about calling anymore. It is more likely to think in terms of career. Yet, for many people a career becomes the altar on which they sacrifice their lives... A calling, which is something I do for God, is replaced by a career, which threatens to become my god. A career is something I choose for myself; a calling is something I receive. A career promises status, money or power; a calling generally promises difficulty and even some suffering – and the opportunity to be used by God. A career is about upward mobility; a calling generally leads to downward mobility.*

I hope you have a sense of calling. God calls his people to work in every area of society, be it in the realms of education, business, media, the arts, or elsewhere. It doesn't have to be the few who feel called to their field. The value of feeling called rather than simply pursuing a career is that you may retire from your job eventually, but not from your calling. Or sometimes you might go through a period of unemployment, but no one ever becomes uncalled.

A woman who had attended a mission wrote afterwards to the missioner saying, "Dear Sir, I have come to know Jesus Christ during the mission. I feel he is calling me to preach the gospel. The trouble is, I have twelve children. What shall I do?" The missioner wrote back, "Dear Madam, I'm delighted to hear that God has called you to preach the gospel. I'm even more delighted that he's provided you with a congregation!"

Have you heard God's call? Have you sought it? Do you want it?

Lord, I choose to pursue your call rather than just my career. Amen!

CAREER OR CALLING? (PART 2)

Colossians 3:23

"Whatever you do, work at it with all your heart, as for the Lord, not for men."

Os Guinness writes:

> *Along with the truth of the cross of Christ, the truth of calling has had as much influence in the world as any truth in history – and it will again, when it is rediscovered... Calling is the truth that God calls us to himself so decisively that everything we are, everything we do, everything we have is invested with a special devotion and dynamism lived out as a response to his summons and service.*

Let's immediately disavow the notion that callings are reserved for those people going into so-called "full-time" Christian work. William Wilberforce nearly made that mistake as a new convert back in 1785. He thought he should shelve politics and become a clergyman, as "spiritual" affairs were apparently far more important than secular ones. Thankfully John Newton, a former slave trader who wrote the hymn "Amazing Grace", dissuaded him from leaving politics. "It is hoped and believed that the Lord has raised you up for the good of the nation," said Newton. Wilberforce subsequently wrote in his journal in 1788, "My walk is a public one. My business is in the world; and I must mix in the assemblies of men, or quit the post which Providence seems to have assigned me." The rest is history, as they say.

Wilberforce was called to politics. My mate Craig is called to business. I'm called to raise a new generation of passionate disciples in Burundi. We're all seeking to use our God-given talents for a God-given purpose. What took me out of marketing and into my current field of service was a bold prayer of surrender: "Lord, I'll do anything. I'll go anywhere."

That's essentially what he wants from you today.

Lord, count me in! I don't know what my life will look like, but I trust you as the Caller. Amen!

John 16:33

"In this world, you will have trouble. But take heart, I have overcome the world."

LIFE-SAVING OR LIFE-ENHANCING?

Picture two men on a flight, both of them having been given a parachute. One is told it'll improve his flight, whereas the other one is told he's going to have to jump. Both of them get ridiculed, so the former one takes his off, feeling humiliated and disillusioned. The latter doesn't mind the minor discomfort or mockery, because he knows he's ready to jump.

Imagine an air-steward tripping and pouring scalding coffee down on that second man. He doesn't blame the parachute. No, if anything, he might cling to it even tighter and look forward to the jump.

If the gospel is just about God's "wonderful plan for our life", in all likelihood we'll end up like the first man when the flight gets rocky. The incentive of an improved ride was false, so he ditched the parachute. However, the second man had the right motive, so he stood firm.

Trials and tribulations draw the true believer closer to God rather than pushing him away, but sadly many people who profess to follow Jesus abandon him when things get tough. Why? Because they bought into a "me-centred" gospel, which promised all blessings at no cost.

Our verse above has two parts. Together they provide a balanced understanding of our lives in Christ. If you just believe the first half, you'll be miserable. If you just take the second half, you'll be an annoying triumphalist until things go wrong, and then you'll probably jack it all in.

So if you're going through a tough time at the moment, hang in there. Be encouraged. You're probably on track. Jesus didn't say it'd be easy. He didn't promise an easy journey. But he does guarantee a safe arrival.

Lord, help me take heart today because you have overcome the world, and so likewise your Word says we are more than conquerors through Jesus. Amen!

MINORITY OR MAJORITY?

1 John 4:4

"The one who is in you is greater than the one who is in the world."

8

FEBRUARY

David Watson wrote, "Christians in the West have largely neglected what it means to be a disciple of Christ. The vast majority of western Christians are church members, pew fillers, hymn singers, sermon tasters, Bible readers, even born-again believers or Spirit-filled charismatics, but not true disciples of Jesus."

That is not a majority I aspire to be a part of! However, it's usually more comfortable to be in the majority. Standing out from the crowd on a matter of principle or faith is difficult. You need to be brave and prepared to face scorn and rejection, but it is hopefully some consolation to know that many people who prefer to remain in the crowd are lost in the crowd! My remarkable granny said to me once, "Don't worry about being in the minority. If God's with you, he makes you the majority!" Or, as Paul wrote, "If God is for us, who can be against us?"

The fact is, you are most likely in the minority as a follower of Jesus once you step out of your front door each morning. But don't worry. It is minorities who end up transforming situations, not majorities. The minority sect of the first century exploded all across the Roman Empire. The small and ridiculed Clapham Sect (which included Wilberforce) transformed the sociological landscape of Britain through their dogged determination to infuse godly standards in society. They lived out the truth that anthropologist Margaret Mead famously voiced, "Never doubt that a small group of thoughtful, committed citizens can change the world. Indeed, it is the only thing that ever has."

Lord God, I choose today to be a true disciple of Jesus, to proudly align myself with you, happy to be in the minority knowing that you are with me. Amen!

Matthew 25:12, 41

"I tell you the truth, I don't know you… Depart from me, you who are cursed."

SHEEP OR GOATS?

During the Soviet era when the church endured fierce persecution, a secret prayer meeting was underway. Suddenly, the doors burst open, and two fully armed guards shouted at those present: "Get out of this place if you're not willing to die for your faith." About half of the professing Christians got up and left, fleeing to safety. Once the doors were closed again, the guards put down their guns, took off their coats and hats, sat down, and said, "Praise the Lord! We were just sorting out the sheep from the goats before we'd risk fellowship!"

Sheep and goats don't always look that different, particularly in warmer climes where sheep are shorn of their wool all the time due to the heat. In Jesus' parable of the sheep and the goats, he differentiates them based on their response to when he (or one of the least of these) was hungry, thirsty, a stranger, needing clothes, or in prison – i.e. based on what they did.

In Matthew 7:15–23, he talks about what fruit a tree bears, and then warns his listeners that only those who do the will of his father will enter heaven. "Many will say to me on that day 'Lord, Lord,… did we not in your name drive out demons…" Then I will tell them plainly, 'I never knew you. Away from me, you evildoers!'"

His words may sound incredibly harsh and shocking, but it shows how important to Jesus it is that we don't just talk a good game, but are willing to live out our words. There's always a cost to getting our hands dirty. How are you doing on that level? You will most definitely come across someone who needs your help today. Too busy? Watch out!

Lord, help me to walk the walk and not just talk the talk today. Amen!

ASSURANCE OR UNCERTAINTY?

1 John 5:13

"I have written these things to you who believe in the name of the Son of God so that you may know you have eternal life."

Under the old covenant there was no assurance of forgiveness, because there were endless sacrifices for sin. Every year 113 bullocks, 37 rams, 30 goats, and 1,093 lambs were sacrificed at the temple in Jerusalem. However, in Hebrews 10:12 we read that when "this priest (Jesus) had offered for all time *one* sacrifice for sins, he sat down at the right hand of God". Under the old covenant, God was saying essentially: "If you keep my laws, I will bless you", whereas under the new covenant, he says: "You can't keep my laws, therefore I offer you salvation as a free gift through Jesus."

This central biblical truth is profoundly liberating. How many of us live under crushing burdens of guilt because we fail to meet even our own standards, let alone God's? One lady couldn't forgive herself and her counsellor took her to 1 John 1:7, which says that "the blood of Jesus purifies us from *all* sin." She read the verse aloud but unconsciously left out the "all". He made her repeat it several times, but each time she missed the "all". When he highlighted it, she paused and then screamed with delight as the penny truly dropped for her.

After Sunday school a young boy said to his father, "Do you know what God can't see?"

"God can see everything, son."

"No," his son replied, "God cannot see my sins when they are covered by the blood of Jesus."

God loves us to bits. It's no namby-pamby touchy-feely love, it's the tested costly love that sent his Son to the cross for us, to give us *total* assurance that he accepts us *fully*, forgiving us *all* our sin. Live in that glorious freedom today!

Thank you Jesus! I choose today to live in the total freedom you bought for me. Amen!

Matthew 5:29

"If your right eye causes you to sin, gouge it out."

TOLERATE OR OBLITERATE?

Two American women were returning from their vacation across the Mexican border when they saw a sick animal in the ditch beside their car. They had a soft spot for the poor little Chihuahua, so they risked smuggling it under a blanket in the back seat. Arriving home, one of them nursed it tenderly and even allowed it to sleep in bed with her so she could stroke and reassure it intermittently. The following morning, she took it to the vet, only to be told that it wasn't a cute little dog but a Mexican water rat dying of rabies!

That's a great urban legend! Maybe it didn't literally happen, but it illustrates an important truth. It's tragic how often we don't treat sin for what it is. We fool around, compromise, self-justify, treating sin as if it is a puppy to be played with, when in fact we've allowed ourselves to get in bed with a deadly rat. Sin can appear to be fun, but actually it's a sugar-coated venom.

Our relativist culture has redefined sin so as to justify almost anything – so long as it doesn't harm anyone else. How affected have you been by that lie? How sensitive are you to the Holy Spirit? What compromise are you justifying? I remember hating a friend who quoted the following verse to me, because he knew I was heading off to have sex with my girlfriend: "But among you there must not be even a hint of sexual immorality, or of any kind of impurity, or of greed, because these are improper for God's holy people" (Ephesians 5:3).

I've been very honest there. Will you be too? We're not talking only sex, as the verse says. And it's very exacting. It talks about there not being even a "hint" of those things. God's grace for us is free, but it's not cheap. Let's be ruthless with sin. Time for heart surgery?

God, forgive me for times when I've tolerated sin in my life. I choose today to deal ruthlessly with it. Amen!

MENTAL ASSENT OR ACTIVE ENGAGEMENT?

James 1:22

"Do not merely listen to the word, and so deceive yourselves. Do what it says."

A little fellow in the ghetto was getting teased by an older boy: "If God loves you, why doesn't he take care of you? Why doesn't God tell someone to bring you shoes and a warm coat and better food?" The little lad thought for a moment before replying with tears welling up in his eyes: "I guess he does tell somebody, but somebody forgets."

Shane Claiborne did a survey on people's misconceptions of Jesus. He asked participants who claimed to be "strong followers of Jesus" whether Jesus spent time with the poor. Nearly 80 per cent said he did. Later in the survey, he sneaked in another question to those same people. Did *they* spend time with the poor? Less than 2 per cent said they did. He concluded:

> *I learned a powerful lesson: we can admire and worship Jesus without doing what he did. We can applaud what he preached and stood for without caring about the same things. We can adore his cross without taking up ours. I had come to see that the great tragedy in the Church is not that rich Christians do not care about the poor but that rich Christians do not know the poor.*

Many a church pastor knows about the 80–20 rule. Briefly stated, 20 per cent of your congregation does 80 per cent of the work. He might be too charitable to say that 20 per cent of his people cause 80 per cent of his headaches as well! Here's a direct invitation to be a positive member of the 20 per cent club. We may lead busy lives with multiple demands on our time, so all the more we need to be strategic and disciplined to prioritize what we do. What will that look like for you?

Lord, I agree today that something needs to be done, and that I'll be the somebody to do it. Amen!

1 Corinthians 7:23

"You were bought at a price."

FREE OR CHEAP?

The danger of receiving something for free is that you don't value it. During the war out here, churches were looted for the metal sheeting that made up their roofs. Interestingly, where the sheets had been donated, the local population allowed the looting to take place; whereas where the locals had bought those sheets sacrificially, they resisted the looting. Unless you contribute to the cost of something, you don't treasure it.

When it comes to our salvation, because we didn't contribute to the cost, the danger is that likewise we can easily not value it. If that happens, the free gift is cheapened. Similarly it is cheapened if we reduce the gospel to forgiveness of sins alone or limit salvation to personal fire insurance against hell.

David Pawson writes, "Salvation may be free, but it is not cheap, either for the Lord or us. For him, the cost was the death of his only Son on a cross. For us it is to take up the cross daily and follow him. So the entrance fee is nothing, but the annual subscription is everything."

C.T. Studd understood that as he set off to lay down his life across the lake from where I am now. He reasoned, "If Jesus Christ is God and died for me, then no sacrifice can be too great for me to make for him." Free grace, but not cheap. Or maybe "cheap grace" would be better referred to as "costly faithlessness".

Have we lowered the bar and diluted the gospel? I fear we're busy proving to the world that they can have all the benefits of the gospel without any inconvenience to their way of life. We can't afford to craft ourselves a more comfortable cross.

Father, forgive me where I've opted for cheap grace. Fill me afresh with gratitude and zeal to live and work for your praise and glory. Amen!

STRESSED OR SERENE?

Matthew 6:27

"Who of you by worrying can add a single hour to his life?"

14

FEBRUARY

The following statistics were published in a business magazine. Stress management experts say that only 2 per cent of our "worrying time" is spent on things that might actually be helped by worrying. The figures below illustrate how the other 98 per cent of this time is spent:

- 40 per cent on things that never happen;
- 35 per cent on things that can't be changed;
- 15 per cent on things that turn out better than expected;
- 8 per cent on useless, petty worries.

So honestly, take the advice from the film *The Lion King*: "Hakuna matata!" That's right: "Ain't no worries for the rest of your days. It's a problem-free philosophy, hakuna matata!" Jesus repeatedly tells us not to worry – three times in Matthew 6 alone – be it worries about food, clothing, or the future. He doesn't belittle our problems, but he calls us deeper into trust. Worries can be transformed into opportunities to grow as we hand them over to God in prayer.

Otherwise, worry becomes the darkroom in which negative thoughts can develop and, as Corrie Ten Boom put it, "Worry does not empty tomorrow of sorrow; but it empties today of strength." Away with stress, in with serenity! And I'm preaching that to myself. I have plenty to get stressed about. I have several hundred people whose very livelihood and families look to me. There is huge pressure involved. But God is Jehovah Jireh, I am not!

One thing I do when I'm stressed might work for you. When I come home, I consciously touch my "worry tree" – could be any old tree, bush, or anything else for that matter – before entering the house. I pray and leave my worries on that tree. That way I can be free to enjoy the family. And then you know what? When I come back out the next morning to pick up those worries again, usually they're not quite as heavy. Could that work for you? Just an idea.

Lord, I choose today to cast all my anxieties on you, because you care for me. Amen!

DISTANT OR INCARNATE?

John 1:14

"The Word became flesh and made his dwelling among us. We have seen his glory."

Søren Kierkegaard tells the story of a prince who fell madly in love with a beautiful peasant maiden in his kingdom. He wanted to marry her, but how? He could order her to marry him, but that coercion would not be love. He could make a grand entrance in his carriage, but her response then might simply be one of overwhelmed awe. So instead he gave up his kingly robe, moved into her village, and lived as a peasant. In time she grew to love him for who he was and because he had first loved her.

This story simply and beautifully illustrates the incarnation. God came and lived among us. Why is that so important? Because it shows that God is with us, he's on our side, and he loves us. And, further, it gives us a glimpse into the mind of God. When we're asked what God is like, we can point to the person of Jesus. The Creator of the whole universe was willing to enter into our world, speak our language, eat our food, share our suffering. The reason? So that you, I, our colleagues, and friends might be rescued and come to a living relationship with him.

God is not distant. One of his names is Emmanuel, which means "God with us". He sees your hopes and dreams, your disappointments and hurts, your fears and hang-ups. He knows the good and the bad about you. He wants to journey with you.

And in the physical absence of Jesus, he gives us the privilege and responsibility to be his hands and feet in our broken world – to incarnate his message of love, acceptance, mercy and sacrifice. Think how you might do that today.

Heavenly Father, thank you that you chose to live with me. I choose today to live with you. Amen!

ACTION OR INACTION?

Ephesians 5:15, 16

"Be very careful, then, how you live... making the most of every opportunity."

16

FEBRUARY

One of my life goals is to live such that I don't have any significant regrets at the end of my life. Two Cornell psychologists called Gilovic and Medvec did some detailed research on the relationship between time as a key factor in regrets. We tend to regret our actions in the short term, whereas in the long term we regret our inactions. So, for example, in the short term a person might regret getting drunk last night and saying what they did; but more profoundly, in the long term they regret not reconciling with their father before he died.

Gilovic and Medvec's study found that in an average week, the number of action regrets was slightly higher than inaction regrets: 53 per cent to 47 per cent. However, when people looked back at end of their lives, inaction outnumbered action regrets by 84 per cent to 16 per cent. So, because many of us are totally risk-averse, we might reach the end of our lives having made only few mistakes but with huge regrets at the risks we didn't take.

Don Herold wrote the following late in life:

> *If I had my life to live over again, I'd try to make more mistakes next time. I would relax, I would limber up, I would be sillier than I have been this trip. I would take more trips. I would be crazier. I would climb more mountains, swim more rivers, and watch more sunsets. I would eat more ice cream and less beans. If I had to do it over again I would go places, do things, and travel lighter. I would ride on more merry-go-rounds. I'd pick more daisies.*

How about you? Take some time to reflect on this today – and then choose to do something about it.

Lord, help me make the most of every opportunity that comes my way today. Amen!

Isaiah 6:8

"Whom shall I send? And who will go for us?"

SPEAK UP OR SHUT UP?

I remember being on a train once and a drunk man urinated in the corner. Everyone kept their eyes down and pretended to ignore it. I was disgusted and challenged him. He got extremely aggressive. It was a difficult situation to deal with, and as I left the train, I felt frustrated because although I wanted him to be punished, I didn't want my ongoing journey to be inconvenienced, so I let him get away with it. In a small way, I've reflected on that incident many times. I spoke up, but didn't follow through, so I might just as well have shut up.

There are many people who are weak and marginalized who can't speak up for themselves. There are many situations that need challenging. There are injustices and abuses of power that need campaigning about – both in our nation and overseas.

Edmund Burke's famous quote that "all it takes for evil to prosper is for good people to do nothing" has never been more true.

Martin Niemöller was a pastor in the German Confessing Church who spent seven years in a concentration camp. He was attributed with writing:

First they came for the communists, and I did not speak out
because I was not a communist.
Then they came for the socialists, and I did not speak out
because I was not a socialist.
Then they came for the trade unionists, and I did not speak out
because I was not a trade unionist.
Then they came for the Jews, and I did not speak out
because I was not a Jew.
Then they came for me, and there was no one left to speak out for me.

Who might you speak up for today? Pick a fight, a cause, a campaign. Don't just be a good person who does nothing.

Lord, thank you that you spoke up loud and clear for humanity in being willing to die on the cross for us. May we similarly speak up and actively get involved in your kingdom causes. Amen!

DULLNESS OR ASTONISHMENT?

Psalm 139:6

"Such knowledge is too wonderful for me, too lofty for me to attain."

Before going to university, I spent my year out teaching in a rural school in South Africa. I lived by myself in the middle of nowhere. Zebras and antelope would graze around my thatched rondavel. Baboons tore down my roof. I woke up with a rat in my armpit. Yet it was so beautiful and idyllic, and very quickly became completely normal for me. Visitors would come to stay and stand in awe at the beauty, but I had become dull to it. Familiarity had bred contempt.

I think sometimes something similar happens in our relationship with Jesus. Robert Capon explores this brilliantly:

> *We are in a war between dullness and astonishment. The most critical issue facing Christians is not abortion, pornography, the disintegration of the family, moral absolutes, MTV, drugs, racism, sexuality or school prayer. The critical issue is dullness. We have lost our astonishment. The good news is no longer good news, it is okay news. Christianity is no longer life-changing, it is life-enhancing. Jesus doesn't change people into wide-eyed radicals anymore; he changes them into "nice people". If Christianity is simply about being nice, I'm not interested.*
>
> *What happened to radical Christianity, the un-nice brand of Christianity that turned the world upside down? What happened to the kind of Christians who were filled with passion and gratitude and who every day were unable to get over the grace of God? I'm ready for a Christianity that "ruins" my life, that captures my heart and makes me uncomfortable. I want to be filled with an astonishment which is so captivating that I am considered wild and unpredictable and… well… dangerous. I want a faith that is considered "dangerous" by our predictable and monotonous culture.*

God, rid me of dullness, replace it with astonishment, and recapture in me a fire to be who you've called me to be today. Amen!

Job 19:25

"I know that my Redeemer lives, and that in the end he will stand upon the earth."

CERTAINTY OR AMBIGUITY?

Job was a righteous man, but found all his blessings wrenched away from him – his health, his wealth, and his children. Amidst conflicting accusations from his so-called friends, he knew how to wrestle with ambiguity, while clinging to the certainty of God's sovereignty. "I know that my Redeemer lives... And after my skin has been destroyed, yet in my flesh I will see God... How my heart yearns within me!" (Job 19:25–27)

U2's Bono once said:

> *Belief and confusion are not mutually exclusive; I believe that belief gives you a direction in the confusion. But you don't see the full picture. That's the point. That's what faith is – you can't see it. It comes back to instinct. Faith is just up the street. Faith and instinct, you can't just rely on them. You have to beat them up. You have to pummel them to make sure they can withstand it, to make sure they can be trusted."*

Has your faith been pummelled, like Job's? If you've followed Christ for any length of time, your earlier certainties will no doubt have been at the very least seriously shaken and challenged. Our self-assured dogmas are easily maintained until death, sickness, or some other impostor rocks our tidy conclusions. Maybe as we move towards spiritual maturity, we come to the same conclusion as Job that it's less about possessions, order and success, and more about an ability to live with uncertainty, loss and mess?

Professor Matt Cartmill quipped: "As an adolescent I aspired to lasting fame, I craved factual certainty, and I thirsted for a meaningful vision of human life – so I became a scientist. This is like becoming an archbishop so you can meet girls!"

Lord, grant me the certainty of Job as I live out life's ambiguities in my faith journey today. Amen!

SAVE OR LOSE?

Mark 8:35

"Whoever wants to save his life will lose it, but whoever loses his life for me and for the gospel will save it."

20

FEBRUARY

More than a millennium ago, the Celtic saint Columbanus pointed out that: "It is the end of the road that travellers look for and desire, and because we are travellers and pilgrims through this world, it is the road's end that we should always be thinking about." He concluded with an exhortation: "Don't let us love the road rather than the land to which it leads, lest we lose our homeland altogether."

How are we going to live? There are two approaches to life: playing to win and playing not to lose. It sounds contradictory to what our verse is saying (which sounds contradictory itself!), but Jesus is saying that you play to win by losing yourself for him. If you play not to lose, you're trying to save yourself but are doomed in that pursuit.

Dietrich Bonhoeffer left the safety of exile in America to return to his native Germany and try to overthrow Hitler. He was eventually caught and executed. What he'd written a few years earlier in *The Cost of Discipleship* became his own authentic reality:

> *Suffering is the badge of true discipleship. The disciple is not above his master… That is why Luther reckoned suffering among the marks of the true church… if we refuse to take up our cross and submit to suffering and rejection at the hands of men, we forfeit our fellowship with Christ and have ceased to follow him. But if we lose our lives in his service and carry our cross, we shall find our lives again in the fellowship of the cross with Christ.*

Are you playing to win, or playing not to lose? What does that mean in light of Jesus' words in Mark 8:35, and the words of Columbanus and Bonhoeffer?

Lord, I choose to lose my life for you today. Amen!

Psalm 27:14

"Wait for the Lord; be strong and take heart and wait for the Lord."

DELAY OR DENIAL?

I'm sure you've had times of desperately crying out to God for something, and there's been nothing but resounding silence. Sometimes we've simply asked for the wrong thing, and so the answer's no. Sometimes we're asked for the right thing and there's been an immediate yes. The difficulty comes when we think we've asked for the right thing but it seems like the answer thus far is no. Well, with God, delay is not always denial.

Picture Columbus: somewhere in the Atlantic Ocean, with a restive crew threatening mutiny, and no end in sight week after week. Most of that famous voyage was mired in problems. He could have given up, but at the end of each day, after much anguished praying, he penned his final log entry: "Today we moved *westward*!" He must have been tempted to give up, but eventually he made it. Delay is not always denial.

Many supermarket tomatoes are picked completely green and unripe so they won't bruise, and then are sprayed with carbon dioxide to turn them instantly red just before they're put on display. In appearance they're fine, but a gas-ripened tomato is no match for one that has been allowed to mature slowly and naturally. We worry how fast we can grow, while God is much more concerned with healthy growth.

Similarly when God wants to make a mushroom, he does it overnight, but with oaks, he grows them over a hundred years. Maybe today you need to remember how far you've come, not just how far you have to go. We want immediate fruit in our lives, but healthy growth is usually gradual growth.

Lord God Almighty, thank you that you know what's best for me. Guide me as I seek to do your will today. May I know when to wrestle through in prayer and know when to let go. Amen!

SEEKER OR FINDER?

Psalm 63:1

"O God, you are my God, earnestly I seek you."

My six-year-old went to his first football lesson and came back saying: "Daddy, I've learned to play football now. I don't need any more lessons." He thought he'd arrived because he could connect his foot to the ball. He didn't know there was a little more to it than that. He needed to go a whole lot deeper.

Some people can be like that with God as well. Tozer warns of us being among the number of those who think they've got it nailed. Whereas

> *[the apostle] Paul was a seeker and a finder and a seeker still, they seek and find and seek no more. After "accepting" Christ they tend to substitute logic for life and doctrine for experience. For them the truth becomes a veil to hide the face of God; for Paul it was a door into his very Presence. Paul's spirit was that of the loving explorer. He was a prospector among the hills of God searching for the gold of personal spiritual acquaintance.*

That last paragraph is worth re-reading. Paul alluded to heavenly visions that he shouldn't even share with people (2 Corinthians 12:2), such was his privileged and intimate relationship with Jesus, and yet he still prayed "I want to know Christ." Of course he already knew him, but how much deeper there was to go in that experiential knowledge!

Sadly I sometimes have to question how much of my spiritual activity boils down to managing God instead of seeking him. How about you? And for some of us, the turning point of our lives will come when we stop seeking the God we want, and start seeking the God who is.

So take heart today! God wants to be found. He promises we can find him. As Jeremiah 29:13 says: "You will seek me and find me when you seek me with all your heart."

Lord, whatever I go through today, I choose to seek you with all my heart. Amen!

VISIBLE LOVE OR EMPTY WORDS?

James 2:14

"What good is it if a man claims to have faith but has no deeds?"

The history of individual lives, families, and even whole communities often swings on seeing the authentic gospel fleshed out in real life.

In 1883, a young clergyman called Joe Roberts went to work with the Indians of Wyoming. Things were tense because the son of Chief Washakie had recently been shot by a soldier in an altercation. Washakie had vowed to kill the first white man he met. Seeking to nip a potentially long-running feud in the bud, Roberts hiked fifteen miles into the mountains to Washakie's tepee, opened his shirt, and called out, "I have heard of your vow. The other white men have families, but I am alone. Kill me instead." The chief couldn't believe Roberts's courage, so invited him in to talk. By the time Roberts left a few hours later, the chief of the Shoshones had renounced his vow to kill and resolved instead to become a follower of Christ. Soon other Shoshones took the same step. They had seen love in action.

People are watching us. Actions invariably do speak louder than words. Empty words are very cheap. Love is never invisible in its outworking. The unreached tribal community we have worked with in Burundi was strongly resistant to hearing about Jesus. So we didn't preach. We asked them what they needed, and responded to those needs. Six months later, the previously antagonistic leader said, "I've seen enough, I want your Jesus." Love in action is a powerful thing.

Offering to pray for someone is OK, but how about following through beyond prayer? Expressing sympathy is one thing, but putting yourself out for someone speaks a lot louder. Most days we will come across someone who needs a listening ear or a helping hand. Let's not be too busy for them today.

Lord, please use me today to be the gospel to someone, in Jesus' name. Amen!

LIPS OR HEART?

Mark 7:7

"These people honour me with their lips but their hearts are far from me."

Jesus reserved his harshest words for those who should have known better – the religious establishment – calling them among other things a "brood of vipers". You can't expect those on the outside to behave any better if they don't acknowledge a higher power, but for those of us who do, we are answerable and accountable to God. Sadly many of us pay lip service to the King of Kings while giving every other kind of service to the Prince of this World.

That is what Brennan Manning meant when he wrote: "The greatest single cause of atheism in the world today is Christians who acknowledge Jesus with their lips and walk out the door and deny him by their lifestyle… That is what an unbelieving world simply finds unbelievable."

One of the most memorable and painful times the Lord spoke to me was through a friend of mine after he had heard me preach. He said: "The content may have been good, but I couldn't really listen to what you were saying because I know what you are really like." Ouch, that cut deep…

How about you? Most people we interact with who don't already know Jesus are never going to read the Bible – or if you like, the only "Bible" they're going to read is you. Nobody likes a hypocrite, and most people can spot a fraud pretty quickly. If there are areas of your life that are inconsistent with what you believe deep down, don't harden your heart. Face up to them today, keep short accounts, confess, and resolve to be true to your convictions. Authenticity is very attractive.

Hebrews 4:12 says that the Word of God is "sharper than any double-edged sword… and it judges the thoughts and attitudes of the heart". We can fool others, but God sees our heart. Be true to him today.

Lord, I choose to honour you with both my lips and my heart today. Amen!

Philippians 3:8

"I consider everything a loss compared to the surpassing greatness of knowing Christ Jesus my Lord."

PRIVILEGE OR SACRIFICE?

In Korea during the last century, a businessman and a missionary were driving along together. As they passed by a field, the trader saw an old man with his son dragging a plough painstakingly through the earth, and exclaimed, "Wow, these folks are so desperately poor." The missionary replied, "Yes, those two men are believers. During the church building project, they were committed to contributing something towards it, but they didn't have any money. So they sold their one and only ox and gave the proceeds to the church. This harvest they're having to pull the plough themselves." The businessman was silent for a moment. Then he said, "That must have been a real sacrifice." The missionary replied, "Yes, but they didn't call it that, because they considered themselves fortunate to have an ox to sell."

People often say to me how hard it must be to lay so much down to go to Africa. I find I can echo David Livingstone's words from his journal:

> *People talk of the sacrifice I have made in spending so much of my life in Africa. Can that be called a sacrifice which is simply paying back a small part of the great debt owing to our God, which we can never repay? Is that a sacrifice which brings its own blest reward in healthful activity, the consciousness of doing good, peace of mind and a bright hope of glorious destiny hereafter? Away with the word in such a view and with such a thought! It is emphatically no sacrifice. Say rather it is a privilege.*

Do you see your journey with Jesus as a privilege or a sacrifice today? Maybe a bit of both. There is most definitely a cost, but the benefits are even greater. So whatever you're going through with Jesus, know that it's worth struggle.

Lord, I choose a positive attitude today, knowing that with you I'll get through whatever comes at me. Amen!

HARBOUR OR HIGH SEAS?

Galatians 5:25

"Let us keep in step with the Spirit."

The Spirit is always on the move. We can easily run ahead or lag behind, so the challenge for us is to keep in step with him. Because most of us want to be in control and fear change, more often than not our greater danger is to lag behind and play it safe.

However, although a ship may be safe in the harbour, to fulfil its purpose it has to take on the high seas; and no new land was ever discovered without the ship's commander agreeing to lose sight of the shore he'd embarked from. Anticipating future regret, Mark Twain warned us: "Twenty years from now you will be more disappointed by the things that you didn't do than by the ones you did do. So throw off the bowlines. Sail away from the safe harbour. Catch the trade winds in your sails. Explore. Dream. Discover."

A survey was taken of people who were over 95 years old. They were asked an open-ended question: if you could live your life over again, what would you do differently? The three most common replies were:

1. *If I could live my life over again, I would reflect more.*
2. *I would risk more.*
3. *I would do more things that would live on after I'm dead.*

So let's learn some lessons from them! We must choose freedom from our natural inclination towards safe convention. We don't want to look back with regret at what could have been. Just after his college days at Cambridge, the journalist Malcolm Muggeridge scribbled his own epitaph to a fellow student: "Here lieth one whose soul sometimes burned with great longings, to whom sometimes the curtain of the Infinite was opened just a little, but who lacked the guts to make any use of it." What tragic candour!

Lord, give me both the wisdom and the guts to keep in step with your Spirit today. Amen!

Genesis 50:20

"Joseph said to his brothers, 'You intended to harm me, but God intended it for good to accomplish what is now being done.'"

STUMBLING BLOCK OR STEPPING STONE?

Bad experiences, such as Joseph's, don't have to define us – or more positively, they can be redeemed for God's glory. Our most famous old boy at school was Winston Churchill. Once he was asked by a journalist in an interview what experience had best equipped him to deal with Hitler leading up to and during the Second World War. To the interviewer's amazement, Churchill recalled the time he'd been forced to repeat a year at school:

"You mean you failed a year at school?"

"I never failed anything. I was given a second opportunity to get it right."

As John Ortberg writes, "Failure is not an event, but rather a judgment about an event. Failure is not something that happens to us or a label we attach to things. It is a way we think about outcomes."

Was Winston Churchill a failure? Or how about Hillary? Ortberg continues:

> *Sir Edmund Hillary made several unsuccessful attempts at scaling Mount Everest before he finally succeeded. After one attempt he stood at the base of the giant mountain and shook his fist at it. "I'll defeat you yet," he said in defiance. "Because you're as big as you're going to get – but I'm still growing."*
>
> *Every time Hillary climbed, he failed. And every time he failed, he learned. And every time he learned, he grew and tried again. And one day he didn't fail.*

So we embrace the fact that progress in any sphere comes through repeated attempts – "failures" – followed by renewed and modified approaches. Maybe for years you've defined yourself – or something you did – as a failure and God wants you to be released to reappraise that experience through a new lens today. Instead of seeing apparent failures as stumbling blocks, they can be transformed into stepping stones.

Lord, help me to transform former failures into victories for your glory. Amen!

WADDLE OR FLY?

Mark 10:27

Jesus said to his disciples, "With man this is impossible, but not with God; all things are possible with God."

28

FEBRUARY

You and I, we follow the God of the impossible. For me, a mere man, with all my hang-ups and weaknesses, my dreams will be impossible to fulfil. But not for God – with him all things are possible! So we have a realistic vision of who we are, but also a real vision of who the LORD is.

Have you heard the parable of the waddling ducks? In a certain town of ducks, each Sunday morning all the ducks waddle out of their homes and waddle down the road into church. They waddle towards their favoured pews and sit down. The duck choir waddles in and performs a few duck songs, before the pastor duck waddles to the pulpit and delivers a thundering exhortation: "Dear ducks, God has given each one of us wings! These wings enable us to fly. Yes, we can fly anywhere, anytime. Our Scriptures even tell us we can soar on wings like eagles. Nothing can hold us back. So let's get out there and fly!" The gathered congregation of ducks give a hearty "Amen!"... and then waddle home.

Nobody wants to waddle home if there's the option to fly. And there is:

Jesus said,
"Come to the edge."
"It is too high."
"Come to the edge."
"We might fall."
"Come to the edge."
And they came
And he pushed them
And they flew.

So here's to flying today, whatever that will look like! It will mean standing firm on the promises of God and then launching out into the purposes of God. Remember, "the One who calls you is *faithful*, and *he will do it*." (1 Thessalonians 5:24)

Lord, as I hesitate on the edge, help me to trust you today, and fly. Amen!

James 5:17

"The prayer of a righteous man is powerful and effective."

POWERFUL OR PUNY?

Andrew Murray wrote: "Jesus never taught his disciples how to preach, only how to pray. To know how to speak to God is more than knowing how to speak to man. Power with God is the first thing, not power with men. Jesus loves to teach us how to pray."

Robert Murray McCheyne grasped the above. He was a young Scotsman who died in his prime, aged twenty-nine, but not before shaking his beloved homeland. Many people wanted to know the secret behind his spiritual power. One such enquirer embarked on a pilgrimage to McCheyne's church, and asked the sexton, "Would you mind telling me what was the secret behind Robert Murray McCheyne's work?" So the sexton led him into McCheyne's former study and invited him to be seated in the great man's chair. The sexton then said plainly: "Now drop your head on that book and weep, for that's what Robert Murray McCheyne always did before he preached."

How is your prayer life going? Most of us find it discouraging to analyse our prayer lives. Don't be. It's self-defeating. Just resolve today to involve God in everything you do: the mundane, the important, work and play, in your problems and in your planning. Pray for yourself, for those you love, for those you come across. Worship him, seek his forgiveness, thank him for all his gifts, ask him for what you need.

C.H. Spurgeon once said, "Prayer pulls the rope down below and the great bell rings above in the ears of God. Some scarcely stir the bell, for they pray so languidly; others give only an occasional jerk at the rope. But he who communicates with heaven is the man who grasps the rope boldly and pulls continuously with all his might."

Lord, it's time for me to grasp the rope boldly! Teach me to pray. Amen!

Genesis 32:26

"Jacob replied, 'I will not let go unless you bless me.'"

INSIDE OR OUTSIDE?

I sometimes wonder how many blessings I might have missed out on because I let go too soon and didn't fight long enough. Jacob fought with God, and picked up a limp in the process, but it was worth it for the incomparable blessing he received.

We go through different stages in our lives. There are times when I've been both hungrier and less hungry for God than right now – that's the nature of an undulating journey. But today I want to invite you to step inside the circle. You can't do it in a few minutes like one of these daily devotionals. That would be undervaluing the experience. This is an invitation to encounter God in unspeakable intimacy and power. What do I mean by stepping inside the circle? Read on:

This man was born in a gypsy tent, of humble origins, and yet ended up being invited to the White House by two presidents. Rodney "Gypsy" Smith came into the world in 1860 in Epping Forest, just outside London. Forty-five times he crossed the Atlantic to preach the gospel to millions of people on both sides. His passion was almost unparalleled, and there was great fruit in what he did. What was his secret? Private prayer. His praying was even more powerful than his preaching.

A delegation once came to him to enquire how they might experience personal and mass revival as he had. They wanted to be used the way Gypsy was. Without hesitating, he said, "Go home. Lock yourself in your room. Kneel down in the middle of the floor, and with a piece of chalk draw a circle round yourself. There, on your knees, pray fervently and brokenly that God would start a revival within that chalk circle."

Too busy? Too dry? Too battered? Too sinful? He's heard all the excuses and is still inviting you. Step inside!

Lord, this is so much more than a one-line prayer…

VELVET HATS OR CRASH HELMETS?

Acts 1:8

*"You will receive power (*dynamis*) when the Holy Spirit comes, and you will be my witnesses… to the ends of the earth."*

2 MARCH

Dynamis is Greek for power. Obviously it's where we get the word "dynamite" from. At Pentecost, a ragtag, fearful bunch of disciples were transformed into fearless, passionate firebrands who went out and laid their lives down in costly surrender. Within three centuries, the seemingly impregnable Roman Empire had been brought to its knees by the explosive *dynamis* of the gospel.

Two millennia later, that power is still available, and is certainly being manifest in some parts of the world, but sadly it seems to be less evident in our part of the world as much of church life has morphed into something quite removed from its initial expression. Be honest, did you go to church last Sunday with any significant expectations of encountering the Living God?

I love Annie Dillard's imagery in *Teaching a Stone to Talk*, as she describes the church coming together:

> *On the whole, I do not find Christians, outside of the catacombs, sufficiently sensible of conditions. Does anyone have the foggiest idea what sort of power we so blithely invoke? Or as I suspect, does no one believe a word of it? The churches are children playing on the floor with their chemistry sets, mixing up a batch of TNT to kill a Sunday morning. It is madness to wear ladies' velvet hats to church; we should all be wearing crash helmets. Ushers should issue life preservers and signal flares; they should lash us to our pews. For the sleeping God may wake someday and take offence, or the waking God may draw us out to where we can never return.*

I don't know about you, but I'm desperate for my own regular Pentecost, and for my church's. I'm sick to death of settling for low expectations so I don't end up disappointed. I need some serious *dynamis* in my life. How about you?

God Almighty, send us out in the power of your Spirit today. Amen!

Galatians 5:16

"So I say, live by the Spirit, and you will not gratify the desires of the sinful nature."

SPIRIT OR FLESH?

A cruel man with two dogs – one black and one white – organized regular fights between the two in a lucrative illegal operation in the backstreets of Birmingham. They were equally ferocious animals, and it was hard to predict which one would win each time. It seemed uncanny, though, week by week, that whenever more bets were placed on the white dog, then the black dog would win – and vice versa – which meant that the owner kept on making good profits. Eventually the punters discovered his secret. He starved both dogs all week, and once the bets were in, he quickly fed the dog that had less money placed on him.

There are two dogs slugging it out within each of us. Whichever one we feed the most will win.

Do read Galatians 5:16–26. Remember, what goes in comes out. If you feed the black dog, the sinful nature, it results in "impurity, hatred, discord, fits of rage, selfish ambition, envy, drunkenness" and the list goes on. The stakes are high because "those who live like this will not inherit the kingdom of God" (verse 21).

Feed the white dog, the Spirit, and here's the fruit: "love, joy, peace, patience, kindness, goodness, faithfulness, gentleness and self-control" (verse 22). It's a no-brainer in theory, but how about in practice? We don't want a list of "thou shalt nots", but when you realize that if you feed on trash, it's going to kill you, then here are a few questions:

- Is what I'm reading, listening to, or watching on TV good for my soul?
- Are my relationships with certain people dragging me down and making me compromise?
- Am I more attentive to the lies of the prevailing culture or to the voice of God in my spirit?

What are you feeding on? Which dog is in the ascendancy?

Lord, help me choose to live by the Spirit today. Amen!

BELIEF OR UNBELIEF?

Mark 9:24

"The boy's father exclaimed, 'I do believe; help me overcome my unbelief!'"

An Indian woman in South America was dying and a few Indian Christians and missionaries gathered to pray for her. She slipped into a coma and looked like a lost cause. When the missionaries had left, the Indian Christians organized another time of prayer for the woman, but this time without the missionaries. The sick woman was completely healed. Later, one missionary asked why they had not been invited to the second prayer meeting. "Because you don't really believe, and you cannot heal by God's power when you have unbelievers in the circle."

The missionary who shared this story, which highlighted his own weaknesses, later wrote, "I am now deeply aware that my western spiritless culture has given me an acute hearing defect to the voice of the Holy Spirit."

I can relate to him. I know God is Almighty, yet I'm so often cynical, doubting, and sceptical, as a by-product of my background. You too, no doubt. One of my friends was deaf, dumb, blind, and curled up in a ball for seven years. Everyone knew Agnes as the village vegetable. But one day some young people prayed for her. She uncurled herself, and regained her sight and hearing. She still couldn't speak, but joined the church choir by faith... and three weeks later, the Lord released her tongue to sing his praises, and she will not shut up! She's been on the radio telling the world.

You can't deny a story... or can you? Are you struggling to believe what happened to Agnes? I've got lots more of those stories. Or maybe they're reserved for Africa? No! God is the same the world over. Maybe the difference out here is there's more faith and expectancy and openness. There are no easy answers or guaranteed formulae, but the best place to start is where the boy's father quoted above did.

Lord, help me overcome my unbelief today. Amen!

Proverbs 16:3

"Commit to the Lord whatever you do and your plans will succeed."

PLANNED OR SPONTANEOUS?

Choosing to live life spontaneously sounds appealing, but it won't get you far. A fool or a sluggard fails to plan. He "does not plough in season; so at harvest time he looks but finds nothing" (Proverbs 20:4); he wastes his time, his talents, his treasure. God help us to avoid that trap!

I'm not naturally wired to write lists, mission statements, and goals, but I have come to see the benefits of them. The following research profoundly influenced me:

Only 3 per cent of people have goals and plans that are thought through and written down. Ten per cent of people do have goals and plans, but they're not written down, just stored somewhere in their brains. The remaining 87 per cent drift through life without clear goals or plans, being "spontaneous" if you like. They are reactive, allowing circumstances to dictate their behaviour rather than their behaviour being guided by clearly defined principles and goals.

Which group are you in? The mind-blowing discovery was that the 3 percenters achieved between 50 and 100 times in their lives what the... not the 87 percenters – that's what you're expecting to hear – but no, what the 10 percenters achieved. I have an issue with how they work out the 50 or 100 times greater achievement, but it makes an extremely powerful case for joining the 3 per cent club, if you want to make the most of your life.

As philosopher poet Ralph Waldo Emerson said: "The world makes way for the man who knows where he's going." I've got the best map to show me the way to go, so I'm confident I'll get there. How about you? Please don't be an 87 percenter, or even a 10 percenter. Join the 3 per cent club! Set aside some time to pray, seek God, and then commit your goals to writing, making them personal, specific, achievable (with him), measurable, and time-sensitive. Go for it!

Lord, I choose today to be a 3 percenter and to maximize my life for your glory. Amen!

REALITY OR VISION?

Philippians 1:6

"… being confident of this, that he who began a good work in you will carry it on to completion until the day of Christ Jesus."

The apostle Paul embraced both reality and vision as he wrote to his disciples. They were the unfinished article – that was the reality; but completion would come in God's time – that was the vision.

Sometimes it's discouraging to see where we've got to. We still struggle in the same areas and don't see the progress we'd hoped for. Or our life hasn't panned out as we'd wanted. Things shouldn't have turned out like this. Such thoughts are common, but take heart, God's not finished with you yet.

Don Quixote has a vision in the musical *The Man from La Mancha*. As he stands with his armour-bearer Sancho Panza, they observe a run-down shack in the distance. Don Quixote describes in extravagant terms the grandeur of the elegant castle that lies ahead of them. But Panza simply sees a run-down shack, and says so as he sees it. However, Don Quixote interrupts him sharply, "Stop! Stop right there! I won't allow your facts to interfere with my vision!"

If you're feeling down on yourself today, I suspect God would say the same as Don Quixote to you. There's your reality, and then there's his vision. Don't give up!

Helen Keller was both blind and deaf. In an interview she was asked if there could be anything worse than being blind. She replied: "Oh, yes! There is something worse than being blind. It's being able to see and not having any vision." Poor eyes may limit our sight, but worse than that, poor vision will limit our deeds.

Listen, you may have taken some knocks along the way, but thank God you can see – and beyond that, today, know that reality doesn't preclude vision. Don't allow poor vision to limit your deeds. He believes in you.

Thank you, Lord, that you will complete the good work you started in me. I choose to embrace your vision for my life today, even if it's not all clear to me right now. Amen!

FOCUSED OR DISTRACTED?

Luke 10:40

"But Martha was distracted by all the preparations that had to be made."

Martha's motives may have been laudable, but Jesus is clear that ultimately her sister got it right. The Son of God was in the house! Mary was focused on him; Martha was distracted from him.

It's very easy to lose focus with so many competing distractions in our lives. What is your focus?

A man was eager to try out his new hunting dog, so he took him out to track a bear. Once in the forest, the dog quickly picked up the bear's scent and sped away. Suddenly it detected the scent of a deer and veered off in a new direction. Again a new scent, that of rabbit, distracted the dog so it pounded off on a new path. Eventually the hunter caught up with his dog. It was barking triumphantly down the hole of a field mouse.

Can you relate to that hunting dog? You can start out with bold and noble intentions and then quickly get diverted to totally inconsequential activities. We want to keep Christ central in our lives but he so easily gets displaced.

A key life skill is to discern the difference between the urgent and the important (Martha again). Distraction is a common temptation to keep us from doing what is most important. Lesser things may be important, but we can easily find ourselves drifting aimlessly from one project to another. We need to be focused. For example, I don't have to answer my phone when it rings just at the critical moment when my friend is pouring his heart out to me. The former seems urgent, but the latter is actually more important. We need to learn to say "no" to things of lesser importance, or we'll never accomplish what we were made to do.

So back to that question: what is your focus today?

Lord, I choose to keep my focus on you today, and on what you want me to do. Amen!

LEGACY OR WASTE?

Romans 9:17

"I raised you up for this purpose, that I might display my power in you and that my name might be proclaimed in all the earth."

Evariste Galois might have been as well-known as Albert Einstein, so why is it that this is probably the first time you've ever heard of him? On 29 May 1832, Galois sat down and wrote a sixty-page mathematical masterpiece from start to finish without taking a single break. That one night's work contributed more to his field than most of his esteemed colleagues could ever hope to. "What he wrote in those desperate long hours before dawn," wrote Eric Bell, "will keep generations of mathematicians busy for hundreds of years."

Why did he do it? He wanted to leave a lasting legacy and he knew he might die the following morning. Pescheux d'Herbinville had challenged Galois to a duel. Foolish as it was, Galois wanted to defend his honour. He scrawled several times around his formulae: "I have not time, I have not time!" Shortly before dawn, he finished, went to meet his foe, and died of gunshot wounds shortly thereafter.

Galois' life embodied both legacy and waste. How much more he could have achieved… I can relate to his situation in that I've faced death many times in war-torn Burundi. Its prospect brings a sense of clear definition to life. Faced with time running out, you want to maximize every moment.

Hopefully you're not going to die anytime soon, but what legacy will you leave? What do you wish to be remembered for? Will you waste your life in pursuit of things that don't really matter? I want to leave a lasting legacy in the lives of others. How about you? Your answer to the above questions will most definitely affect how you choose to live today.

Lord, with your help I choose to invest my life in what amounts to a lasting legacy to the benefit of others. Amen!

SHREWD OR UNSCRUPULOUS?

Matthew 10:16

"I am sending you out like sheep among wolves. Therefore be as shrewd as snakes and innocent as doves."

After stopping at an illegal drinking den, a Zimbabwean bus driver was dismayed to discover that the twenty mental patients he was supposed to be transporting from Harare to Bulawayo had escaped. Not wanting to lose his job, he went to a nearby bus stop and offered everyone waiting there a free ride. He then promptly delivered the passengers to the mental hospital, telling the staff that the patients were very excitable and prone to strong delusions. It took three days before the whole mess got sorted out.

I don't think Jesus would endorse that highly creative piece of deception, but he might have laughed! In his tricky parable of the shrewd manager, Jesus commends the manager for somewhat questionable behaviour, "for the people of this world are more shrewd in dealing with their own kind than are the people of the light. I tell you, use worldly wealth to gain friends for yourselves, so that when it is gone, you will be welcomed into eternal dwellings" (Luke 16:8, 9). The manager was shrewd enough to use the means at his disposal to plan for his future well-being.

In David's song of praise to the Lord in 2 Samuel 22:27, he says: "To the pure you show yourself pure, but to the crooked you show yourself shrewd." If, as Jesus makes clear, we are sent out by him into the world like sheep among wolves, we desperately need his guidance in many ambiguous or downright potentially compromising situations so that we maintain our integrity ("innocent as doves") while exhibiting streetwise judgment ("shrewd as snakes"). It's a fine line sometimes. I've been there; no doubt you have as well.

Father God, I choose to be a person of integrity. Help me to live above reproach in difficult situations, and grant me the discernment to act in ways that always honour your name. Amen!

LIFE WASTED OR WELL SPENT?

1 Corinthians 15:58

"Always give yourselves fully to the work of the Lord, because you know that your labour in the Lord is not in vain."

10

MARCH

Last century a young man felt the call of God on his life to go to China. William Borden came from an affluent family and attended the prestigious Yale University. His prospects were as good as anyone's, and a successful career would surely follow in whichever field he set his mind to excel. So his family and friends were horrified when he chose to give up everything and head for China. "If you want to do good things, then surely there are plenty of needs here. Don't waste your life in a foreign country!" they remonstrated with him. But he knew what he had to do.

He boarded a ship for China, full of faith and hope. By the time he had reached Egypt, however, it was clear to everyone that he was a dying man. It was at this point that he might have slipped into self-pitying despair. Thoughts could have entered his mind such as, "What a waste of my life! They were right. I should have stayed back home and had a respectable life, enjoying my family and friends." But no, as he lay dying in the port of Suez, he scribbled a brief note to his loved ones in America which made a powerful epitaph – just six words: "No reserve, no retreat, no regrets."

What a waste, surely?! My grandfather was the top mathematician of his year at Cambridge University and was given the prestigious title "Senior Wrangler". His professors despaired when he went to the mission field rather than into academia: "What a waste of such a brain!" But his life's work touched maybe hundreds of thousands of people. And through the likes of him and Borden, hopefully we are inspired to give God our all.

Have you decided what you'll spend your life on?

Lord, I choose to spend and even "waste" my whole life on you today. Amen!

USELESS OR USEFUL?

Hebrews 11:8

"By faith Abraham… obeyed and went, even though he didn't know where he was going."

We all want a sense that our lives have purpose and direction, and that we are ultimately "useful" in some way. But what is the difference before God between being useful and useless? Oswald Chambers explains:

> *The aim of the missionary is to do God's will, not to be useful, not to win the heathen; he is useful and he does win the heathen, but that is not his aim. His aim is to do the will of his Lord… Notice God's unutterable waste of saints. According to the judgment of the world, God plants His saints in the most useless places [I think of friends slogging their guts out faithfully in the inner city, or in the Middle East, both with apparently very little tangible fruit over many years]. We say, "God intends me to be here because I am so useful". God puts His saints where they will glorify Him, and we are no judges at all of where that is.*

Hopefully that is a profoundly liberating reality. God calls us. We either respond or don't. If we do step out in obedience and faith, God delights in us, and the fruit in essence is irrelevant. It is his responsibility; the ball is in his court. We are doing our part. It doesn't mean following Jesus is easy. Sometimes the lack of fruit is deeply discouraging, but we plod on faithfully. Joss Billings wrote: "Consider the postage stamp; its usefulness consists in the ability to stick to one thing till it gets there!"

Abraham stepped out in obedience. He didn't know where he would end up. He teaches us in turn not to focus on "What is God's will for my life?" but rather "How can I give my life to fulfil God's will?"

Lord God, use me today, in whatever way you choose. Here I am, send me. Amen!

OBEDIENCE OR VICTORY?

2 John 6

"And this is love, that we walk in obedience to his commands."

12

MARCH

Jerry Bridges wrote:

> *God wants us to walk in obedience – not victory. Obedience is oriented toward God; victory is oriented toward self... This is not to say God doesn't want us to experience victory, but rather to emphasize that victory is a by-product of obedience. As we concentrate on living an obedient, holy life, we will certainly experience the joy of victory over sin.*

Jesus "became obedient to death, even death on a cross" (Philippians 2:8). Notice the order: his obedience came first, which then led to ultimate victory: "Although he was a son, he learned obedience from what he suffered and, once made perfect, he became the source of eternal salvation for all who obey him" (Hebrews 5:8, 9).

Our obedience to God is the very best proof of our love for him – nothing else. Obedience involves humility, submission, and acknowledgment that God calls the shots. "You are not your own; you were bought at a price. Therefore honour God with your body" (1 Corinthians 7:19, 20).

Be encouraged today if you've been getting discouraged after faithfully seeking to follow and obey the Lord. Bernard of Clairvaux wrote, "Only by desertion can we be defeated. With Christ and for Christ victory is certain. We can lose the victory by flight but not by death. Happy are you if you die in battle, for after death you will be crowned. But woe to you if by forsaking the battle you forfeit at once both the victory and the crown!"

Many a time I've been tempted to throw in the towel and settle for doomed compromise. Thankfully I've hung on thus far with no regrets. Although victory is assured, we're still in the thick of the battle. We need to just keep on that steady road of obedience. You can do it!

God, I choose to be steady on the long road of obedience today, wherever that may take me. Amen!

SHALLOW OR DEEP?

Psalm 42:7

"Deep calls to deep in the roar of your waterfalls; all your waves and breakers have swept over me."

Richard Foster writes:

> *Perhaps you have had the experience of hearing someone talk about faith and confidence and victory. In one sense all the words are right and the stories certainly sound good, but somehow something does not ring quite true. The problem is that you are listening to someone who is living on the fluff side of faith, someone who has not been baptized into the sacrament of suffering. Augustine notes wryly: "How deep in the deep are they who do not cry out of the deep?" But we have a Saviour who was "a man of sorrows, and acquainted with grief" (Isaiah 53:3). Jesus, we are told, "offered up prayers and supplication, with loud cries and tears" (Hebrews 5:7).*
>
> *I ask you: is the servant any better than the Master? There is a victory that is in Christ, but it goes through suffering, not around it. The triumphant note of the apostle Paul is no triumphalism. His "we are more than conquerors" comes on the other side of hardship and distress and persecution and famine and nakedness and peril and sword (Romans 8:35–39). The trenchant words of William Penn ring true to life: "No cross, no crown". For disciples of Jesus, suffering simply comes with the territory. Thomas Kelly notes: "God, out of the pattern of His own heart, has planted the cross along the road of holy obedience.*

It is my experience that God always answers in the deep, never in the shallows of our soul. I write this during an extended time of bed rest with something resembling chronic fatigue. It's no fun at all, but it draws me deeper, away from the shallows of my usual frenetic lifestyle.

So whatever negative stresses or strains you are under today, may you experience the positive flip side of them giving opportunity for you to be taken deeper with God himself.

Lord, I don't want to settle for the shallows. Take me deeper today. Amen!

SUCCESS OR FAILURE?

Daniel 4:29, 30

"As the king was walking on the roof of the royal palace of Babylon, he said, 'Is not this the great Babylon I have built as the royal residence, by my mighty power and for the glory of my majesty?'"

Those brazenly self-exalting words led to an immediate humbling as God struck Nebuchadnezzar with madness. The king learned the hard way that claiming the glory for himself rather than deflecting it to God was the pathway to ruin. His apparent success became cataclysmic failure as he was driven from his people and ate grass like cattle, until eventually his sanity was restored; and failure became success again as the humbled king now correctly attributed all glory to where it was due: "Now I praise and exalt and glorify the God of heaven, because everything he does is right and all his ways are just. And those who walk in pride he is also able to humble" (Daniel 4:37).

Rudyard Kipling's famous poem "If" was written as a birthday gift to his son. It includes the following lines:

If you can meet with Triumph and Disaster
And treat those two impostors just the same;
Yours is the Earth and everything that's in it.
And – which is more – you'll be a Man, my son!

Paul Tournier put it this way:

It is extremely difficult to define failure and success. The line between them is so elusive. Today's failure may turn out to be tomorrow's success and today's success, tomorrow's failure. The infinite value of Biblical perspective, is that it changes our attitude to the events of life… It is no longer a matter of whether they constitute success or failure, but rather what they mean in God's purpose.

So let's not worry about whether we're being successes or failures, let's concentrate on seeking God's purposes in all our activities.

Lord Jesus, I choose to be obedient to your call to walk a humble path today as I follow you. Amen!

Colossians 4:2

"Devote yourselves to prayer."

PRAYER OR ACTION?

When you are devoted to something, it means you give (devote) a lot of time to it, because it is very valuable and important to you. You can't be devoted to too many things, because our time is finite, but the apostle Paul makes clear that prayer should be one of those few things worthy of our devotion.

At the turn of the twentieth century, two pastors' wives were sitting mending their husbands' trousers. One of them said to the other: "My poor Andrew, he's totally discouraged in his work at church. He told me yesterday he was thinking of packing it all in." The other replied: "Well, for my husband it's the complete opposite. He's so vibrant and on fire, things are going great." There was a subdued stillness as they continued to mend their husbands' trousers – the first one patching the seat and the other the knees.

James O. Fraser was a remarkable man who became largely forgotten as he laboured for many years in isolation behind the great mountain ranges of China's far west. In areas steeped in witchcraft, he fasted and prayed for years with hardly any tangible spiritual fruit. Through dark times he contemplated suicide, but he clung on to God's promises, until the day came in God's time, and there was a massive outpouring of the Holy Spirit in revival power. In village after village where previously the inhabitants had been hardened to the gospel, families responded en masse.

As Fraser reflected on his work, he reached the following conclusion: "I used to think that prayer should have the first place and teaching the second. I now feel that prayer should have the first, second and third place, and teaching the fourth."

Do re-read the above and let the lesson sink in. How often I just get on with things without praying first! You're probably the same. God help us slow learners!

Lord, teach us to pray sufficiently before we act. Amen!

WILLING OR UNWILLING?

Romans 12:1

"Therefore, I urge you, brothers, in view of God's mercy, to offer your bodies as living sacrifices."

Some of you will have watched my thirteen short films on radical discipleship called "More Than Conquerors". One of the films involved me taking a lamb and a goat up a mountain to slaughter them as sacrifices to God. At the base of the mountain I tied some rope around each of their necks and started dragging them along with me. The purpose of the film was to show that we cannot be forced into sacrificing ourselves. It has to be, as our verse says, a freewill offering. Paul urges us "to offer" our bodies as living sacrifices.

I used the lamb and the goat to illustrate how traditionally when animals were sacrificed, some went willingly (the lamb), and some needed to be tied up (the goat). It soon became apparent as we headed up the mountain that I didn't need any rope for the lamb at all. I thought I'd need it to get him up the mountain when we were off camera and then just film him without any rope. But no, he simply pootled along next to me all the time while I had to keep on yanking the poor goat every step of the way. I won't ruin the climax for you, but it's worth watching right to the end. (See it at www.more-than-conquerors.com.)

Jesus was led like a lamb to the slaughter. Not a goat, but a lamb. He was the Lamb of God who came to take away the sins of the world. Similarly we are to offer ourselves willingly to God. He won't force us. This is the purest kind of voluntary service. So in our very self-consumed and self-obsessed age, here's a good question: is God going to help himself to me or am I so taken up with what I want to make of my life?

Lord, I'm willing. Have your way in my life today. Amen!

INNER OR OUTER?

1 Samuel 16:7

"The Lord does not look at the things man looks at. Man looks at the outward appearances but the Lord looks at the heart."

The website www.beautifulpeople.com was hacked recently. It's a website for beautiful people. There is a strict rating process enforced by members to keep ugly people out. The screening process failed for a short while because of the glitch, and 30,000 "ugly" people were wrongly admitted to the site. Managing Director Greg Hodge said: "We got suspicious when tens of thousands of new members were accepted over a six-week period, many of whom were no oil painting. We have sincere regret for the unfortunate people who were wrongly admitted to the site and who believed, albeit for a short while, that they were beautiful. It must be a bitter pill to swallow, but better to have had a slice of heaven than never to have tasted it at all."

How do we get sucked in by such piffle?! That outward beauty won't last. Their different body parts will sag, wrinkle, fall out, change colour, no matter how much they try to arrest their decline! Two per cent of Western women are happy with their bodies. How tragic is that? And it's because we buy into the lies of advertising that define us by such shallow superficial external criteria. And men preening themselves like peacocks in front of the mirror in the gym, you make me laugh! Wake up, beauty is way deeper!

If some of us put as much effort into our inner being as we do into our outer shell, we'd be a whole lot more meaningfully beautiful. As Elizabeth Ross wrote; "People are like stained-glass windows. They sparkle and shine when the sun is out, but when the darkness sets in, their true beauty is revealed only if there is a light from within."

Lord, free me from society's crass definition of beauty to live a beautiful life that points others to you. Amen!

YESTERDAY OR TOMORROW?

Matthew 6:34

"Therefore do not worry about tomorrow, for tomorrow will worry about itself. Each day has enough trouble of its own."

18

MARCH

Robert Burdette wrote this piece called "God's Days":

> *There are two days in the week upon which and about which I never worry – two carefree days kept sacredly free from fear and apprehension. One of these days is Yesterday. Yesterday, with its cares and frets and pains and aches, all its faults, its mistakes and blunders, has passed forever beyond my recall. It was mine; now it is God's.*
>
> *The other day that I do not worry about is Tomorrow. Tomorrow, with all its possible adversities, its burdens, its perils, its large promise and performance, its failures and mistakes, is as far beyond my mastery as its dead sister, Yesterday. Tomorrow is God's day; it will be mine.*
>
> *There is left, then, for myself but one day in the week – Today. Any man can fight the battles of today. Any woman can carry the burdens of just one day; any man can resist the temptation of today. It is only when we willfully add the burdens of these two awful eternities – Yesterday and Tomorrow – such burdens as only the Mighty God can sustain – that we break down.*
>
> *It isn't the experience of Today that drives people mad. It is the remorse of what happened Yesterday and fear of what Tomorrow might bring. These are God's Days… Leave them to God.*

Leave them to God indeed! And thank him that our mess of yesterday can become our message for today and tomorrow. Our test of yesterday can be our testimony for today and tomorrow.

So live today as a gift. As George Bernard Shaw said, "Yesterday is the past, tomorrow is the future, today is a gift – that's why it's called 'the present'."

Lord, I choose to live life to the full today, free from the remorse of yesterday or the fear of tomorrow. Amen!

ALONE OR ACCOMPANIED?

Psalm 23:4

"Even though I walk through the valley of the shadow of death, I will fear no evil, for you are with me; your rod and your staff, they comfort me."

During the Holocaust, prisoners in concentration camps would usually be worked to exhaustion and were eventually executed once they couldn't contribute to the cause any more. One couple had two children, one of whom was severely mentally disabled. The father worked each day separately from the others, and when he returned one night he found only his healthy son. "What happened?" he asked. The surviving child told how the guards had decided to execute his brother, as he wasn't doing anything productive. The disabled brother had sobbed and grabbed his mother's skirt. She said, "Don't be afraid. I'll go with you." And they had walked hand in hand peacefully into the gas chamber.

David in Psalm 23 knew that the Lord was his shepherd and would always take care of his sheep, even in the valley of the shadow of death. However dark and desperate our circumstances may seem, God promises to go through them with us. As D.L. Moody said, "The valley of the shadow of death holds no darkness for the child of God. There must be light, else there could be no shadow. Jesus is the light. He has overcome death."

My little kids recently started a new school in a new country in a new language. I was so concerned on their behalf. So we began learning some key verses together which we went through on our way to school: "The one who is in me is greater than the one who is in the world" (1 John 4:4) and "The Lord is with me, I will not be afraid. What can people do to me?" (Psalm 118:6). Difficult times, but they got through.

Remember you are never alone. "I will never leave you, I will never forsake you" (Hebrews 13:5).

Lord Jesus, thank you that you accompany me in every situation. Give me confidence today to walk with you. Amen!

CONTEMPLATIVE OR RESTIVE?

Psalm 23:2

"He leads me beside quiet waters, he restores my soul."

20

MARCH

In the business of life, I try to have a weekly day of prayer, skipping food to make time for being in God's presence. The crazy thing is, because my identity is so tied up in "doing", I often get to the end of that day and think it wasn't a "productive" day, as if that time spent with God was somehow wasted. Can you relate? How many of us do a quick devotional out of duty so we can then just get on with our day? Listen to the piercing words of Henri Nouwen:

> *To live a life that is not dominated by the desire to be relevant but is instead safely anchored in the knowledge of God's first love, we have to be mystics. A mystic is a person whose identity is deeply rooted in God's first love. If there is any focus that the Christian leader of the future will need, it is the discipline of dwelling in the presence of the One who keeps asking us, "Do you love me? Do you love me? Do you love me?" It is the discipline of contemplative prayer. Through contemplative prayer we can stop ourselves from being pulled from one urgent issue to another and from becoming strangers to our own and God's heart. Contemplative prayer keeps us home, rooted and safe, even when we are on the road, moving from place to place, and often surrounded by sounds of violence and war. Contemplative prayer deepens in us the knowledge that we are already free, that we have already found a place to dwell, that we already belong to God, even though everyone and everything around us keeps suggesting the opposite.*

If those words don't rock your soul, you've read them too fast. Try again. It took me until the third reading to breathe more deeply and process the incredible reality that I am already free, home, rooted, and safe, without any of my "doing"...

Lord, I choose to slow down, breathe deeply, and listen to you today. Amen!

JOURNEY OR DESTINATION?

Jeremiah 6:16

"Stand at the crossroads and look; ask for the ancient paths, ask where the good way is and walk in it, and you will find rest for your souls."

A Chinese proverb tells us that "the journey is the reward". The verse above tells us that we will find rest for our souls as we choose to journey along the ancient paths, the tried and true ways that God had revealed to his people. Our journey with Christ requires that we be fully present *in the present,* not obsessing about how things will eventually turn out.

John Eldredge writes:

> *Thinking of life as a journey reminds me to stop trying to set up camp and call it home. It allows me to see life as a process, with completion somewhere down the road. Thus I am freed from feeling like a failure when things are not finished, and hopeful that they will be as my journey comes to its end. I want adventure, and this reminds me I am living in it. Life is not a problem to be solved; it is an adventure to be lived.*

There are two kinds of mountain climbers. Both journey along the same path in the same direction to the same place. But the "frantic-achiever-climber" misses the whole experience. The stunning vistas wash right over him. The smells, the sounds, the camaraderie are often wasted on him as he pursues his goal. Robert Pirsig says of him, "His talk is forever about somewhere else, something else. He's here but he's not here. What he is looking for, what he wants, is all around him, but he doesn't want that because it is all around him."

The destination matters, and it helps orient and direct our daily steps; but there's no need to run ahead and miss the blessings of the journey today.

Lord, help me to relish the joys of today's journey without obsessing about the destination. Amen!

CIVILIZED TEDIUM OR ENERGIZED PASSION?

John 2:15, 16

"Jesus made a whip out of cords, and drove all from the temple area... 'Get these out of here! How dare you turn my Father's house into a market!'"

Sometimes God wants us to get angry. Often the status quo needs challenging. How attractive is Jesus in his violent indignation over the misuse of his Father's house! What does his example teach us for today? Dorothy Sayers wrote:

> *The people who hanged Christ never, to do them justice, accused Him of being a bore – on the contrary, they thought Him too dynamic to be safe. It has been left for later generations to muffle up that shattering personality and surround Him with an atmosphere of tedium. We have very efficiently pared the claws of the Lion of Judah, certified Him "meek and mild", and recommended Him as a fitting household pet for pale curates and pious old ladies.*

In *Rocky 3*, Stallone's character is going soft and losing his edge. The fire in his belly is disappearing as he enjoys the fame and adulation that have come his way. In one scene, his manager says to him: "The worst thing happened that could happen to any fighter – you got civilized." Might Jesus say that to us today? Shane Claiborne challenges us: "We should be the most passionate people on the planet, enthused with passion. The word enthusiasm comes from two Greek words, 'en' and 'Theos', which together mean in God. The more we get into God, the more passionate we become."

If we've become civilized, the first step is to recognize it. Then we can pray for that enthusiasm, that state of becoming more and more "in God", i.e. passionate for his kingdom. And then we can offer up that energized passion to God and look around us to see where he wants to use us.

Lord, I don't want to settle for civilized tedium. Stir up something in me today that simply has to burst out into concerted action for your glory. Amen!

MINE OR YOURS?

Romans 6:11, 13, 14

"Count yourselves dead to sin but alive to God in Christ Jesus… Offer yourselves to God, as those who have been brought from death to life; and offer the parts of your body to him as instruments of righteousness… because you are not under law, but under grace."

John Wesley went as a missionary to America before he was converted. He didn't understand the above verses (indeed much of Romans), and so he ended up returning to England feeling completely discouraged and defeated. It was in his broken state in Aldersgate Street, London that he described his heart as being "strangely warmed" as he came to understand more how Christ's sacrifice on the cross brought us life in him. The founder of Methodism was one of the most influential men of the eighteenth century and beyond, and he called on his people to embrace the following as a "Covenant Prayer":

I am no longer my own, but Yours.
Put me to what You will,
Rank me with whoever You will.
Put me to doing.
Put me to suffering.
Let me be employed for You,
Or laid aside for You.
Exalted for You, or brought low for You.
Let me be full
Let me be empty.
Let me have all things,
Let me have nothing!
And now, O Father,
You are mine and I am Yours. So be it.
And the covenant I am making on earth,
Let it be ratified in heaven. Amen.

Why not re-read the covenant and try to say "Amen" after each line? Some lines might be easier than others. Will you make it your own? What is holding you back? Bring those areas, concerns, fears, or idols to the Lord today.

Lord, the above covenant is so deeply challenging. In my spirit I know it's right to pray. Help me get to the place of making it my own and living it out. Amen!

LIGHT OR HEAVY?

Matthew 11:30

"My yoke is easy and my burden is light."

A man was trudging down a dusty road in rural Kentucky in the heat of the day, loaded up with a cumbersome backpack and a suitcase in either hand. The driver of a pick-up truck took pity and offered him a ride in the back. A few minutes later the driver looked in his rear-view mirror to see the man standing in the truck, still wearing the backpack and still carrying both suitcases.

Have we climbed aboard the truck of faith, but still insist on carrying all our baggage, not realizing we can lay them down and take it easy for a while?

Jesus said, "Come to me, all you who are weary and burdened, and I will give you rest. Take my yoke upon you and learn from me, for I am gentle and humble in heart, and you will find rest for your souls" (Matthew 11:28, 29).

I remember doing an epic team-building exercise up some mountains. I carried a very heavy backpack for hours on end. Eventually a friend wanted to give me a break, so I swapped with his much lighter one. The sensation was remarkable, because although I was obviously more weighed down than if I was carrying nothing, I actually jumped and skipped along for a while because it was so much lighter than my previously crushing backpack.

If we team up with Jesus, he takes our backpack and shares the workload with us. There'll always be some load to carry – that's life – but with him alongside us it's more bearable, and hopefully even enjoyable. In the daytime wind and rain on the mountain face, it wasn't much fun, but later around the camp fire with a mug of hot chocolate, it was fabulous. I found rest for my soul!

Lord, I choose to lay down unnecessary burdens today and to yoke myself with you. Amen!

What about John the Baptist?

INDIVIDUAL OR TEAM?

Luke 10:1

"The Lord appointed seventy-two others and sent them two by two ahead of him to every town and place he was about to go."

A team is never fewer than two, and usually it's more than that. Whatever the number, we need each other. Your strengths compensate for my weaknesses, and our gifts complement each other. When I'm discouraged, you can lift my spirits, and vice versa. "We" beats "I". Lone rangers seldom get far, and neither do they leave a lasting legacy – not a positive one, at least.

We've all seen geese flying through the sky in a V-formation. They do this for a number of reasons. Scientists have shown that those flying in the slipstream have their range increased by 71 per cent through the efforts of the ones in front. The lead goose obviously doesn't have the benefit of anyone else's help, so when it feels tired, it simply swaps with one of the others. The ones at the back make all the loud noises, honking away to encourage the one at the front. If one goes off and flies out of formation, it encounters strong resistance and finds it much more difficult to progress. Working together is far more effective.

Jesus knew that meaning is found in community, not individualism. He knew that there was strength in numbers. He demonstrated the value of a team as he selected his small band of disciples to invest in over a number of years. Notice how the individual disciples messed up when they found themselves isolated: Judas went to betray Jesus alone, Peter denied Jesus when he found himself alone.

Are you plugged in with your local community of faith, in a small group of fellow stragglers and strugglers who are committed to modelling kingdom values together? Or are you isolated? Are you a lone ranger for Jesus? Get on a team, fly in formation, or you won't make it!

Lord, I choose today to be intentional in journeying with others as I follow you. Amen!

RESOLUTE OR WAVERING?

Luke 9:51

"As the time approached for him to be taken up to heaven, Jesus resolutely set out for Jerusalem."

Jesus knew that heading to Jerusalem meant going to the cross. Despite that he was resolute in obeying his Father. Even in the garden at Gethsemane, his anguished praying was not a wavering but an embracing of God's costly will for his life. Back in Elijah's day, the authorities were similarly antagonistic and God's people similarly reticent in embracing the cost of loyalty to him. Elijah assembled the prophets of Baal and the people of Israel on Mount Carmel and challenged the latter: "How long will you waver between two opinions? If the Lord is God, follow him; but if Baal is God, follow him" (1 Kings 18:21). We read of Abraham's resolute faith in Romans 4:20, 21: "Yet he did not waver through unbelief regarding the promise of God, but was strengthened in his faith and gave glory to God, being fully persuaded that God had power to do what he had promised."

Are you wavering today, or resolute and steadfast in your pursuit of Christ's mission?

In 1519 colonist Hernan Cortez set sail from Cuba on a bold mission to conquer Mexico. So when he disembarked at Vera Cruz with 700 men, he promptly ordered them to set fire to the fleet of 11 ships. Then all 700 men watched as their only exit strategy sank in the depths of the Gulf of Mexico. The only course of action left was to press on resolutely into the interior and fight for their commander.

Whatever we're faced with in life, we can choose to do it with or without God. There are no guarantees that it'll be easy. In fact, Abraham, Elijah, and Jesus all show us that it will be costly. Count the cost today, and choose not to waver.

Lord, help me not to waver but to live resolutely surrendered to your cause today. Amen!

RIGOROUS OR SOGGY?

Psalm 139:23, 24

"Search me, O God, and know my heart. Test me, and know my anxious thoughts. See if there is any offensive way in me, and lead me in the way everlasting."

Eugene Peterson, as both a pastor and a writer, provided this bleak diagnosis of the state of the people in his care:

> *I was living in classic suburbia, and not liking it very much. The people who gathered to worship God under my leadership were rootless and cultureless. They were marginally Christian. They didn't read books. They didn't discuss ideas. All spirit seemed to have leaked out of their lives and been replaced by a garage-sale clutter of clichés and stereotypes, securities and fashions. Dostoevsky's sentence hit the target: the "people seem to be watered down… darting and rushing about before us every day, but in a sort of diluted state". No hard ideas to push against. No fiery spirit to excite. Soggy suburbia…*
>
> *I had no idea that an entire society could be shaped by the images of advertising. I had lived, it seems, a sheltered life. The experiments of Pavlov accounted for the condition of these people far better than anything in the four Gospels. They were conditioned to respond to the stimulus of a sale price, quite apart from need, as effectively as Pavlov's dogs were trained to salivate at the bells' signal, quite apart from hunger.*
>
> *These were the people for whom I was praying and for whom I was writing, these spirits who had taken early retirement, whose minds had been checked at the door. Suburbia-lobotomized spirituality… They left their houses for several hours each day to make what they call a "living". What, in fact, they make is money. It is the only thing they make, if you can call what they do making it. Everything else they buy or borrow, after which they abuse or waste it. Not everybody. There are exceptions. But this was classic American suburbia, repetitive, predictable, featureless.*

Ouch! Any truth in the above for me?

Lord, I choose decisively to reject the above critique for how I live my life. Amen!

SLOGANS OR SCARS?

Galatians 6:14, 17

"May I never boast except in the cross of our Lord Jesus Christ, through which the world has been crucified to me, and I to the world... for I bear on my body the marks of Jesus."

Adoniram Judson's proposal to his future wife was no soft sell: "Give me your hand to go with me to the jungles of Asia, and there die with me in the cause of Christ." They reached Rangoon, Burma, in 1813. They spent six years language-learning before he preached his first sermon. It was seven years before he saw his first convert. He translated the whole Bible over twenty years. He was twice widowed, and six of his children died before him. He returned just once to the USA in thirty-seven years. At his death there were 7,000 baptized Karen believers, and now there are over 3 million.

At one stage earlier in his life he was caught up in the Anglo-Burmese war. During a seventeen-month stint in Ava Prison, his mistreatment was horrific and he picked up some ugly scars made by the chains and iron shackles that cruelly bound him. When released, he sought permission to take the gospel to yet another province, but the antagonistic ruler indignantly denied his request, saying, "My people are not fools enough to listen to anything a missionary might *say*, but I fear they might be impressed by your *scars* and turn to your religion!"

What a life! Hearing about such spiritual heavyweights can inspire on the one hand or discourage on the other as we see what total lightweights we are in comparison. Choose to be inspired rather than discouraged. We live in a different era and a different context, but we serve the same God who issues the same call, to live and die for him. Let's not settle for bumper stickers and slogans when he is calling us to scars.

Lord, by your grace help me to choose the path of scars rather than slogans. Amen!

ON THE GOAL OR ON THE OBSTACLE?

Hebrews 12:2

"Let us fix our eyes on Jesus, the Author and Perfecter of our faith, who for the joy (goal) set before him, endured the cross, scorning its shame, and sat down at the right hand of throne of God. Consider him…"

Someone once wrote: "Obstacles are those frightful things you see when you take your eyes off the goal." It's easy to be distracted from the goal when so many things compete for our attention. We're bombarded with apparently urgent tasks which need doing.

My teammate in our Evangelism Department at Scripture Union is called Leonidas. Back in 1996, he had to flee from university because he was from the "wrong" tribe. Students from the other tribe had thrown a grenade into his room as he was praying, and he narrowly escaped with his life, needing several operations to remove shrapnel from his eye. He has no bitterness towards them and often includes the incident as part of his testimony of grace. He was forced to go and live in the bush, and used to walk eighteen miles each day to teach at a distant school. The believers met each week on his only day off, so even then he walked all that way, through mud, rain, sunshine, whatever; and all these years on, the fruit is obvious as the whole area seems to be experiencing extraordinary times. God is faithful. Leonidas's eyes – damaged but still shining – are on the goal: to change the nation through the powerful message of the risen Christ.

Jesus "endured the cross" because he kept his eye on the goal. That was quite an obstacle. Whatever you're facing, don't lose hope today. So if obstacles are those frightful things you see when you take your eyes off the goal, I guess you and I need to ask ourselves:

1. *What's my goal?*

And, irrespective of any obstacles:

2. *Who or what are my eyes focused on?*

Lord, I choose to keep my eyes firmly fixed on the goal today. Amen!

FRIEND OR FOE?

John 6:33

"In this world you will have trouble. But take heart! I have overcome the world."

Over the last seventy years, the Chinese church has experienced both extremes of persecution and explosive growth. A friend of mine was ministering in the underground church. He was with a group of seasoned followers – and by seasoned that meant they had spent at least three years in prison for their faith. He'd been speaking to an impressively fiery evangelist when one of the leaders took him aside and said: "That young man shows great promise... but we don't know how much we can trust him, because he hasn't been to prison yet." By that he meant that only once people had endured prolonged mistreatment in prison could their faith be recognized as genuine. He went on: "In the West you go to seminaries for three years to learn about God. Here in China, the prisons have been our three-year seminaries!"

Thank God that the persecution nowadays is less severe than it used to be in China – although one pastor cautioned believers in the West: "Please don't pray for an end to persecution in our nation. Persecution is not our foe, it's our friend. More persecution means more growth."

How can he say that? How did this situation evolve? Tony Lambert writes:

> *The reason for the growth of the church in China and for the outbreak of genuine spiritual revival in many areas is inextricably linked to the whole theology of the cross... the stark message of the Chinese church is that God used suffering and the preaching of a crucified Christ to pour out revival and build his church. Are we in the West still willing to hear? The Chinese church has walked the way of the cross. The lives and deaths of the martyrs of the past have borne rich fruit.*

Lord, I ask that you comfort and sustain my brothers and sisters in the persecuted church today. And teach me here to walk the way of the cross rather than seek comfort. Amen!

Acts 13:3

"So after [the church leaders] had prayed and fasted, they placed their hands on Barnabas and Saul and sent them off."

COURTSIDE OR CENTRE STAGE?

Hoosiers is a film about a small-town basketball team that amazingly made it to the state championship. During one tight game, the team coach brought a new player off the bench and into the action. The young lad, who was clearly religious, dropped to his knees to pray before going out on the court. Everyone waited, and waited... until eventually the coach leaned down and said, "Son, God wants you out on the court now."

Some of us are like that: God has promised to be our strength, but we're paralysed by fear into inactivity on the sidelines and still praying for him to strengthen us. A team effort involves those both courtside and centre stage. We all work together. Praying and going are both important. But sometimes we are praying as a justification for not entering the bustling fray of battle.

Barnabas and Saul left the safety of Antioch to journey far and wide into uncharted spiritual territory. They knew the importance of praying themselves, of being supported in prayer, and of course that the people they were going to needed them to come themselves to present the truth claims of Christ to the lost. That principle applies to all of us – as we send out missionaries to the nations, but also as we get out into our community or workplace or club (or wherever else) and share our hope in Jesus.

I remember back in my first job praying for months for a natural opening to share my faith with my suspicious housemates. When it eventually came, I was caught off-guard and blabbered away incoherently. Continuing with the above analogy, I needed to be keeping warmed up on the sideline ready at any moment for action.

Who are you praying for today? Are you ready for action?

Lord, use me today to pray and then enter the fray for you. Amen!

2 Chronicles 16:9

"For the eyes of the Lord range throughout the earth to strengthen those whose hearts are fully committed to him."

FULL OR PARTIAL?

Garibaldi, the great patriot who led Italy many years ago to unification and freedom, said to those who would follow him: "I promise you forced marches, short rations, bloody battles, wounds, imprisonment and death, but let him who loves home and fatherland follow me." It wasn't an attractive political manifesto, but he was a realist. He needed full commitment from people who had counted the cost in order to have any chance in his aim to liberate his countrymen.

The Lord is looking for similar commitment from us. Today's verse gives a beautiful picture of the Lord's desire to strengthen and empower his people. His eyes are searching out people he can use. Are you one of them? Is your heart *fully* committed to him?

A chicken and a pig were chatting by the farm fence when a commercial truck pulled up. Emblazoned on the side was a photo of some crispy bacon rashers and a few lightly fried eggs. The chicken salivated and said, "That looks so tasty!" The pig replied, "No way! For you it's just a small contribution but for me it requires my very life!"

In a similar vein, a Greek shipping magnate wanted to demonstrate his loyalty to the king. So he asked the king's secretary, "Would His Majesty like me to give him one of my ships as a gift?" The secretary's reply shocked him: "No! The king doesn't want that really. He wants you to give *yourself* as the gift. Then he will have all your ships as well."

Will I present myself as a living sacrifice to God (Romans 12:2)? That includes my hopes and dreams, my frustrations and disappointments, my bank account, hobbies, relationships, career, health, time, and more. He calls for, and is worthy of, full commitment.

Lord, help me to surrender control willingly of every area of my life to you today. Amen!

PIERCE OR HEAL?

Proverbs 12:18

"Reckless words pierce like a sword but the tongue of the wise brings healing."

Never has a saying been more untrue than "Sticks and stones may break my bones but words will never hurt me". Usually a crushed spirit takes longer to heal than a broken bone. Words can sting and cut deep, often leaving wounds and insecurities that last a lifetime. No doubt like me you can think back to an incident in your life that the other person involved has long forgotten, but what they said was so hurtful, that those reckless words did indeed "pierce like a sword", leaving a lasting wound.

When I receive hundreds of responses to a piece of writing, it's the few negative ones that I tend to re-read and dwell on. Why are we like that? One thing I've learned is that words are so powerful and there will always be a negative one, a biting criticism, an accusation, be it justified or not. Our motives will be misunderstood and questioned. And it cuts deep.

"... but the tongue of the wise brings healing."

Encouragement is likewise a powerful thing. Mark Twain once said, "I can live for two months on a good compliment." I made it a resolution last year to intentionally write one email of encouragement a day to someone, knowing how much it blesses the recipient. The apostle Barnabas was a great encourager, and we can all be one; it doesn't cost us much. Resolve to be one today, and then God will use you to bring healing. What a privilege!

Most people's opinions of us don't matter. Supremely only God's does. And he offers you today the most profoundly affirming, energizing, empowering, life-giving endorsement that, no matter what you're going through: "I BELIEVE YOU'VE GOT WHAT IT TAKES TO BE WHO I'VE CALLED YOU TO BE!"

Lord, I receive that word – it's so healing! And I choose both to receive that encouragement and to offer it to others today. Amen!

BEGINNER OR PRO?

1 Peter 5:10

"And the God of all grace… will himself restore you and make you strong, firm and steadfast."

Well-known pianist Ignace Jan Paderewski's concerts were sold out for six straight months in New York. One night, a mother brought her nine-year-old son, hoping to inspire him to continue with his lessons. Shortly before the concert was to begin, she looked up to the stage and to her horror saw he had climbed up and was opening up the huge Steinway piano. The audience grew tense, and some people shouted at the boy to get off the stage. But he calmly began to play "Chopsticks". As the ushers began moving toward the young boy, Paderewski himself came out on stage and stopped them. He tiptoed up behind the boy and whispered in the child's ear, "Don't give up. Keep on playing. You're doing great!" As the boy continued, Paderewski put his arms around him and began to play a concerto based on the tune of "Chopsticks".

By God's standards, our best efforts are like that little boy's attempt at "Chopsticks", and yet the beauty is that he can take hold of them and turn them into something exquisite. We can get frustrated with our own lack of progress in various areas, but Thomas Merton provides a comforting thought: "We do not want to be beginners. But let us be convinced of the fact that we will never be anything else but beginners all our life!"

God sees our heart, our desire, our motivation. We know whether we've tried our hardest or have coasted along in compromise. So if we feel like we're bumbling along with little obvious sense of progress but actually we've given it our best in whatever pursuit for his glory, God draws near to us and whispers: "Don't give up. Keep on playing. You're doing great!" Can you hear him?

Lord, I hear you. Thanks. I choose to team up with you today. Amen!

NOISE OR VOICE?

Matthew 17:5

"This is my son, whom I love… listen to him!"

4

APRIL

During the First World War, a government department was recruiting Morse code operators. One young man saw the advert in a paper and went for an interview. He entered the noisy office, took the application form from the receptionist, and began filling it out with several others in the waiting area. A few minutes later, the man opposite him stood up with his form and entered the inner office. The other applicants wondered why he'd gone unprompted, and began complaining that they'd waited longer than him. A few minutes later, the employer came out with that same man and said: "Gentlemen, thank you very much for coming but we've now made an appointment." The other applicants complained vociferously: "Wait a minute, that's not fair. He was the last to come in and we never even got a chance to be interviewed. Yet he got the job." The employer replied, "I'm sorry, but all the time you have been sitting here, the telegraph has been ticking out the following message in Morse code: 'If you understand this message, then come right in. The job is yours.' None of you heard it or understood it. This young man did. The job is his."

I sometimes envy others who seem more attuned to God's voice, but I don't think it's an accident that they hear him more clearly. They have taken the time to learn to listen. They have set aside time to spend with him. They have embraced a disciplined thirst for meditating on his Word and waiting on him in quietness and submission.

Try to make some time to really listen to him today. Above the clatter and busyness of your life, learn to move beyond hearing to listening. He's talking all the time, if we will only stop to listen. Don't complain that he never speaks to you. He has, he is, and he will. Just slow down and listen!

Speak, Lord, your servant is listening. Amen!

MOUNTAIN OR VALLEY?

Exodus 34:29, 30

"When Moses came down from Mount Sinai… he was not aware that his face was radiant, because he had spoken with the Lord… and the people were afraid to come near him."

Moses' intense encounter on the mountaintop was unique. God met with him in a powerful way, and then sent him back down into the valley to get on with his mission. Occasionally you might come across someone who simply radiates God's glory, but it's unusual. I'm fairly confident my face has never shone quite like Moses', but I have had a few mountaintop experiences of my own during which time stands still, the sense of intimacy and awe are breathtaking, and you never want it to end… but then it does end… and you have to get down into the thick of things in the valley below.

C.S. Lewis wrote of the real but limited value of such glorious mountaintop experiences:

> *But God never allows this state of affairs to last long. Sooner or later He withdraws, if not in fact, at least from their conscious experience, all those supports and incentives. He leaves the creature to stand up on its own legs – to carry out from the will alone duties which have lost all relish. It is during such tough periods, much more than during the peak periods, that it is growing into the sort of creature He wants it to be.*

Whether you've had a mountaintop experience or not is immaterial. In Moses' context, he was the only one to have one, while the overwhelming majority didn't. Don't waste time hunting for a hilltop experience. Remember, it is in the valley that the true battle is played out. Where you are is where you are. So don't be discouraged if you're going through a hard time. As Oswald Chambers said: "Trials are God's vote of confidence in us."

Lord, please strengthen me for today's battles in the valley, for your glory. Amen!

YOUNG OR OLD?

Isaiah 40:30, 31

"Even youths grow tired and weary, and young men stumble and fall; but those who hope in the Lord will renew their strength. They will soar on wings like eagles; they will run and not grow weary, they will walk and not be faint."

Our oldest supporter, Alison Hall, died a few years ago. Well into her nineties she was still baking cakes to sell and raise funds for us at the weekly market down the road from her. My granny went back out to Africa to work with widows when she was eighty-three years old, once Grandpa died, and she was still full of zest to keep on going as long as God would grant her. Both those ladies were seriously wrinkly and physically decrepit, but age is a state of mind – you're as old as you feel – and they were young at heart.

General Douglas MacArthur wrote:

> *Youth is not a period of time. It is a state of mind, a result of the will, a quality of the imagination, a victory of courage over timidity, of the taste for adventure over the love of comfort. A man doesn't grow old because he has lived a certain number of years. A man grows old when he deserts his ideal. The years may wrinkle his skin, but deserting his ideal wrinkles his soul. Preoccupations, fears, doubts, and despair are the enemies which slowly bow us toward earth and turn us into dust before death. If one day you should become bitter, pessimistic, and gnawed by despair, may God have mercy on your old man's soul.*

So if age is a state of mind, what state is yours in? So much of life has to do with our attitude. Don't blame it on which side of the bed you got out this morning, choose to be hopeful in the Lord today, and he will renew your strength.

God Almighty, I indeed choose to be hopeful and young at heart today. Amen!

CYNICISM OR ACTION?

Romans 5:3–5

"We rejoice in our sufferings, because we know that suffering produces perseverance; perseverance, character; and character, hope. And hope does not disappoint us..."

Why doesn't hope disappoint us? "... because God has poured out his love into our hearts by the Holy Spirit, whom he has given us" (Romans 5:5b)

You might think in our cynical age that the antidote would be optimism, but no! It's action! It's action that is born out of hope! Cynicism gives up on believing the world can be changed, and that becomes a self-fulfilling prophecy. What a relief that Paul is such a realist. There is no pretence! He acknowledges that suffering is part of the package, as God uses it to develop in us perseverance and character, and ultimately lived-out hope.

Jim Wallis writes:

> *Ultimately, cynicism protects you from commitment. If things are not really going to change, why try so hard to make a difference? And if you have middle-class economic security (as many cynics do), things don't have to change for you to remain secure. That is not intended to sound harsh, just realistic. Cynics are finally free just to look after themselves... Perhaps the only people who view the world realistically are the cynics and the saints. Everybody else may be living in some kind of denial about what is really going on and how things really are. And the only difference between the cynics and the saints is the presence, power, and possibility of hope... Hope is not a feeling; it is a decision. And the decision for hope is based on what you believe at the deepest levels. You choose hope, not as a naïve wish, but as a choice, with your eyes wide open to the reality of the world – just like the cynics who have not made the decision for hope.*

Lord, I believe that the world can be changed, and that you're wanting to involve me in the process. I choose to live a hope-filled life today. Amen!

SELF-PITY OR SENSE OF PERSPECTIVE?

2 Corinthians 4:8–10

"We are hard pressed on every side, but not crushed; perplexed, but not in despair; persecuted, but not abandoned; struck down, but not destroyed. We always carry around in our body the death of Jesus, so that the life of Jesus may also be revealed in our body."

These words from the apostle Paul's pen could be echoed by millions of followers of Jesus in the world today. I'm sitting here typing away on my laptop with graphic pictures in front of me of mutilated bodies in yet another country where an aggressive Islamist agenda is being enacted. I lived there for a while in the 1990s with a remarkable pastor called Pierre. His house is currently overrun with fearful members of his congregation, his children are traumatized, and they don't know who, if any of them, will survive.

Why do I tell you that? Because this morning I woke up and was tempted to feel sorry for myself. I've been sick for months with some undiagnosed tropical ailment, and I've had enough. But knowing what Pierre is going through right now (and he might be dead by the time you read this, or he might be fine, but be assured that there are plenty of Brother Pierres going through similarly grim trials right now around the world), how can I possibly slip into self-pitying mode? If in some small way I can relate to the above verses of being "perplexed, but not in despair, struck down but not destroyed", that's but a glimpse of what others are going through.

God doesn't belittle our problems. They are real. He cares about them. But a healthy sense of perspective is an antidote to self-pity. I count my blessings every day: freedom to worship, support of loved ones, access to healthcare, clean water, food, education, the list goes on. How blessed I am! Thank you, Lord.

Lord, help me to keep things in perspective and trust you with all my problems today. Amen!

TOPSY OR TURVY?

1 Corinthians 1:27, 28

"God chose the foolish things of the world to shame the wise; God chose the weak things of the world to shame the strong. He chose the lowly things of this world and the despised things – and the things that are not – to nullify the things that are."

God's ways are sometimes topsy-turvy. With him, things work differently. The first are last and the last are first. God in heaven becomes a baby on earth. Our life comes through his death. His cross provides our crown. Foolish shame wise. Weak shame strong. His ways are most definitely not our ways.

But thank God his ways aren't ours. In our sophistication, we've learned how to make a living but not how to live; we have higher incomes, but lower morals; we have more acquaintances but fewer friends; we have fancy houses but broken homes. The list goes on…

Topsy-turvy… his ways right, our ways wrong.

And when it comes to praying, you might think it reasonable to pray for comfort, peace, joy and wisdom, but this Franciscan prayer offers us the total opposite.

May God bless you with discomfort
At easy answers, half-truths, and superficial relationships,
So that you may live deep within your heart.

May God bless you with anger
At injustice, oppression, and exploitation of people,
So that you may work for justice, freedom and peace.

May God bless you with tears
To shed for those who suffer pain, rejection, hunger and war,
So that you may reach out your hand to comfort them and
To turn their pain into joy.

And may God bless you with enough foolishness
To believe that you can make a difference in this world,
So that you can do what others claim cannot be done.
To bring justice and kindness to all our children and the poor.

Lord, I choose – maybe with some hesitation, but convinced it is your will – to embrace this benediction for my life today. Amen!

SUCCESSFUL OR FAITHFUL?

1 Thessalonians 5:24

"The one who calls you is faithful, and he will do it."

We mustn't confuse success with faithfulness. There is nothing wrong with being successful, but it doesn't mean you've been faithful. Or maybe we simply need to redefine or qualify what success is. Mother Teresa of Calcutta was once asked, "How do you measure the success of your work?" She looked puzzled for a moment and then replied, "I don't remember that the Lord ever spoke of success. He spoke only of faithfulness in love. This is the only success that really counts."

Today's short verse says three things: God calls us. He's faithful. He'll do it. If we respond to his call, he will be faithful, and he'll accomplish what he wants. That's what Mother Teresa is getting at when she rejects success for "faithfulness in love".

Are we faithful in what God has entrusted us with – in terms of our talents, our finances, our relationships, our ambitions? Are our priorities aligned with his? Whether we're involved in business, politics, education, or the arts, are we blindly pursuing personal glory and success, or seeking to be Christ's ambassador where he has placed us?

Oswald Chambers writes, "We are not called to be successful in accordance with ordinary standards, but in accordance with a ear of wheat falling into the ground and dying, becoming in that way what it never could be if it were to abide alone."

The nature of faithfulness in love is that it is sacrificial. Christ laid down his life for us. In turn what will that look like for you this week?

Lord, I choose to be faithful to your call on my life today, in the big things and in the little things. Amen!

1 John 3:1

"How great is the love the Father has lavished on us, that we should be called children of God! And that is what we are!"

HEIRS OR DOGS?

A new convert approached Watchman Nee in deep anguish of soul, saying, "No matter how much I pray, no matter how hard I try, I simply cannot seem to be faithful to my Lord. I think I'm losing my salvation." Watchman Nee replied, "Do you see this dog here? He is my dog. He is house-trained; he never makes a mess; he is obedient; he is a pure delight to me. Out in the kitchen I have a son, a baby son. He throws his food around, he fouls his clothes, he's a total mess. But who is going to inherit my kingdom? Not my dog. My son is my heir! And you are Jesus Christ's heir because it is for you that He died."

It's deeply liberating to know we are Christ's heirs not through our strivings for perfection, but simply by means of his grace. It's difficult for us to grasp fully the concept of grace. Maybe this illustration will help: A burglar broke into a house and killed a sleeping baby. If the father tracked down the burglar and killed him, that would be revenge. If the law took its course and the burglar was sent to prison, that would be justice. If the father forgave the burglar, took him into his home, and treated him as his own son, that would be grace. It sounds an absurd scenario, yet that's what God did for us, even though it was we who killed his son.

How about spending some time meditating on that for a while?

Lord God Almighty, as an undeserving recipient of your grace, I choose to live today as an heir, extending that same grace to others and modelling the freedom of knowing my status and security in you. Amen!

LIFE OR DEATH?

Colossians 3:1–4

"Since, then, you have been raised with Christ, set your hearts on things above, where Christ is seated at the right hand of God… For you died, and your life is now hidden with Christ in God. When Christ, who is your life, appears, then you also will appear with him in glory."

George Mueller was known by people around the world for the extraordinary answers to his prayers on a continual basis. One day he was urged to share the secret of the effectiveness of his ministry and prayer life. In his answer he spoke of his "secret death". "There was a day," he said, "when I died; utterly died." He spoke deliberately and quietly, bending lower until he nearly touched the floor. "I died to George Mueller, his opinions, preferences, tastes and will; died to the world, its approval or censure; died to the approval or blame even of my brethren and friends; and since then I have studied only to show myself approved of God."

As Peter writes, "He himself bore our sins in his body on the tree, so that we might *die* to sins and live for righteousness" (1 Peter 2:24). The dying to self is the pathway to life, as Paul wrote to Timothy: "If we *died* with him, we will also live with him" (2 Timothy 2:11). So Christ's death has huge consequences on our outlook and motivation for life. "For Christ's love compels us, because we are convinced that one *died* for all, and therefore all *died*. And he *died* for all, that those who live should no longer live for themselves but for him who *died* for them and was raised again" (2 Corinthians 5:14–15).

Dying to one's own opinions, preferences, tastes, and will – and everything else Mueller talks about – is supremely costly and challenging… but so undoubtedly worth it! Count the cost today and choose well.

Lord, help me to seek to show myself approved by you alone. Amen!

Philippians 1:21

"For to me, to live is Christ and to die is gain."

WIN OR LOSE?

So often we encounter situations in our lives that are win/lose. For me to win, somebody else has to lose. Or vice versa. Or sometimes, nobody's going to come out on top, and it's lose/lose. But the best scenario is win/win, and that is what the apostle Paul is talking about in Philippians 1. To live is Christ is to win, and to die is gain, which is an even bigger win.

Dietrich Bonhoeffer wrote, "When Christ calls a man, he bids him come and die." Why should we listen to him? Because Bonhoeffer was willing to pay the ultimate price for following Jesus. During the Second World War, he left the safety of exile in America and returned to suffer with his people and fight for liberation from the yoke of the Nazis, who eventually caught and executed him shortly before the end of the war. His choosing life meant literally embracing death. For most of us it won't involve physical martyrdom. But Bonhoeffer himself knew – and calls us in turn – to embrace the challenge that if you haven't found something worth dying for, you haven't found something worth living for.

In John Chrysostom's final sermon, which led to his exile and death in AD 407, he thundered:

> *The waters are raging and the winds are blowing but I have no fear for I stand firmly upon the rock. What am I to fear? Is it death? Life to me means Christ, and death is gain. Is it exile? The earth and everything it holds belongs to the Lord. Is it loss of property? I brought nothing into this world and I will bring nothing out of it. I have only contempt for the world and its ways and I scorn its honours.*

Lord, help me to align my perspective on life to yours as illustrated by Paul, Bonhoeffer and Chrysostom. Amen!

WORLDLY HOPE OR BIBLICAL HOPE?

Hebrews 11:1

"Faith is being sure of what we hope for and certain of what we do not see."

14

APRIL

Shortly before Moody graduated to glory, he said, "Someday you'll read in the papers that D. L. Moody is dead. Don't you believe it! At that moment I'll be more alive than I am now; I'll have gone up higher, that's all! I was born of the flesh in 1837; I was born of the Spirit in 1856. That which is born of the flesh may die, but that which is born of the Spirit will live forever!"

Biblical hope is a confident expectation that we can depend upon. This is in sharp contrast to today's usage, which seems to almost assume uncertainty. People "hope" that things will work out, but there's often little confidence that it will. For such people who are "separate from Christ", they are "foreigners to the covenants... *without hope* and without God in the world" (Ephesians 2:12). Concerning their future after death, they "grieve like the rest of men, who have *no hope*" (1 Thessalonians 4:13); whereas the Christian can echo the confidence expressed by Paul to Titus, "We wait for the *blessed hope* – the glorious appearing of our great God and Saviour, Jesus Christ" (Titus 2:13).

In my own life in Burundi, it's this hope which keeps me keeping on. Things can appear so bleak, unfair, desperate, and hopeless. A recurring prayer over the years at our daily team times of devotion, particularly during periods of more intense fighting, has been, "*Imana yacu, turagushimiye kuko watuzigamye kugez' uyu musi*" [Our Lord, we praise you that you have protected us until today]. Yet it's the hope of heaven which has sustained my brothers and sisters through the horrors of war. They're ready to die. And so am I.

Biblical hope brings total security and assurance. Are you hopeful?

Thank you, Lord, that my hope in you is sure. Help me live a hope-full life today. Amen!

EARTH OR HEAVEN?

Matthew 6:19–21, 24

"Do not store up for yourselves treasures on earth, where moths and rust destroy, and where thieves break in and steal. But store up for yourselves treasures in heaven… For where your treasure is, there your heart will be also… You cannot serve both God and money."

Jesus is not against the rich, but as he quickly exposed in his encounter with the young ruler, riches are a dangerous threat in supplanting loyalty and commitment to him. Money can so easily enslave us, and diminish our eternal perspective. Treasures on earth or treasures in heaven? What will we give our lives to? C.S. Lewis wrote that "anything which isn't eternal is eternally out-of-date".

Neil Hannon of the band Divine Comedy wrote the following lyrics in his song "Eye of the Needle":

The cars in the churchyard are shiny and German
Distinctly at odds with the theme of the sermon
And during communion I study the people
Squeezing themselves through the eye of the needle.

I was preaching in an affluent suburb in Chicago a few years ago. The congregation was all white apart from one African sitting at the back. He came up to me afterwards and said, "Guillebaud! God used your grandparents to lead me to Christ!" Why do I tell you that? Because my grandparents were gifted people who could have been very successful in worldly terms, but they laid their lives down in order to store up treasures in heaven. In monetary terms, when they died they left us grandchildren virtually nothing. They'd "spent" everything on the kingdom of God; all we got were a few tasteless hand-knitted jumpers! But as this chance encounter demonstrated, they'd left a living inheritance in thousands of lives scattered across the globe. That's what I want as well!

Take an inventory of what you're investing in. I suspect much of it is "eternally out-of-date". Time for any changes?

Lord, I choose to serve one master, and that's you! Help me choose to invest in what lasts today. Amen!

FRIENDLINESS OR FRIENDSHIP?

1 Thessalonians 2:8

"We loved you so much that we were delighted to share with you not only the gospel of God but our lives as well, because you had become so dear to us."

In my early twenties, I began taking my fourteen-year-old sister and three of her friends to a lively church each week to help them get connected to a vibrant Christian community. Like most teenage girls, they were shy and self-conscious, but they wanted to be plugged in. I was going through my hippie phase with turbocharged long curly hair and bright ethnic clothing, so I was probably quite hard to miss! Being more confident as well, I found it easy enough to get to know people. My sister and her three friends continued going week by week through the term while I was away at university. When I came back in the holidays, I took them again. Immediately someone came up to me, greeted me, and then turned to the girls: "Hey nice to have you back again!" My sister replied, "Actually we've been here every week." None of those four girls, now women, has a relationship with Jesus any more, as far as I know. There's only so much of being ignored, week by week, that anyone can put up with…

When people come to church, it is not *friendliness* they need but *friends*. Let's not do the handshake out of duty but rather let's show genuine interest in others, hang out and do life with them. Often we're good at inviting outsiders into our meetings but not so good at sharing our lives with them. My Mum is a great role model in this respect, always greeting newcomers and inviting them around for food.

Sharing our lives – our victories and defeats, our fears and concerns, our laughter and our tears – that's what Paul did and what he's calling us to do. Who can you reach out to this week, offering not just friendliness but true friendship?

Lord, help me to open up and share my life with others today. Amen!

WHAT IF OR WHAT IS?

17 APRIL

Isaiah 41:10

"So do not fear, for I am with you; do not be dismayed, for I am your God. I will strengthen you and help you; I will uphold you with my righteous right hand."

Fear is such a common emotion that it is addressed almost 400 times in the Bible. Many of us live lives full of fear – some legitimate, others totally unnecessary. Henri Nouwen observed,

> *Look at the many 'if' questions we raise: What am I going to do if I do not find a spouse, a house, a job, a friend, a benefactor? What am I going to do if they fire me, if I get sick, if an accident happens, if I lose my friends, if my marriage does not work out, if a war breaks out? What if tomorrow the weather is bad, the buses are on strike, or an earthquake happens? What if someone steals my money, breaks into my house, rapes my daughter, or kills me?*

On the back of all those "what ifs", Brennan Manning noted, "Once these questions guide our lives, we take out a second mortgage in the house of fear."

So instead of living shackled by the weight of *what if*, let's look at *what is* true and live accordingly: The verse above says God is with us. He is our God. He will strengthen, help, and uphold us. That being the case, there's no need to fear. I remember years back being in a nightclub, and a dance-floor altercation looked like escalating into a violent brawl with me caught in the middle – until my brawny friend jumped next to me and diffused the situation. How much more is God able to come alongside us in whatever circumstance to strengthen, help, and uphold us!

Take a look at your own life today: are there any fearful "what ifs" that need replacing by God's promises *of what is true*?

Lord, I choose freedom from fear today, knowing that you are with me. Amen!

PRIVATIZED OR UNFETTERED?

Romans 1:16

"I am not ashamed of the gospel, because it is the power of God for the salvation of everyone who believes."

Paul wasn't ashamed, so why am I?

One of our biggest problems has arisen out of the privatization of our faith. The result of a privatized faith is that Christ's lordship is restricted to certain times and places in our compartmentalized lives. We may hang him on the coat peg with our jacket as we enter the office, or in the locker in the changing room before training on the team, and only pick him up at the end of the day's work or after the training session. People aren't attracted by the hypocrisy of Sunday religion; they want the reality of a consistent and dynamic 24–7 relationship which transcends the suffocating pressures and ambitions of day-to-day existence.

Often our problem doesn't lie in the fact that we're in the wrong place – rather we're not living out the reality of our faith where we are.

How can we make sure we are what we should be where we are?

We need to immerse ourselves afresh in the Scriptures, to be struck anew by the all-encompassing nature of Christ's call on the original disciples' lives. Jesus wants to turn us into wide-eyed radicals. If being "nice" is our highest aspiration, the gospel is emasculated and becomes simply life-*enhancing* instead of life-*transforming*. Nice people are never offensive, and yet at some stage the gospel must offend, because it highlights areas of inconsistency and hypocrisy in my own life, as well as in the lives of those who reject Jesus for who he claims to be. If our greatest virtue is that we don't offend anyone, then there will be no potency or passion in our message or movement, which ends up being OK news instead of the best news in the world.

Lord, I choose to be totally unashamed about you. Use me to share this great news today. Amen!

1 Corinthians 1: 25

"For the foolishness of God is wiser than man's wisdom."

COMMON SENSE OR RECKLESS FAITH?

Oswald Chambers wrote:

> *The simplicity that comes from our natural common sense decisions is apt to be mistaken for the witness of the Spirit, but the Spirit witnesses only to his own nature and to the work of Redemption, never to our own reason. If we try to make him witness to our reason, it is no wonder that we are in darkness and perplexity. Fling it all overboard, trust in God, and he will give the witness.*

We need to be clear what he's not saying: he's not advocating an abandoning of our critical faculties, a spontaneous embarking on ill-conceived adventures, or a jeopardizing of the safety and well-being of others. Neither is he saying that common sense is wrong or to be jettisoned as conflicting at all times with the life of faith. Common sense is a God-given faculty, an endowment without which we couldn't survive. However, common sense wouldn't advocate sending Jesus to the cross. Common sense would preclude adhering to or implementing much of what Jesus said. Common sense rationalizes away most of the dynamics of faith, because it operates on a different plane. That's why the message of the cross is "foolishness to those who are perishing" (1 Corinthians 1:18). It's quite simply an absurd message – unless it's a historical reality.

Chambers continued, "Never let common sense obtrude and push the Son of Man to one side. Common sense is a gift which God gave to human nature; but common sense is not the gift of his Son. Supernatural sense is the gift of his Son; never enthrone common sense."

Once we embrace the message of the cross as the absolute truth, the call to authentic discipleship will involve reckless faith that sometimes overrides common sense.

Lord, I want to live fully surrendered to you. Show me the difference between common sense and reckless faith, which way is appropriate, and when. Amen!

FULL OR PART TIME?

Colossians 3:23

"Whatever you do, work at it with all your heart, as for the Lord, not for men."

Some people believe all Christians are born equal, but "full-time" Christians are born more equal than others. What do you think?

We need to completely reject that way of viewing things. All vocations are equal, and so-called "secular work" is a vocation. The Bible doesn't differentiate between the physical and spiritual parts of human life in the same way that we tend to, and God doesn't distinguish or compartmentalize "work" and "worship" – indeed the Hebrew words for both "work" and "worship" are derived from the same root.

One cannot overestimate the insidious effect that such a misrepresentation of the validity of "secular" work has had on committed believers. Mark Greene highlights the danger, saying that

> *the impact on Christians of effectively robbing their work of spiritual and ministry value is to produce a sense of guilt. The working Christian comes home at the end of a fifty-hour week and thinks, "I haven't done any evangelism. I haven't done any ministry. I'm not serving God. I must make time outside work to do all these things, otherwise I'm not leading an obedient Christian life." So perhaps he or she gets involved in neighbourhood evangelism, or accepts the invitation to serve on whichever committee, and tries to squeeze a hundred commitments into a seven-day week. The result can simply be exhaustion and discouragement.*

In seeking to be disciples of Jesus, our aim is to live in any and every situation as he would live if he were us. It's not *what* I do, but *how* I do it. Otherwise, if my job isn't a supposedly "full-time" one, I'll be spending a large proportion of my waking hours excluding Jesus' relevance and primacy in it. Thankfully that is not the case.

Lord, I choose to sign up: full-time, whole-hearted, single-mindedly yours, in whatever task you assign to me in this world. Amen!

WORRY OR TRUST?

Philippians 4:6, 7

"Do not be anxious about anything, but in everything, by prayer and petition, with thanksgiving, present your requests to God. And the peace of God, which transcends all understanding, will guard your hearts and your minds in Christ Jesus."

Worry has been described as the interest we pay on tomorrow's troubles, and it severely curtails the extent to which we can act out our dreams and maximize our lives for Jesus.

A widow was telling her story to a reporter about how she had managed to raise a huge family, which included six of her own and another twelve adopted children. Not only did they grow up into fine young men and women, but she had retained her own sanity and spirit through several tiring decades. Answering his question as to the secret of her success, she replied, "I managed so well because I'm in a partnership!" The reporter was confused by her answer, and asked, "I don't understand. Please explain what you mean." The woman replied: "Many years ago I said, 'Lord, I'll do the work and you do the worrying.' And I haven't had an anxious care since."

Worrying seldom helps. For each one of us, we can be certain that God's call will never take us where his grace won't keep us. Be it in the workplace or with family, we acknowledge the Lord's control and right to do with us as he wills. We trust his character and constancy. For Lizzie and me, taking our three little children to Africa, where the quality of healthcare is decidedly ropey, takes trust that God will watch over them. For you there will be other issues, but our verse today shows us how to deal with all our potential worries. Obey verse 6, and then acknowledge verse 7 – that peace is truly priceless.

Lord, thank you that I can bring all my worries to you… I hand them over to you, and I receive your transcending peace for today. Amen!

SPRINTER OR PLODDER?

James 1:2–4

"Consider it pure joy, my brothers, whenever you face trials of many kinds, because you know that the testing of your faith develops perseverance. Perseverance must finish its work so that you may be mature and complete, not lacking anything."

William Carey is often attributed the title "father of modern missions". He was born into a desperately poor family and consequently obtained a poor education. He was apprenticed as a shoemaker, but simply didn't make the grade. He tried his hand at running a school, but it was a flop. His marriage was an unhappy one, during which his daughter died early – an event which left him bald for life. He was a deeply committed believer, but his subsequent attempt at pastoring a small church lessened his chances of ordination, because by common consent his sermons were too boring for words!

Despite such an apparently flawed track record, Carey formed a missionary society, with himself as the first candidate setting sail to India. This feeble individual translated the Bible into Bengali, Oriya, Marathi, Hindi, Assamese, and Sanskrit, as well as portions into twenty-nine other languages. At one stage, he lost ten years' translation work in a fire. What did he do? He just started again. Then there were his contributions to literature, education, literacy, agriculture, getting infanticide outlawed, and more. This man's obedience and perseverance were used to impact the lives of literally millions of people.

Before dying, knowing that one of his supporters wanted to write about his life, Carey conveyed his wishes: "If one should think it worth his while to write my life, I will give you a criterion by which you may judge of its correctness. If he gives me credit for being a plodder, he will describe me justly. Anything beyond this will be too much. *I can plod. I can persevere in any definite pursuit.* To this I owe everything."

Lord, give me strength today to plod where necessary. Amen!

PULLING OUT OR FINISHING STRONG?

2 Timothy 4:7

"I have fought the good fight, I have run the race, I have kept the faith."

My first spiritual mentor left his dying wife and four children for a young man. The teacher I idolized most at Bible college left his wife and daughter for a younger woman. Both of these men had been much used by God in many different settings in a number of countries – but right now it doesn't look as though they are planning to finish well.

John Akhwari was a Tanzanian marathon runner at the Mexico Olympics of 1968. Over an hour after the winner had crossed the line, as the day's activities had just come to an end, people were emptying out of the stands and heading home. Just then Akhwari entered through the tunnel and embarked on his last lap in the stadium after just under twenty-six miles around the city. His cramped feet shuffled along, and his face was contorted in agony as he pushed through the pain barrier, having dislocated his knee in a fall at the 19km point. Gradually the crowd caught on and started cheering wildly. When Akhwari crossed the finishing line, the noise was deafening. At a press conference afterwards, he was asked by the interviewer: "You were so far behind. Why didn't you just give up?" He replied, "My country, Tanzania, of which I am very proud, didn't send me here to start the race, but to finish it."

In seeking to finish the race, and finish well, we will need persistence and determination. We will press on through trials and difficulties. Finishing strong is not a matter of talent or genius – there are plenty of gifted and talented men and women who never finish the Christian race. It's not a matter of education or social standing, but of disciplined, dogged, tenacious persevering, walking closely in Jesus' footsteps, heeding his call, obeying his commands, fulfilling his commission.

Lord, I am desperate to be able to echo Paul's words at the end of my life too. Help me to remain humble, disciplined, and finish strong. For your glory, Amen!

TOO BUSY TO OR TOO BUSY NOT TO PRAY?

1 Thessalonians 5:17

"Pray continually."

Most of us are too busy to pray, but our excuses illustrate our fundamental misunderstanding of the primacy of prayer. If we grasp the importance of prayer, it will undergird our very existence and act as the engine-room for all our activities, such that we will be too busy not to pray, as the title of a book on the subject suggests. R.A. Torrey gave this critique: "We have a great deal of activity but we accomplish little; many services but few conversions; much machinery but few results."

Jesus placed prayer right at the heart of his ministry. He modelled the life of prayer and exhorted his disciples to follow his example. As a matter of fact, he never taught his disciples to preach, but he made sure they were well taught in the school of prayer. We need to access power from God before we can wield power with men. Hence speaking with God will come before speaking with men. It's said that Francis of Assisi spent 75 per cent of his active hours in prayer and 25 per cent in preaching and apostolic service; yet although he's primarily remembered nowadays for the impact of his preaching, the latter was only the result of many hours spent in the Father's presence, before being sent out empowered, envisioned, energized, and equipped by the Holy Spirit.

It's sometimes hard to set aside a chunk of time every day for dedicated prayer and Bible study, but I want to encourage you that it's not so hard to "pray continually", as Paul exhorted the Thessalonians. It just means being in constant communion with God. So, for example, you could put up post-it notes of verses on your bathroom mirror, on the fridge door, on the dashboard of the car, as constant reminders to talk to God throughout the day. It works. Never say you're too busy to pray. It's not true, and you'll be the loser for it.

Lord, I choose to cultivate a habit of praying continually today. Amen!

2 Corinthians 11:25, 26

"Three times I was beaten with rods, once I was stoned, three times I was shipwrecked, I spent a night and a day in the open sea..."

LAWNMOWER OR MOTORCYCLE?

Paul's life was one of incredible variety, challenge, adventure, and suffering. The last thing you would say about it was that it was dull. As we follow Christ faithfully, our life may have some dreary patches but in general it won't be dull either.

Wes Seliger is an Anglican priest and also a petrol head. One day he was checking out a beautiful Honda 750 on display at a bike shop and regretting that his career path meant he couldn't afford to buy it. A salesman saw the look in his eyes and started on his pitch with gusto, mentioning the head-turning growl of the pipes, the speed, acceleration, excitement, the potential to woo beautiful women, and more. Then he asked Wes what he did for a living, and the sales patter suddenly changed! In an instant the bike had become practical, with good mileage, and would be a sensible choice.

Reflecting on the incident, Wes observed: "Lawnmower salesmen are not surprised to find clergymen looking at their merchandise; motorcycle salesmen are. Why? Does this tell us something about clergymen and about the church? Lawnmowers are slow, safe, sane, practical, and middle-class. Motorcycles are fast, dangerous, wild, thrilling." Then Wes asked: "Is being a Christian more like mowing a lawn or like riding a motorcycle? Is the Christian life safe and sound or dangerous and exciting?" He concluded: "The common image of the church is pure lawnmower – slow, deliberate, plodding. Our task is to take the church out on the open road, give it the gas, and see what the old baby will do!"

Is my faith a lawnmower faith or a motorcycle faith? And is my church a lawnmower church or a motorcycle church? Maybe it's time we took more risks for God.

Lord, more motorcycle less lawnmower please! Amen!

WARTIME WALKIE-TALKIE OR DOMESTIC INTERCOM?

2 Corinthians 10:4

"The weapons we fight with are not the weapons of the world. On the contrary, they have divine power to demolish strongholds."

Paul frequently used the metaphor of war to convey the urgency and purpose of prayer. We're in a battle, and the realm of warfare we're engaging in isn't the material world, rather the spiritual one (Ephesians 6:10–18), which is why he exhorts us to "put on the full armour of God, so that when the day of evil comes, you may be able to stand your ground, and after you have done everything, to stand" (verse 13). In turn he calls us to appropriate every available weapon in God's spiritual armoury (verses 14–18). The list of weapons culminates with prayer: "And pray in the Spirit on all occasions with all kinds of prayers and requests. With this in mind, be alert and always keep on praying for all the saints. Pray also for me..." (verses 18–19).

So we need to wake up to the fact that our prayers have power; they can have eternal consequences! Each of us has a key role to play in God's army and it is prayer that underpins everything. If we don't grasp that, then our prayers will be sluggish, apathetic or just won't happen.

John Piper hits the nub of it:

Probably the number one reason why prayer malfunctions in the hands of believers is that we try to turn a wartime walkie-talkie into a domestic intercom. Until you know that life is war, you cannot know what prayer is for... But what have millions of Christians done? We have stopped believing that we are in a war. No urgency, no watching, no vigilance. No strategic planning. Just easy peace and prosperity. And what did we do with the walkie-talkie? We tried to rig it up as an intercom in our houses – not to call in fire power for conflict with a mortal enemy, but to ask for more comforts in the den.

Challenging words...

Lord, I choose to pray with a greater sense of urgency today. Amen!

Philippians 4:19

"And my God will meet all your needs according to his glorious riches in Christ Jesus."

NEEDS OR GREEDS?

I might wish verse 19 promised that God would meet all my "wants", but no, it says "needs": he will meet all my (and your) needs according to his glorious riches in Christ Jesus. You can be sure of that. It's a comfort to know that he sees what we're going through and knows what we need. Trust him today.

Dr Helen Roseveare was a missionary in what is now the Democratic Republic of Congo, across the lake from me. She tells of a young mother dying at the mission station shortly after having given birth prematurely. The medical staff needed a makeshift incubator for the premature baby, but the only hot water bottle they had leaked. During team prayers that morning, the children were asked to pray for the baby and her little sister who was now orphaned. So one young girl prayed, "Dear God, please send a hot water bottle today. Tomorrow will be too late because by then the baby will be dead. And, dear Lord, send a doll for the sister so she won't feel so lonely."

Although parcel deliveries were rare, a large one did arrive that afternoon. They opened it and were overjoyed to find a hot water bottle! The little girl who had prayed so earnestly pounced on the parcel and rummaged among the contents, exclaiming, "If God sent that, I'm sure he also sent a doll." She was right! A beautiful doll was there, in response to the little girl's petition. Five months earlier, the Sovereign Lord had prompted a group of ladies to pack a parcel of just the right things to arrive on just the right day in just the right place – a remote mission station in Africa thousands of miles away! What perfect timing! God surely holds the whole world in his hands!

Few stories of God's provision are that dramatic, but how about learning that verse today, and standing on its promise for the rest of your life. I have, and I'm still standing!

Lord, I choose to take you at your word today. You see my needs. Amen!

TURN TOWARDS OR TURN AWAY?

Isaiah 45:22

"Turn to me and be saved, all you ends of the earth; for I am God and there is no other."

Many people we come across refuse to turn to God or even acknowledge his existence. On one occasion, a barber said to the man whose hair he was cutting: "I don't believe that God exists." "Why do you say that?" asked the customer. "Well, you just have to go out in the street to realize that God doesn't exist. Tell me, if God existed, would there be so many sick people? Would there be abandoned children? If God existed, there would be neither suffering nor pain." The customer stayed quiet to avoid an argument. Once finished, he paid and left.

Out on the street, he saw a man with long, matted hair and an untrimmed beard. He was filthy and smelly. The customer went back into the barber shop again and he said to the barber: "You know what? Barbers don't exist!" "How can you say that?" asked the surprised barber. "I'm here, and I'm a barber. And I just cut your hair!" "No!" the customer went on: "Barbers don't exist because if they did, there would be no people with dirty long hair and untrimmed beards, like that man outside." "But barbers *do* exist! That's what happens when people don't come to me." "Exactly!" said the customer. "That's the point! God, too, *does* exist! That's what happens when people don't go to him and don't turn to him for help. That's why there's so much pain and suffering in the world."

It's a pithy story, but maybe one worth sharing with your atheist or agnostic friends. If you're reading this, you've probably already committed your life to God, but we still manage to turn elsewhere so often in search of solutions to our problems. Turn to him today.

Lord, you are God, and there is no other. I choose to turn to you for guidance today, rather than anywhere else. Amen!

SIT THERE OR DO SOMETHING?

Deuteronomy 30:19

"This day I call heaven and earth as witnesses against you that I have set before you life and death, blessings and curses. Now choose life!"

Larry Walters was a 33-year-old truck driver living near Los Angeles. On weekends he used to just sit around and watch TV. But this particular Saturday, he was bored with his usual routine, so he decided he wanted to *do* something. He went shopping and bought forty-two weather balloons and a deck chair. Returning home, he anchored the chair to the ground with some ropes, and then tied the weather balloons to it. When all was ready, he ensconced himself in the chair, with his air gun nestled in his lap. He then cut the ropes, and rose steadily into the sky. Within minutes he had attained an altitude of 16,000 feet. The air traffic control tower at LA airport reported receiving a number of garbled and incredulous messages from different pilots along the lines of, "You're not going to believe this, but there's a man floating up here in a deck chair!" Soon Larry's thirst for action seemed quenched, and he decided it was time to return to planet earth. He shot a number of balloons with his air gun and gradually floated downwards. Forty-five minutes later he landed at Long Beach, about seven miles from where he had taken off. His excursion made front-page news, resulting in a Timex ad and an interview on *The Tonight Show*. Quizzed as to his motivation for doing it, Larry Walters replied, "I couldn't just sit there – I had to do something!"

I'm not sure the outworking of Larry's need to "do something" was the best, but I resonate with his dissatisfaction of just sitting there! Let's switch off the TV, get off the couch, and work out what choosing life looks like for us.

Father, that urge to "do something" is from you. Show me what to do today, and in my life in general. Amen!

FLICKERING OR FLOODED?

Psalm 8:4

"What is man that you are mindful of him, the son of man that you care for him?"

30

APRIL

So many people aspire to being "successful", yet find that when/if attained, success simply doesn't deliver the desired sense of wholeness. The brilliant but tragic Ernest Hemingway wrote shortly before committing suicide, "I live in a vacuum that's as lonely as a radio when the batteries are dead." Bob Geldof's autobiography is entitled *Is That It?* Actor Kenneth Williams wrote in his diary on the day of his death, "What's the bloody point?" Jean-Paul Sartre noted, "This world isn't the product of intelligence. It meets our gaze as would a crumpled piece of paper… what is man but a little puddle of water whose freedom is death?" A. E. Matthews joked sadly of his own life, "In the end I got so old and tired and weary of living, that I looked in *The Times'* obituary column each morning and if I wasn't there, I got up!"

Taken together, they're enough to make anyone depressed! Contrast the words of Professor Joad, who was converted from atheism to Christianity. He said, "trying to find happiness from this world is like trying to light up a dark room by lighting a succession of matches. You strike one, it flickers for a moment, and then it goes out. But when you find Jesus Christ, it's as though the whole room's suddenly flooded with light."

Maybe you can relate to the flickering light of fleeting pleasures sought outside of God's will for your life. I hope you can all the more relate to Joad's imagery of a room being flooded with light when Christ comes in. He is the source of all meaning, purpose, and fulfilment. Look to him!

Lord, thank you that you are indeed mindful of man, that you do care for us. May I derive all my sense of worth and purpose from you today. Amen!

Matthew 5:16

"Let your light shine before men, that they may see your good deeds and praise your Father in heaven."

SWITCHED ON OR SWITCHED OFF?

If you did an honest self-assessment of your life, would you say that you let your light shine?

A family friend writes about a documentary on five young Australian lads who had just done a 1,800-mile cycle ride through Outer Mongolia. They were interviewed about their time – how they had handled injuries, conflicts, and other unforeseen difficulties. The interviewer then asked, "Why did you do the trip?" The last boy said that, when he was younger, he had a dream, and in the dream, he stood at the end of his life before five judges who were there to pass judgment on his life. After a long silence, one of the judges threw down the gavel and said, "Guilty of a wasted life!" He said that the dream had a massive impact on him and he didn't want to hear that verdict pronounced at the end of his *real* life.

The friend concludes, "This young man wasn't a Christian. Are the children of the world more switched on than the children of light? Do we forget that one day we'll all stand before a Judge, not just in a dream, but in reality, and we'll be required to give account of all the deeds we've done and how we've used our talents?"

Ouch! Are the children of the world more switched on than the children of light? I take that challenge on the chin. I don't want to be guilty of a wasted life, and I'm pretty sure you don't either. We're accountable for how we use our God-given talents, our time, and our willingness to shine God's light in this dark world. Jesus is the light of the world. He lives in you. So let him shine through you today.

Lord, use me today to bring light into a dark situation for your glory. Amen!

TRIVIAL OR ESSENTIAL?

Mark 8:35

"Whoever wants to save his life will lose it, but whoever loses his life for me and for the gospel will save it."

2

MAY

The basic essence of life in Christ is self-abandonment. Tullian Tchividjian writes, "Jesus said we must die in order that we might live. Daily Christian living, in other words, is daily Christian dying: dying to our trivial comforts, soul-shrinking conveniences, arrogant preferences, and self-centred entitlements, and living for something much larger than what makes us comfortable and safe."

Back in 1996, I was part of a team that drove a truck for a mission organization from Wales to Kenya. We travelled through thirteen countries and had many eventful experiences over several months. Having returned to the UK, one of the women on our team wrote to me with the following reflections:

> *To me the calling I left Africa with wasn't just a call to evangelism, it was surpassing that call – it was a call to live for Jesus. Whatever country I'm in, I know God calls me to live for him. Not for a car, a job, family, church, Bible study, security, romance, friendships, or anything else I might want to live my life for. That's how God has started to change me since our trip. It used to be important what I ate, how much sleep I had – such trivial things I'd revolve my life around.*

What am I revolving my life around? What should I revolve my life around? What is essential to my life? What should be essential in my life? It's sobering to really take stock and analyse how I allow myself to get distracted and corrupted, such that the trivial often displaces the essential. How about you? May God show us what needs addressing and changing.

Lord, enough trivialities and banalities! Draw me back to the essence of what life is about. I choose to lose my life for you and for the gospel today. Amen!

Hebrews 10:31

"It is a fearful thing to fall into the hands of the living God." (ESV)

SAFE OR DANGEROUS?

My friend Mark Buchanan has written a book entitled *Your God is Too Safe*. He insists that God is not at all safe, but dangerous: "And yet there is something far more fearful and dangerous than to fall into His hands: to not fall into His hands."

Historically, the growth of the cult of Mary came into being as a reaction against how God was perceived as too angry and cruel, like an aggressive domineering Father. So the masses needed a more gentle, tender, and motherly influence to shelter them and intervene on their behalf. Contrasting this Catholic tendency, Buchanan continues:

> *In Protestantism, I think we've simply substituted the safe god. But the biting irony is this: neither the safe god nor the tyrant god are the real God. The God who truly is, who seeks you and me, who desires our holiness, is far more loving and comforting than the safe god. And the true God is far more fierce and fearsome than the bullying and petulant god of our imaginations. But His anger is not irritability: it is the distillation of His justice, His hatred of evil. It is what we would want, even demand, from a good God.*

Having given the Israelites the Ten Commandments on God's behalf, Moses said to them: "Do not be afraid... so that the fear of God will be with you to keep you from sinning" (Exodus 20:20). As Tozer remarked, we take refuge *from* God *in* God. Such a God inspires awe and wonder in us, and only a God we fear and yet do not need to be afraid of can set our hearts ablaze for him.

Familiarity can breed contempt, or at the very least complacency. Spend some time today thinking about this dangerous, fearful, awesome God whom you can call Father.

God Almighty, I take refuge from you in you today. Rid me of any notions that you are safe, and use me for your glory. Amen!

CONTENTED OR COMPLAINING?

Philippians 4:12–13

"I have learned the secret of being content in any and every situation, whether well fed or hungry, whether living in plenty or in want. I can do everything through him who gives me strength."

I remember feeling chastened on one occasion when I had recently come out to Africa as a single man. I was feeling lonely and homesick, and a firebrand called Livingstone came to visit me. As I wallowed in self-pity, he gently reminded me of his own situation. He had fled civil war in his homeland but then got caught up in the Congolese troubles, so had walked for thirty days through hundreds of miles of jungle. He had a bullet wound in his back to show for it, and hadn't seen or heard of his wife and children for six years. As a refugee he had minimal rights, no job, a hovel to sleep in, and a seemingly bleak future. Yet despite his personal circumstances, Livingstone was truly alive, counting his blessings, full of the Holy Spirit; and *he* had come round to encourage *me*, even though I had so much more than him. I realized that he was one of many African men and women who, through the crucible of suffering, had been elevated to loftier heights of intimacy with their heavenly Father.

Livingstone's attitude taught me (and can teach each one of us) that we can choose to be content and grateful for what we've been given rather than to complain about what we don't have. And in choosing either the former or the latter response, it will become a habit for life. Speaking as an Englishman, our national pastime is moaning! Let's zip it, and may God help us to choose to be grateful and contented people, because such people are joyful people, whose joy can defy personal circumstances.

Lord, forgive my moaning and ingratitude. I choose to be content today, counting the many blessings you've poured out on my life. Amen!

Ecclesiastes 3:13

"That everyone may eat and drink, and find satisfaction in his toil – this is the gift of God."

NUT-JOB OR ENLIGHTENED?

Russian author Fyodor Dostoevsky was arrested by the Tsar's soldiers as a dissident and rebel, and was sentenced to death. The Tsar enjoyed toying with his prisoners by having them blindfolded and lined up in front of a firing squad. But only blanks were used, so the blindfolded prisoners heard the shots but weren't killed. They were left traumatized. The effect on Dostoevsky was life-transforming. His senses were sharpened such that every mouthful became more tasty, the songs of the birds more beautiful, the diverse shades of the leaves more delectable; it was this very experience which enabled him to see things more deeply and convey them more richly in his writings. Having faced death threats myself and expected to get killed, I can totally relate to him.

Comedian and chat-show host Jonathan Ross surprised me with what he said in an interview recently:

> *I learned the secret of happiness from Swiss musician Dieter Meier. He told me, "I make sure I enjoy everything I'm doing. For example, today I was washing up, and I stopped and looked at the bubble on a glass, and enjoyed the sensation of my hand in the water." At the time, I thought, "You're a nut-job!" But actually, what a lovely way to go through life! You can spend your time getting angry and xxxx-ed off about things, or you can be a little bit more accepting and think, "What have I done that's nice today?" which sounds trite, I know – but it's all I've got.*

He's so close. It's all he's got, because he's missing the last piece of the puzzle: the Source of all goodness to be able to express thanks towards. You know the Source. Enjoy all that comes from him today.

Thank you, Lord, that you are that Source. I choose to live joyfully today. Amen!

EARTH OR HEAVEN?

1 Peter 1:3, 4

"Praise be to God! In his great mercy he has given us new birth into a living hope through the resurrection of Jesus Christ from the dead, and into an inheritance that can never perish, spoil or fade – kept in heaven for you."

Today's verse talks clearly about how Christian hope is both for this life and for the next. But many of us aren't living today in light of eternity. J.I. Packer puts it well:

> *For today, by and large, Christians no longer live for heaven, and therefore no longer understand, let alone practise, detachment from the world... Does the world around us seek profit, pleasure and privilege? So do we. We have no readiness or strength to renounce these objectives, for we have recast Christianity into a mould that stresses happiness above holiness, blessings here above blessing hereafter, health and wealth as God's best gifts, and death, especially early death, not as thankworthy deliverance from the miseries of a sinful world, but as the supreme disaster... Is our Christianity out of shape? Yes it is, and the basic reason is that we have lost the New Testament's two-world perspective that views the next life as more important than this one and understands life here as essentially preparation and training for life hereafter.*

It's important to note in the above that Packer is redressing an imbalance which he observes in many of us nowadays. But we mustn't create a false dichotomy and swing too far the other way either, ending up "so heavenly minded that we're no earthly good". As the Christian Aid motto states: "We believe in life *before* death." Jesus provides not only hope for the after-life, but hope through our day-to-day trials, challenges, disappointments, and hurts. Let's grasp hold of both dimensions of this "living hope" and share it with people around us today.

Thank you, Lord, for the gift of hope – for now and into eternity. I choose to embody that hope today. Amen!

PEACE OR FEAR?

John 20:21, 22

"Again Jesus said, 'Peace be with you! As the Father has sent me, I am sending you.' And with that he breathed on them and said, 'Receive the Holy Spirit'."

"The disciples were together with the doors locked for fear of the Jews" (John 20:19) when Jesus appeared to them. He was preparing his disciples for tough times ahead. Soon he would ascend to heaven, and they would be left to fend for themselves – but not quite by themselves because the promised Holy Spirit would be given to empower them to live out their God-given mandate to change the world.

Back in 1520, Ferdinand Magellan spent a whole year trying to find a passage around South America. There at the southernmost tip of the continent, he and his crew were overwhelmed by towering ice floes, raging seas, and bitter gales. The crew threatened mutiny, but eventually they made it, and quickly the violent weather was replaced by peaceful waters. The straits they had just been through are named after him to this day – the Straits of Magellan – but he also chose the name of the new body of water that his ship had now entered. Having praised God for their deliverance, he named the new ocean "The Peaceful One – the Pacific Ocean".

Oswald Chambers wrote:

> *When you really see Jesus, I defy you to doubt Him. When He says "Let not your hearts be troubled," if you see Him I defy you to trouble your mind, it is a moral impossibility to doubt when He is there. Every time you get into personal contact with Jesus, His words are real. "My peace I give you," it is a peace all over from the crown of the head to the sole of the feet, an irrepressible confidence. "Your life is hid with Christ in God," and the imperturbable peace of Jesus Christ is imparted to you.*

Lord, I receive your Holy Spirit and choose to live from the place of peace today, not fear. Amen!

SEEN OR UNSEEN?

James 5:16–18

"The prayer of a righteous man is powerful and effective. Elijah was a man just like us. He prayed earnestly that it would not rain and it did not rain on the land for three and a half years. Again he prayed, and the heavens gave rain."

There's a certain type of bamboo in Asia that grows to prodigious heights and at prodigious speed – sometimes as much as sixty feet in six weeks. However, before that growth spurt, the seed lies in the dark beneath the ground for up to five years. Those farmers who make a profitable living from this bamboo know what it is to be patient. They would have given up long ago and changed crops if they weren't confident that plenty was going on beneath the surface even though there was no visible sign to encourage their perseverance. Every bit of watering and waiting is worthwhile. No prayer is wasted. Elijah had learned that, and may we do so too.

I was challenged once by a Bolivian called Carlos. He had decided to follow Jesus at significant personal cost, experiencing alienation and antagonism from various family members. But God was at work! Slowly, over several years, one by one, each member of Carlos's family decided to surrender their lives to God. What was his secret? "Three times a day, year after year, I got down on my knees and pleaded with the Lord for all my family."

I've prayed for family members and friends for a few decades now, and some have come to faith, while others have not yet. Sometimes there is clear visible progress, but most of the time it's unseen – but I can be confident that plenty is going on beneath the surface, just like those bamboo shoots.

Whether it's loved ones you want to see converted; a debilitating long-term illness, a crushing disappointment, or whatever other issue you've battled with and wrestled over in prayer for years, don't give up! God has heard every single prayer.

Lord, I choose to trust your wisdom and timing today for… Amen!

Ecclesiastes 5:4

"When you make a vow to God, do not delay in fulfilling it."

APATHY OR URGENCY?

There's a pithy parable about the devil's training academy for his demonic minions. On the day of the graduation ceremony, he was mingling with the new graduates and questioning them about what they had learned. He approached one group of three demons and engaged them in conversation. He asked them, "Now that you're ready to start your mission of leading as many earthlings away from the path of God and into my clutches, what strategy will you use?" The first demon replied, "Sir, I'll tell them there's no God." "Rubbish! That won't work. Creation's so beautiful that it points to the fact that surely there is a Creator. You won't dupe many with that one." The second one replied, "Sir, I'll tell them that there's no judgment." "No chance! Come on, we all know that those pathetic earthlings have been endowed with a conscience so that they inherently have a conception of right and wrong. Most know and recognize a coming judgment. That's not going to work." Finally, the third demon replied, "I'll tell them that yes, there is a God, and yes, there is a judgment, but also that there's still plenty of time." "Excellent! You've studied well. Many will be suckers for that lie. Get to it!"

Satan is described in the Bible as "the father of lies", who "was a murderer from the beginning", and when "he lies, he speaks his native language, for he is a liar" (John 8:44). He is a thief who "comes only to steal and kill and destroy" (John 10:10). He "prowls around like a roaring lion looking for someone to devour" (1 Peter 5:8).

So in light of the parable above, can you think of anything you've been putting off that you need to deal with? Satan hates it when we boldly advance in obedience to Jesus' commands. Just do it!

Lord, I choose to live with a sense of urgency and mission today. Amen!

MUGS OR MODELS?

Philippians 3:17

"Join together in following my example, brothers and sisters, and just as you have us as a model, keep your eyes on those who live as we do."

Dallas Willard highlights how mistaken we've become in thinking that imparting information is the best means of learning and discipleship:

> *It is a peculiarly modern notion that the aim of teaching is to bring people to know things that may have no effect at all on their lives. In our day learners usually think of themselves as containers of some sort, with a purely passive space to be filled by the information the teacher possesses and wishes to transfer – the "from jug to mug model". The teacher is to fill in empty parts of the receptacle with "truth" that may or may not later make some difference to the life of the one who has it. The teacher must get the information into them. We then "test" the patients to see if they "got it" by checking whether they can reproduce it in language rather than watching how they live.*

Jesus spent three years living out his message and modelling how to live for his disciples. Paul pursued the same strategy. He wrote: "Be imitators of me, as I am of Christ" (1 Corinthians 11:1). Both wanted their disciples not only to be biblically literate, but biblically obedient. Spiritual maturity was gauged by application, not contemplation only.

Some questions to consider: are you a mug? If so, then stop! But presuming you want to be a model, do you know how to go about it? Do you have someone to mentor you and help you learn how to live as a disciple of Christ? Are you part of an intentional community of disciples *and disciple-makers*? If your answer is no, then do something about it today. Seek out like-minded people. It's critical to your effectiveness.

Lord, help me identify both people to learn from and to invest in, so that I'm an effective model and disciple-maker for your glory. Amen!

ALL THE TIME OR TIME OUT?

James 4:14, 15

"Why, you do not even know what will happen tomorrow. What is your life? You are a mist that appears for a little while and then vanishes. Instead, you ought to say, 'If it is the Lord's will, we will live and do this or that.'"

Plans are all well and good, but James warns us not to be complacent and self-sufficient as we look ahead. Our times are in God's hands.

I came across this obituary:

> *Died, Salvador Sanchez, 23, World Boxing Council featherweight champion and one of the sport's best fighters; of injuries after his Porsche 928 collided with two trucks, just north of Queretaro, Mexico. A school dropout at 16, Sanchez explained, "I found out that I liked hitting people, and I didn't like school so I started boxing." A peppery tactician, he wore opponents down for late-round knockouts. His record: 43–1–1. "I'd like to step down undefeated," he said last month. "I'm only 23 and I have all the time in the world."*

Like many young people, Sanchez considered himself practically immortal. Siegfried Sassoon once said, "At the age of 22, I believed myself to be inextinguishable." Actually, so did I. And such an attitude is representative of many for whom old age seems miles away. But it's dangerous to live that way. Whereas life is uncertain, death is sure. David was right when he said to Jonathan: "As surely as the Lord lives and as you live, there is only a step between me and death" (1 Samuel 20:3). I look back at a number of school friends who have died in the last few years, all of them virile and robust men in their twenties or thirties from highly affluent and privileged backgrounds – we are far from immortal – and so we need to be ready.

Lord, I choose to trust you with all the days in my life. Help me use my time well for you and live ready, for your glory. Amen!

PERSIST OR DESIST?

Hebrews 12:1

"Let us run with perseverance the race marked out for us."

A certain man went into business, but his venture was a total flop. He switched to politics but within only one year that didn't work out either. He tried his hand for a second time at business, but failed again. That meant three failures in three years. He proposed to his fiancée after four years of courtship, but she turned him down. Another woman he was courting died some time later. All these pressures led to a nervous breakdown, which required two years of convalescence, after which he relaunched his aborted political career with a bid to be elected as speaker of the House of Representatives. He failed. He was again defeated two years later for the position of elector. Another three years after this, he was defeated as he ran for a seat in Congress. Another five years passed before he sought office again, but was defeated. Tragically his four-year-old son died during this time. That led to seven years in the wilderness, before running for the Senate – to no avail. Things looked more positive the following year, when he was nominated by his party as their vice-presidential candidate, but he and his running mate were defeated in the general election. He failed two years later when trying again for a seat in the Senate. However, another two years later, in 1860, after twenty-four years of dogged persistence, Abraham Lincoln was elected as the sixteenth president of the United States of America!

I don't know what challenges you face, but keep running your race today. Be encouraged by these words on an office plaque:

> *Press on. Nothing in the world can take the place of persistence. Talent will not: Nothing is more common than unsuccessful men with talent. Genius will not: Unrewarded genius is almost a proverb. Education alone will not: The world is full of educated derelicts. Persistence and determination alone are omnipotent.*

Lord, help me to resist discouragement and persist with whatever you're calling me to today. Amen!

DAYDREAMER OR DREAMER OF THE DAY?

Hebrews 11:13

"All of these people were still living by faith when they died. They did not receive the things promised; they only saw them and welcomed them from a distance."

Lawrence of Arabia said: "Everyone dreams, but not equally. Those who dream by night in the dusty recesses of their minds wake up in the day to find it was vanity. But the dreamers of the day are dangerous people, for they may act out their dreams with open eyes to make it happen." Daydreaming is a waste of time because it doesn't produce anything. But being a dreamer of the day is entirely different. Hebrews 11 talks of the latter kind, mentioning the likes of Abraham and Moses who were world-shaping dreamers in their day.

More recently, Disneyland and then Disney World became hugely successful realities, although Walt Disney himself died before the latter was completed. However, at the opening ceremony of Disney World in Florida, the presiding speaker said, "I wish Walt could've seen this!" Behind him, Walt's wife whispered, "He did!"

Clement Stone was a hugely successful financier and philanthropist. He was once asked, "How have you been able to do so much in your lifetime?" He replied, "I've dreamed. I've turned my mind loose to imagine what I wanted to do. Then I've gone to bed and thought about my dreams. In the night, I've dreamed about them. And when I've arisen in the morning, I've seen the way to get to my dreams. While other people were saying, "You can't do that, it isn't possible", I was well on my way to achieving what I wanted."

How about you? What's your dream? Think about it. Pray about it. Crystallize the vision. Be prepared for opposition. And then "act out your dream with open eyes to make it happen"!

Lord, speak to me so that my dreams and aspirations align with your plans and purposes for my life; and give me the courage to go for whatever you are calling me to. Amen!

SHRINK BACK OR STAND UP?

Hebrews 10:39

"But we are not of those who shrink back and are destroyed, but of those who believe and are saved."

14

MAY

Listen to the words of a persecuted pastor in the Sudan, having gone through decades of oppression, injustice, and pain:

> *St James says: "Resist the devil and he will flee." How do we resist the devil who is threatening us today? Our weapon as Christians is "the sword of the Spirit" – the Holy Bible – and prayer. I don't want to say bad things, but I must say this: our Lord is powerful. But we assure the government that we won't take up stones or guns to defend our schools or churches. We know God is in us. We don't fear those who can kill the body. We fear the one who can kill the body and the soul. Continue praying until this issue is resolved. Those who are afraid to die: go home. Because if you are here and one of us dies, you will run away and frighten the rest. We believe God has a purpose in allowing this to happen at this time. It is for the good of Christians in this country. Some people dream of wiping out the Christian faith by the end of the decade. They are entitled to their dream. Let them continue to dream. I have a different dream. I have a dream that the people of Sudan will soon live together in peace and harmony. I have a dream that all the people of the Sudan will be worshipping the one God, the Lord Jesus Christ, by the end of the next hundred years. Are you ready to dream with me?*

Those words are deeply humbling and challenging… They are a reminder to pray for our persecuted brothers and sisters around the world, and to stand up with and for them. Look up Open Doors, Christian Solidarity Worldwide, Barnabas Fund, and so on and get involved today.

Lord, may I not be among those who shrink back. I choose to stand up today. Amen!

Proverbs 13:12

*"Hope deferred makes the heart sick,
but a longing fulfilled is a tree of life."*

DEFERRED OR FULFILLED?

Hope brings life, purpose, and direction. Without hope, the soul shrivels. I've seen it in the lives of many people languishing in refugee camps where they have lost everything. People often die for lack of hope before they die for lack of medicine.

This was graphically illustrated by a study of concentration camp survivors, which aimed to determine the common characteristics of those who didn't succumb to disease and starvation in the camps. The results showed that it was those who retained hope and dreamed against all odds who pulled through. Victor Frankl epitomized such a man. He was a successful Viennese psychiatrist before being incarcerated by the Nazis. Many years later, while addressing a number of illustrious dignitaries, he declared:

> *There's only one reason why I'm here today. What kept me alive was you. Others gave up hope. I dreamed. I dreamed that someday I would be here, telling you how I, Victor Frankl, had survived the Nazi concentration camps. I've never been here before, I've never seen any of you before, I've never given this speech before. But in my dreams, in my dreams, I have stood before you and said these words a thousand times.*

Hope gives oxygen to our dreams. Hebrews 12:2 encourages us to "fix our eyes on Jesus… who for the joy set before him endured the cross, scorning its shame, and sat down at the right hand of God" – he saw beyond the suffering of the cross because his hope was unshakeable. Whatever circumstances we're going through today, verse 3 further encourages us to "consider him who endured such opposition from sinful men, so that you will not grow weary and lose hope". Are we looking to man or God for hope? Well, man's way leads to a hopeless end but God's way leads to endless hope.

God, I choose to put my hope in you today. Amen!

SELF-ESTEEM OR SELF-LOATHING?

Psalm 139:13, 14

"You knit me together in my mother's womb. I praise you because I am fearfully and wonderfully made."

16

MAY

We live in an age obsessed with image, with popularity, with appearance. Striving for acceptance, it's easy to feel the need to put a mask on and be somebody else. Brennan Manning wrote of his own experience: "When I was eight, the impostor, or false self, was born as a defense against pain. The impostor within whispered, 'Brennan, don't ever be your real self anymore because nobody likes you as you are. Invent a new self that everybody will admire and nobody will know.'"

Actress/comedienne Dawn French said in an interview with chat-show host Michael Parkinson:

> *I've tried to wonder what it was that gave me confidence from early on, and I can only put it down to my dad. I remember that there was a night when I was going to go out to a disco, and I was really ready to have sex with anybody who wanted to ask me. And my father called me into his office and sat me down, and I thought, "I'm going to get the lecture." And instead of giving me a lecture about what time to be home or any of that he just said to me: "You are the most precious thing in our lives and you are beautiful, and you are worthy of anybody who shows you any attention. You shouldn't feel grateful for the scraps that any other girls leave behind: you should have the best." And I went out, and in fact no boy came within ten yards of me! I wouldn't allow them because they were beneath me. He just gave me a bit of self-esteem.*

Self-esteem isn't self-worship. No! Rather, it's a healthy view of oneself as valuable and precious. So whether we're male or female, let's not listen to the impostor's voice but let's listen to our Father, who made us and loves what he has made.

Lord, I choose to live at peace with who I am, fearfully and wonderfully made. Amen!

TEAM SECURITY OR INDIVIDUAL DANGER?

Psalm 66:9–12

"You, O God, laid burdens on our backs… and kept our feet from slipping… You let men ride over our heads; we went through fire and water, but you brought us to a place of abundance."

Psalm 66 is a song of praise to God for saving his people from an enemy attack in which they obviously went through the mill together in a number of difficult circumstances.

In the state of Mississippi, there was a tribe of Indians many years ago who lived next to a swirling river. If anyone fell in, they usually drowned because of the irresistible current. But one day they found themselves attacked and cornered by a hostile group of settlers. Their only escape option was to attempt to cross the rushing river. They quickly identified the stronger and weaker ones, so that the strongest young men could carry the sick, the children, and the elderly. As they waded out into the river, the strong carriers were relieved to discover that the added weight of those on their shoulders gave them greater stability so that they could keep their footing and make it safely across the river.

I remember doing a group hike in the mountains of North Carolina. I separated from the group and went ahead to investigate a river to see if we should cross at that point. I waded in, lost my footing, and was helplessly washed downstream with a soaking backpack. When the others came, they were able to hold onto and support each other in tight proximity and so avoid the same mistake.

Both examples show the strength of working together in a team to overcome whatever challenges might make us lose our footing. That is even more true when we team up with God! As our verse today states, we can hope to make it through "fire and water" to a "place of abundance".

Are you wrestling against the current alone today?

Lord, help me find others to journey alongside. Amen!

CONTENTMENT OR DISSATISFACTION?

1 Timothy 6:6, 7

"But godliness with contentment is great gain. For we brought nothing into the world, and we can take nothing out of it."

Living in Africa, I see a huge amount of physical suffering and poverty on a daily basis. And yet I also see many people with minimal possessions living contented lives of true satisfaction.

The story is told of an old tribal chief in the Congo who asked his chief witchdoctor to help him because although he seemingly had everything, he was still lacking happiness and fulfilment. The witchdoctor told the chief he'd find lasting satisfaction if the shirt of a contented man was brought for him to wear. His subjects set off to find such a person, and after a long search they tracked down a man who was really happy and content. But he didn't even possess a shirt.

In sharp contrast, I read the following article: "A few years ago, the Rolling Stones' most successful tour grossed $80 million. Mick Jagger, their leader, has houses in New York (£2.5m), Richmond (£2.2m), the Loire (£1.5m) and Mustique (£2m). He is a friend of the rich, titled, famous and even royalty. He has had five children by three women, and had bedded some of the most beautiful women in the world. He has fame, money and influence. His friend Keith Richards says: '99% of the world would give a limb to live the life of Mick Jagger, to be Mick Jagger… and he's not happy being Mick Jagger.'" The Elle magazine article concludes: "30 years after the Stones' most defining moment in song, the one certain thing about Mick Jagger is that he is unsatisfied still. And for all that he possesses and has done, he tries and he tries and he tries and he tries…"

Two people, two extremes, neither probably close to your current reality. But the lesson is clear. Who/what/where are you looking to today for your satisfaction?

Lord, I choose to be content with what I have today. Amen!

Philippians 3:19, 20

"Their mind is on earthly things. But our citizenship is in heaven."

IN OR OF?

In 1 Peter, the apostle addresses his recipients as "God's elect, strangers in the world" (1:1). Are we living as strangers in the world, with our true citizenship in heaven, or are we making ourselves a little too comfortable here?

The second-century *Letter to Diognetus* described the Christians' lifestyle in the following way:

> *They live in their own countries, but only as aliens. They have a share in everything as citizens, and endure everything as foreigners. Every foreign land is their fatherland, and yet for them every fatherland is a foreign land… It is true that they are "in the flesh", but they do not live "according to the flesh". They busy themselves on earth, but their citizenship is in heaven. They obey the established laws, but in their own lives they go far beyond what the laws require. They love all [people], and by all [people] are persecuted. They are unknown, and still they are condemned; they are put to death, and yet they are brought to life. They are poor, and yet they make many rich; they are completely destitute, and yet they enjoy complete abundance. They are dishonoured, and in their very dishonour are glorified; they are defamed, and are vindicated. They are reviled, and yet they bless; when they are affronted, they still pay due respect… Christians dwell in the world, but are not of the world.*

What a challenging testimony to their authentic faith! That is why within the first three centuries the pagan Roman Empire was completely transformed, such that when Emperor Constantine declared it Christian, it was out of political expediency – *the battle for the Empire had been won by numerous communities of believers living costly lives of surrender to the King of Kings!*

It's happened before. It can happen again.

Lord God, help me recapture the right understanding of living as a stranger on earth with my citizenship in heaven. Amen!

ABLE OR BOUND?

Matthew 25:40

"I tell you the truth, whatever you did for one of the least of these brothers of mine, you did for me."

20

MAY

God has given us all responsibilities. We are responsible. Break down that word: Response-able. But beyond that, we are, according to Jesus, *response-bound.* Faced with the needs that surround us, we choose either to respond with apathy or with action, with indifference or with intercession. It can seem overwhelming, and we might not think we know where to start, but Mother Teresa provides some guidance:

> *I never look at the masses as my responsibility. I look only at the individual. I can love only one person at a time. I can feed only one person at time. Just one, one, one. As Jesus said "Whatever you do to the least of my brethren, you do it to me." So you begin… I began. I picked up one person… The whole work is only a drop in the ocean. But if we don't put the drop in, the ocean would be one drop less. Same thing for you. Same thing in your family. Same thing in the church where you go. Just begin. One. One. One.*
>
> *At the end of our lives we will not be judged by how many diplomas we have received, how much money we have made, or how many great things we have done. We will be judged by "I was hungry and you gave me to eat. I was naked and you clothed me. I was homeless and you took me in." Hungry not only for bread but for love. Naked not only for clothing but naked of human dignity and respect. Homeless not only for want of bricks, but homeless because of rejection.*

Think about the distinction between being response-able and response-bound. How might that affect your life today?

Father, I accept that I am response-bound in response to your abounding grace. Use me today. Amen!

Romans 12:1

"Therefore, I urge you, brothers, in view of God's mercy, to offer your bodies as living sacrifices."

TO THE FATHER, THE SON, OR THE HOLY SPIRIT?

Walter Lewis Wilson was an American doctor in the nineteenth century. A visiting speaker once asked him, "Who is the Holy Spirit *to you*?" Wilson answered, "One of the Persons of the Godhead –Teacher, Guide, Third Person of the Trinity." The visitor continued, "You haven't answered my question." Wilson opened up with real candour, "He's nothing to me. I have no contact with him and could get along just fine without him." The following year, Wilson heard another speaker, who bellowed from the pulpit, "Have you noticed that our verse in Romans 12 doesn't tell us to whom we should give our bodies? It's not the Lord Jesus. He has his own body. It's not the Father. He remains on his throne. Another has come to earth without a body. God gives you the indescribable honour of presenting your bodies to the Holy Spirit, to be his dwelling place on earth."

Wilson was struck to the core and rushed home to seek the Lord. He fell on his face and pleaded with the Lord: "My Lord, I've treated you like a servant. When I wanted you, I called for you. Now I give you this body from my head to my feet. I give you my hands, my limbs, my eyes and lips, my brain. You may send this body to Africa, or lay it on a bed with cancer. It's your body from this moment on."

The next morning, Wilson was working in his office when two women arrived trying to sell him advertising. He immediately led them to Christ. The previous night's surrender had enabled him to access new power from on high. From that day on his life entered a new dimension of evangelistic fruitfulness. He went on to pioneer a church plant, a mission organization, and a Bible college.

Holy Spirit, I choose to offer you my body today as a living sacrifice. Amen!

STAY IN OR GIVE UP?

James 1:3

"The testing of your faith develops perseverance."

In life, not many of us end up either where we thought we would be, or doing what we thought we would be doing. But we are where we are, and we're somehow still making progress. Georgene Johnson was forty-two years old when she ran the Cleveland marathon… by accident. She thought she'd lined up for the 10km, but she simply kept on going with the others for another 32km to complete in just over four hours. She later said, "This isn't the race I trained for. This isn't the race I entered. But, for better or worse, this is the race I'm in."

We may face situations we feel ill equipped or unqualified to deal with, but the Lord allows us to face them to develop our faith and dependence in him. Charlton Heston was the star of the movie *Ben Hur*. Cecil B. DeMille as producer wanted Heston to learn how to drive a chariot for the all-important chariot race towards the end of the film. It would lend greater authenticity to the production. Heston was willing to take driving lessons, but learning to drive a chariot with horses four abreast was no simple matter. "I think I can drive the chariot all right, Cecil," said Heston, "I'm not at all sure I can actually win the race." DeMille replied with a grin: "Heston, you just stay in the race, and I'll make sure you win!"

That's what God says to you today. You may be way out of your comfort zone, doing things you never thought you'd have to do. You may think others could do it better, so you want to step down and give up. But no, the testing of your faith develops perseverance. He's the Great Director, so listen to him: "Just stay in the race, and I'll make sure you win!"

Lord, help me stay in the race today, for your glory. Amen!

Romans 8:37

"No, in all these things we are more than conquerors through him who loved us."

RESIGNATION OR ACCEPTANCE?

Two scenarios:

- I was driving along the main thoroughfare in downtown Bujumbura when an old lady stepped out into the road. She was hunched over, filthy, and never even looked up. I tooted my horn, slammed on the brakes, and swerved around her. She was "alive", but really she was more like the living dead.
- I was having a meal with my friend David in the slum. He was so poor that there was open sewage around his mud hut. He had once reluctantly asked me for some money to buy a pair of shoes because "every time I preach, I have to borrow a different friend's shoes, and now they're all fed up with me." That's how poor he was. But his face was always radiant with joy. I asked him once, "David, how can you be so happy when you are so desperately poor?" His answer wasn't meant as a rebuke but I felt chastened by it: "Simon, how can I not have such joy when I have my Jesus?!"

Will you choose resignation or acceptance? With resignation, you focus on your problems, completely lose sight of God, and give up – and the door of hope slams firmly shut. But with acceptance, you acknowledge your reality, face up to your problems, and yet look above and beyond them to Jesus who is still on his throne. And with that attitude, the door of hope remains wide open to God's sovereign and creative plans and purposes.

Although probably not in the above two scenarios' league, your and my problems are real. Emmanuel is one of God's names – "God with us" – and he is committed to helping you through. So don't give up! "Cast all your anxieties on him, because he cares for you" (1 Peter 5:7).

Emmanuel, help me never to give up. I accept today's problems and challenges and look to you to help me get through them. Amen!

TIMID OR BOLD?

Hebrews 4:16

"Let us then approach the throne of grace with confidence, so that we may receive mercy and find grace to help us in our time of need."

During the American Civil War, a soldier was granted permission to seek a presidential hearing due to a family tragedy. He went to Washington but was promptly refused entry and dismissed from the White House. He despaired of what to do, and wandered down the road to a park, where a little boy came up to him to ask what was wrong. The soldier poured out his story and woe. To his surprise, the boy replied, "Come with me." He led the soldier back to the White House. None of the guards stopped them as they took a detour around the back. The various medal-emblazoned guards stood to attention as they walked past. The soldier couldn't believe what was happening. When they came to the presidential office, the boy entered without so much as a knock. The Secretary of State was briefing President Abraham Lincoln, who interrupted him and turned to the boy to ask, "What can I do for you, Todd?" Todd said, "Dad, this soldier needs to talk to you."

Hebrews 10:19 says, "Therefore, brothers, since we have confidence to enter the Most Holy Place by the blood of Jesus…" The discouraged soldier had access to the president "through the son". How much more do we have access to God "through the son" – Jesus. Both verses from Hebrews include the key word "confidence". We don't come with shame, fear, or embarrassment. We come with confidence. We need not be timid, but bold – *not because of what we've done but because of who we are.* We are "co-heirs with Christ Jesus" (Romans 8:17) and "children of God" (1 John 3:1).

Enjoy the assurance, confidence, and security that knowledge brings, and petition God boldly today.

Thank you, Lord, for the incredible privilege of being your child. May I act like a child of the King today. Amen!

TOUGH OR TENDER?

Deuteronomy 32:10, 11

"The Lord shielded him and cared for him; he guarded him as the apple of his eye, like an eagle that stirs up its nest and hovers over its young, that spreads its wings to catch them and carries them on its pinions."

God fiercely loves his people. Deuteronomy 32 is a song Moses recited to the whole assembly of Israel to remind them about how God had acted on their behalf. God's love was both incredibly tough and tender.

The toughness can be seen in verses 15 to 38, where we read of judgment, abandonment, rejection, and more. There are consequences to disobedience, apathy, and pride.

The tenderness of his love comes through beautifully in the imagery of today's verses. We read of how the eagle handles its young, which chimes with what we know of mothers teaching their offspring to fly. This is how they go about it: the eaglets are nurtured in the comfortable nest to begin with, while the mother spends much of the time hovering above them so that the eaglets can see what is possible. She progressively removes more and more of the fur and hair from the nest to make it less comfortable for the eaglet, encouraging it to leave the nest for good. If the eaglet doesn't voluntarily leave the nest, the mother eagle nudges it out of its comfort zone so it has to fly. It free-falls a while before the mother swoops under it to pick it up on her wings. This process is repeated until the eaglet learns to fly on its own. Even then, the mother continues alongside the eaglet for a while until it has matured sufficiently to soar on its own.

It's a beautiful picture of God's love for us, both tough and tender at the same time. Both are needed to get us to fly. Can you see how the Lord has been dealing with you in this way?

Lord, I choose to trust you today as you nurture me with both tenderness and toughness. Amen!

OBEDIENCE OR CONVENIENCE?

1 Chronicles 21:19

"So David went up in obedience to the word that Dan had spoken in the name of the Lord."

Obedience is seldom convenient. It usually means doing something in submission to someone else's will or desire. During David's life, he sought God's heart in obedience, even when it was inconvenient, even when the pressures were overwhelming, even when he wanted to quit.

King Henry III of Bavaria understood King David's pressures. In the eleventh century, Henry got to the stage where he couldn't handle the pressures of court life, so he applied to Prior Richard at a local monastery to take him in to spend the rest of his life in prayer and contemplation. "Your Majesty," said Prior Richard, "do you understand that the pledge here is one of obedience? That will be hard because you have been a king." "I understand," said Henry. "The rest of my life I will be obedient to you, as Christ leads you." "Then I will tell you what to do," said Prior Richard. "Go back to your throne and serve faithfully in the place where God has put you."

When King Henry died, a plaque was engraved: "The king learned to rule by being obedient."

There are some difficult and draining days when I just want to throw in the towel and give up my responsibilities. The grass is always greener elswhere so maybe another career will be easier, more fruitful, or more fulfilling. You could be the same, and it could be your job or your marriage or whatever other role or responsibility you're tiring of. Hang on though! Remember God calls us to obedience, not convenience. He didn't say it would be easy, but he did promise to be with us every step of the way. Don't do anything rash. Pray it through. Seek counsel. Walk the path of obedience with him today.

Lord, I choose to live a life of obedience to you, even when it's inconvenient. Amen!

Romans 13:10

"Therefore love is the fulfilment of the law."

LEGALISM OR LOVE?

Jesus opposed the proud but gave grace to the humble. Chief among the proud were the teachers of the Law and the Pharisees – those who should have known better, but were blinded by their own pride and theological sophistication. They were professional legalists. For them, it was all law (what they must do) and no gospel (what Jesus has done). Do we sometimes behave like them?

Mark Driscoll preached a sermon on "How to Become a Legalist". Here's how to go about it: (1) Make rules outside the Bible; (2) Push yourself to try and keep your rules; (3) Castigate yourself when you don't keep your rules; (4) Become proud when you do keep your rules; (5) Appoint yourself as judge over other people; (6) Get angry with people who break your rules or have different rules; (7) "Beat" the losers.

Alternatively, a true understanding of Jesus' message is so liberating. My relationship with God is not determined by my past or my present, but by Christ's past and his present. It's not about turning over a new leaf, it's about receiving a new life. As Tullian Tchividjian writes:

> *We tend to think of the gospel as God's program to make bad people good, not dead people alive. The fact is, Jesus came first to effect a mortal resurrection, not a moral reformation, as his own death and resurrection demonstrate… Progress in obedience happens only when our hearts realize that God's love for us does not depend on our progress in obedience.*

So Martin Luther is right when he says: "It is not imitation that makes sons; it is sonship that makes imitators."

How will the above change how you live? Is the way you live your life rooted in legalism or love? How might your life look like lived under the banner that reads, "It is finished!"?

God Almighty, I choose to live a life of love and freedom today. Amen!

FORWARD OR BACKWARD?

Matthew 5:16

"In the same way, let your light shine before others, that they may see your good deeds and glorify your Father in heaven."

As ambassadors of Christ, when we interact with people, we will either draw them forward towards Jesus or push them backwards away from him. Someone once asked the question: "If the church disappeared tomorrow, would anyone notice?" It's a challenging question and one we can also relate to ourselves. Do our friends, family, and neighbours know the good news that we carry? Do the people we work with know that we have a hope to share, an answer to their longings, a shoulder to lean on or a listening ear? Do we gossip, grumble, and gripe or bring life and love in our dealings with others?

Catherine Ryan Hyde's book *Pay it Forward* tells the story of Trevor McKinney, a twelve-year-old boy who accepts his social studies teacher's challenge to come up with a plan to change the world. His plan is to do a good deed for three people and ask them to "pay it forward" to three others who need help. He envisions a vast movement of kindness and goodwill spreading beyond his small California town and across the world. A film was made of the book and the practice of doing random acts of kindness has brought hope and joy to people across the world. Good deeds spread good seeds! Jesus' sacrifice was the ultimate demonstration of paying it forward when he gave his life for us on the cross, so let's take every opportunity likewise to "pay it forward". As Mother Teresa said, "Spread love everywhere you go. Let no one ever come to you without leaving happier."

I remember one winter cleaning up a grubby inner-city car park with some friends. The people in the surrounding apartments were astonished. They sent out hot mugs of tea, bananas, curry even! It broke down barriers of distrust and fostered community very quickly. What might paying it forward look like for you?

Lord, show me how I might "pay it forward" today. Amen!

Deuteronomy 6:9

"Write them on the doorframes of your houses and your gates."

PENCIL OR MEMORY?

Remembering is crucial. God knew how forgetful his people would be. The Old Testament is a frustratingly consistent cycle of his people forgetting him, disobeying, suffering the consequences, repenting, being restored, and then forgetting again.

In Deuteronomy 6:6–9, God insists: "These commandments that I give you today are to be upon your hearts. Impress them on your children. Talk about them when you sit at home and when you walk along the road, when you lie down and when you get up. Tie them as symbols on your hands and bind them on your foreheads. Write them on the doorframes of your houses and your gates."

There's so much in those verses to apply to our lives today. That last one invariably was at the heart of each cycle of repentance. In brokenness they re-read what had been written down by their forebears as instructed by God. That's why God was so insistent that they write down and record his works.

Catherine Cox researched 300 people from different backgrounds who were significant history-shapers to discover some of their shared characteristics. The one (perhaps unexpected) common denominator among them she found was that they all kept a journal of one kind or another. As Mark Batterson notes, "The shortest pencil is longer than the longest memory!"

I haven't kept a journal my whole life, but certainly for many years. Sometimes I've re-read different sections, and a key life-lesson that I'd managed to forget jumps out at me off the pages and encourages me afresh. If I hadn't written it down, it would be gone forever.

In Old Testament times, God got them to build an altar as a memorial to him – it was a place they could go back to and remember how he had intervened. It strengthened them for tomorrow. Maybe journalling is a modern-day equivalent.

Too busy? Too busy to be blessed? It's your choice…

Lord, I don't want to forget your faithfulness. I choose to remember today. Amen!

LUXURIES OR NEEDS?

Philippians 4:19

"My God will meet all your needs according to his glorious riches in Christ Jesus."

30 MAY

John Wesley's father was an Anglican vicar with nine children who ended up in debtors' prison. So John felt great freedom in being financially self-sufficient when he started earning his own salary. But one cold winter day, a chambermaid came to his door. He had just bought some pictures to decorate his room and showed them to her. She was so poor that he noticed she couldn't protect herself from the freezing wind. He reached into his pocket to get some money to buy her a coat but realized he didn't have enough. He immediately felt the conviction of the Holy Spirit that he had wasted his money on those pictures. He thought to himself: "Will thy Master say, 'Well done, good and faithful steward? Thou hast adorned thy walls with the money which might have screened this poor creature from the cold!' O justice! O mercy! Are not these pictures the blood of this poor maid?"

It was a defining moment in Wesley's life. He recorded his income at that time. It was £30. His expenditure was £28, so he gave away £2. He kept his expenditure the same for the rest of his life, and when his income soared to six times that sum, he gave all the rest away, the equivalent of six figures nowadays.

Was there anything wrong with those pictures? No, but the Lord used them to convict his servant about investing in what really mattered. Can you spend money on non-essentials of beauty and pleasure? Of course! But it's worth reviewing how much we spend, what we spend it on, and why. So often it's a luxury, not a need. May Wesley's sensitive hearing of the Spirit's voice rub off on us. Can you hear him?

Lord, I choose to use my God-given resources wisely for your glory today. Amen!

Hosea 6:6

"For I desire mercy, not sacrifice."

MERCY OR SACRIFICE?

After the end of apartheid in South Africa, a Truth and Reconciliation Commission was set up. During one hearing, in the presence of the victim's mother, a policeman named van de Broek recounted how he had shot an eighteen-year-old boy and burned the body on a fire to destroy all evidence. Eight years later he returned to the same house and seized the boy's father. The wife watched as her husband was tied up, had petrol poured over him, and was then set alight. The courtroom became completely silent as the judge offered the widow the opportunity to respond. "What do you want from Mr van de Broek?" he asked.

She asked van de Broek to go and collect the dust from the place where he'd burned her husband's body, so she could honour him with a proper burial. He was so ashamed he couldn't look her in the eye, but nodded in agreement. Then she added, "Mr van de Broek took all my family away from me, and I still have a lot of love to give. Twice a month, I would like for him to come to the ghetto and spend a day with me so I can be a mother to him. And I would like Mr van de Broek to know that he is forgiven by God, and that I forgive him too. I would like to embrace him so he can know my forgiveness is real."

As the elderly woman pronounced those astoundingly grace-filled words and walked towards him, some people began spontaneously singing "Amazing Grace", but van de Broek didn't hear any of it, because he was so totally overwhelmed that he had fainted.

Lord, I myself am totally overwhelmed by that story of the triumph of mercy over sacrifice. I know it's a picture of what you did for me in Jesus. I praise your name. Help me to model that extraordinary grace in my life towards others today. Amen!

Proverbs 3:5

"Trust in the Lord with all your heart and lean not on your own understanding."

PARTIAL OR WHOLE WEIGHT?

In the nineteenth century, Scotsman John Paton sailed to the south-west Pacific to the New Hebrides as a missionary to the unreached people there. They happened to be cannibals, and the culture there was one of fear, distrust, and suspicion. He settled down despite being in great danger, and began learning phonetics with a view to eventually translating the Scriptures. To his amazement, he discovered that they didn't have any word in their language for "faith", "trust", or "belief". They simply had no concept of those terms. This presented serious challenges to communicating the gospel, and to his translation work. But one day, he had a brainwave. When his worker arrived in the morning, Paton sat back fully into his chair, raised his feet, and asked, "What am I doing now?" His worker used a word that meant, "to lean your whole weight upon". Paton took this expression and used it for "faith" in his translation.

Are you leaning your whole weight on Jesus today? That's what living by faith means. I think we usually only partially lean on him. We hedge our bets, have a plan B in case God doesn't deliver, and make contingency arrangements as back-up. Too often we try to work things out ourselves using logic, or as the verse above says, we "lean on our own understanding". Well, faith is not logical – but neither is it illogical. As Mark Batterson writes, "Faith is theological. It does not ignore reality; it just adds God into the equation. Think of it this way. Logic questions God. Faith questions assumptions. And at the end of the day, faith is trusting God more than you trust your own assumptions."

Lord, I don't see the road ahead. I assume you do. And so I choose to trust you in everything, leaning my whole weight on you today. Amen!

COMPELLED TO GO OR CONTENT TO STAY?

2 Corinthians 5:14

"For Christ's love compels me..."

2

JUNE

How many people are waiting for us to go to them and offer them Christ's liberating all-embracing love?

Sean Litten was working for International Justice Mission in Thailand. He found out about a girl called Elizabeth who was only thirteen who had been forced into prostitution. Various caseworkers made their dangerous undercover investigations to gather sufficient evidence before presenting it to the police. They then raided the brothel. Sean found Elizabeth locked in a dormitory that seemed more like a dank dungeon. When Elizabeth realized Sean was coming to save her rather than abuse her, she said to him:

"I knew you'd come. I knew you'd come."

Well how had she known? Sean was further surprised to see strange writing on the back wall behind her. The script looked different from Thai and as he shone his flashlight at it, he was amazed to read words from Psalm 27: "The Lord is my light and my salvation – whom shall I fear?" It turned out this precious young girl was a Christian and, against all odds, she was still trusting her Lord and Saviour in her living hell. Her family had been praying and praying for nearly a year that God would free her.

I find her words strangely haunting. "I knew you'd come..."

Who else is out there, crying out to God for us to come? It could be in Thailand, or it could just as well be in your neighbourhood. The apostle Paul wrote, "Christ's love compels us." That's the motivation that compels me to go to Burundi, and yet even here I can choose to be content to stay in the safety of my comfort zone. So wherever we are, let's resolve today to reach out to someone. What are we waiting for? We are the ones God is waiting for.

Lord, help me feel afresh that sense of your love compelling me to go in your name. Amen!

PROCESS OR END?

Romans 8:28, 29

"And we know that in all things God works for the good of those who love him, who have been called according to his purpose… to be conformed to the likeness of his Son."

The verse above can easily be, and often has been, misapplied in difficult situations, but it clearly states that God is at work in the believer's life "in all things". Oswald Chambers wrote, "We must never put our dreams of success as God's purpose for us. The question of getting to a particular end is a mere incident. What we call the process, God calls the end. His purpose is that I depend on Him and on His power now. It is the process, not the end, which is glorifying to God."

It's very easy to live life looking ahead – when I finish my studies, get married, have a good job, retire, and so on, then I'll be able to… but in doing so we miss so much of the moment, the now, the experience of living. We need to live for today. As Frederick Buechner wrote, "Today is the first day of your life because it has never been before, and today is the last day of your life because it will never be again."

The verse above says that we "have been called according to his purpose… to be conformed to the likeness of his Son". Elisabeth Elliot, whose husband was murdered by the Auca Indians, wrote, "Our vision is so limited we can hardly imagine a love that does not show itself in protection from suffering… The love of God did not protect His own Son… He will not necessarily protect us – not from anything it takes to make us like His Son. A lot of hammering and chiseling and purifying by fire will have to go into the process."

God, I see that you are less concerned with where I am going than with who I am becoming. I choose today to submit to and embrace the process of becoming more like you. Amen!

DISTURBINGLY AUTHENTIC OR COMFORTINGLY DISTORTED?

Acts 4:32–34

"All the believers were one in heart and mind. No one claimed that any of his possessions was his own, but they shared everything they had. With great power the apostles continued to testify for the resurrection of the Lord Jesus, and much grace was on them all. There were no needy persons among them."

Having translated the book of Acts in 1955, J.B. Phillips wrote:

> *It is impossible to spend several months in close study of this remarkable short book… without being profoundly stirred and, to be honest, disturbed. The reader is stirred because he is seeing Christianity, the real thing, in action for the first time in human history. The newborn Church, as vulnerable as any human child, having neither money, influence, nor power in the ordinary sense, is setting forth joyfully and courageously to win the pagan world for God through Christ…*
>
> *We cannot help feeling disturbed as well as moved, for this surely is the Church as it was meant to be. It is vigorous and flexible, for these are the days before it ever became fat and short of breath through prosperity, or muscle-bound by over-organization. These men did not make "acts of faith," they believed; they did not "say their prayers," they really prayed. They did not hold conferences on psychosomatic medicine, they simply healed the sick. But if they were uncomplicated and naïve by modern standards, we have ruefully to admit that they were open on the God-ward side in a way that is almost unknown today.*

Maybe the above can act as an encouragement to take a fresh examination of the book of Acts. Even in the short verses above we read of the early church's radical unity, sacrificial generosity, boldness, grace and power. Where are we now?

Let's cry out in prayer with Habakkuk the prophet:

Lord, I have heard of your fame. I stand in awe of your deeds, O Lord. Renew them in our day, in our time make them known; in wrath remember mercy. Amen!

1 Timothy 2:1

"I urge, then, first of all, that requests, prayers, intercession and thanksgiving be made for everyone."

FULL CAPACITY OR LOW CAPACITY?

God is interested in every aspect of our lives, both the seemingly trivial and the undeniably important. Nothing is too small for him. He wants us to ask, he's waiting to hear, and he's longing to reply. Andrew Murray said of prayer: "God's giving is inseparably connected with our asking. Only by intercession can that power be brought from heaven which will enable the Church to conquer the world."

George Mueller, who fed several thousand orphans simply in answer to prayer, said that he never came to requests or petitions in prayer until he had "an active and living realization of the presence of God". Hudson Taylor, after so many painful breakthroughs in China, wrote, "The prayer power has never been tried to its full capacity. If we want to see mighty works of Divine power and grace wrought in the place of weakness, failure and disappointment, let us answer God's standing challenge, 'Call to me, and I will answer you, and show you great and mighty things, which you do not know.'"

Maybe I should decide to call out more loudly, boldly and persistently, so that God will show me "great and mighty things" of which I do not know. Maybe I'll pray bigger prayers, as I'm naturally inclined to pray little ones. Maybe I'll pray more risky prayers, as I'm all too good at offering up qualified petitions couched in religious verbiage to lessen my disappointment if my will isn't done. Maybe I'll pray more specific prayers, as I'm an expert at vague ones which are hard to see whether they've been answered or not. Maybe I'll pray more uncomfortable and dangerous prayers, in case I've set the bar at a safe height and am missing out on more lofty exploits for God's glory.

Father, increase my capacity to pray today. Take me deeper. Use me however you like, for your glory Amen!

SELF OR OTHERS?

Philippians 2:4

"Each of you should look not only to your own interests, but also to the interests of others."

A rich man went to his psychiatrist to complain that he was miserable despite all his wealth. The psychiatrist took the man to the window and asked, "What do you see?" The man replied, "I see people walking around." The psychiatrist then took the man to stand in front of the mirror and asked, "Now what do you see?" The man said, "I see only myself." The psychiatrist then said, "In the window there is a glass and in the mirror there is glass, and when you look through the glass of the window, you see others, but when you look into the glass of the mirror you see only yourself. The reason for this is that behind the glass in the mirror is a layer of silver. When silver is added, you cease to see others. You only see yourself."

If we are all caught up in ourselves, we make a very small package. Whether it's the empty promises of material satisfaction or loneliness caused by social dislocation, or whatever other reason, Paul says we should look beyond ourselves and look to others. Dr Karl Menninger once gave a lecture on mental health and at the end did a Q&A with his audience. Somebody asked, "What would you advise a person to do if that person felt a nervous breakdown coming on?" Most people anticipated the answer, "Consult a psychiatrist." To their amazement he replied, "Leave your house, go across the railroad tracks, find someone who is in need, and do something to help that person."

Without discounting the value of seeking professional help in many instances, the point is clear that in an excessively self-obsessed age, Jesus' call is to lay down ourselves for others. It's life-giving on multiple levels.

Lord, help me today to look beyond myself to others. Amen!

James 4: 7, 8

"Resist the devil, and he will flee. Draw near to God, and he will draw near to you."

FLEE OR FACE?

Lions in Africa have a particular strategy in hunting gazelle. The oldest male lion positions himself upwind of the herd of gazelle. He's slow, weak, and toothless, but still has an intimidating roar. The younger more agile members of the pack then sneak downwind and hide in the tall grass. Once all of them are in position, the old man lets out a mighty roar. The gazelles look up, catch his scent, and then flee in the opposite direction, right into the jaws of the hidden lions.

How often the devil seeks to make us flee by sowing fear. But, as James wrote, the devil will flee as we resist him and face our fears. The devil seeks to imitate, so "he prowls around like an angry lion looking for someone to devour" (1 Peter 5:7), but is no match for Jesus who is the "Lion of Judah". So next time you hear the roar and feel your fears, don't flee. Rather go for the roar, move through your fears and you will invariably discover that they don't have as many "teeth" as you thought they would.

As Eleanor Roosevelt wrote, "We gain strength, and courage, and confidence by each experience in which we really stop to look fear in the face… we must do that which we think we cannot."

During the war in Burundi, I thought I would die at some point in an ambush. We regularly used roads that were considered to be the most dangerous in the world at the time. Many others died. But our task was urgent, it was worth dying for, and we faced those fears. One day my colleague looked across at me and said, with a glint in his eye, "Isn't it exciting, we are immortal until God calls us home!"

You too can live free from fear. Face each one down, with the Lion of Judah at your side.

Lord, I choose to face my fears today. Amen!

DAMNED OR SAVED?

2 Corinthians 5:10

"For we must all appear before the judgment seat of Christ."

We tend to feel embarrassed by the whole concept of God judging people, and by the thought that he might even punish them. Often we view hell as a blemish to be covered up by the cosmetic of divine love. John 3:16 is called on ("For God so loved the world that he gave his only Son...") but we can only understand the depth of God's love for us when we appreciate the judgment from which he is rescuing us.

Moody wrote, "It is a great mistake to give a man who has not been convicted of sin certain passages that were never meant for him. The Law is what he needs... Do not offer the consolation of the gospel until he sees and knows he is guilty before God." Moody adds, "Many feel secure in their sins with no fear or worry of Judgment Day because 'God is a God of Love and will overlook my sins'. They forget the fact that love has no place in a courtroom. The purpose of a court is to present evidence and determine guilt or innocence."

Taking this into account, how zealous are we in lovingly taking this message to a lost world?

In a sermon at Exeter Hall in 1860, Spurgeon pleaded with his listeners: "If sinners will be damned, at least let them leap to hell over our bodies; and if they will perish, let them perish with our arms about their knees, imploring them to stay. If hell must be filled, at least let it be filled in the teeth of our exertions, and let not one go there unwarned and unprayed for."

Awesome righteous Judge of all, I choose to live and love with urgency today. Amen!

Matthew 19:26

"With man this is impossible, but with God all things are possible."

INCOMPETENCE OR OMNIPOTENCE?

Hudson Taylor asks us to consider: "How often do we attempt work for God to the limit of our incompetence, rather than the limit of God's omnipotence?"

I am challenged by that today. What is the limit – my incompetence or God's omnipotence? If all things are possible for God, then impossible situations become wonderful opportunities to point people to him. As Tozer said, "God has called us to do the impossible. What a pity we settle for what we can do ourselves."

Sometimes it's helpful to look back and see how far we've come rather than getting discouraged by how far we have to go. Over the last decade, God has truly done "immeasurably more" than I could have asked for or imagined (Ephesians 3:20) in our work out here, with over a hundred thousand people coming to faith, a nation-shaking missionary movement mobilized, schools, theological institutions, and medical clinics built, and more. Yet despite that, I can easily lose sight of God's omnipotence by my myopic self-imposed limitations.

It all comes back to the object of our faith, our hope, and our love – the God of the impossible. As Brother Lawrence wrote, "Many things are possible for the person who has hope. Even more is possible for the person who has faith. And still more is possible for the person who knows how to love. But everything is possible for the person who practises all three virtues."

God help us not to be what C.T. Studd called "nibblers of the possible instead of grabbers of the impossible". God help us to see the invisible so we can do the impossible. God help us pray great things, as John Newton wrote:

Thou art coming to a King
Large petitions with thee bring;
For His grace and power are such,
None can ever ask too much.

God of the impossible, you see where I am at. Increase my faith. Use me today for your glory. Amen!

LASTING OR FLEETING?

Isaiah 55:2

"Why spend money on what is not bread, and your labour on what does not satisfy?"

10

JUNE

God's alternative to the above is "Come to me… Eat what is good, and your soul will delight in the richest of fare" (verses 2, 3). Our perennial problem in seeking lasting satisfaction is that we look to the gifts rather than the Giver. Pleasures derived from material gifts are fleeting if they don't have a spiritual and eternal dimension to them. Indeed at some level we will always experience some dissatisfaction in this life, as C.S. Lewis explains: "If I find in myself a desire which no experience in this world can satisfy, the most probable explanation is that I was made for another world." However, in terms of making the most of our time here on earth, he continues: "I have discovered that the people who believe most strongly in the next life do the most good in the present one."

So what will satisfy? J. Campbell White writes:

> *Most men are not satisfied with the permanent output of their lives. Nothing can wholly satisfy the life of Christ within his followers except the adoption of Christ's purpose toward the world he came to redeem. Fame, pleasure and riches are but husks and ashes in contrast with the boundless and abiding joy of working with God for the fulfillment of his eternal plans. The men who are putting everything into Christ's undertaking are getting out of life its sweetest and most priceless rewards.*

"Working with God for the fulfillment of his eternal plans" – that will look very different for each one of us. It could be in the context of church but for most of us it will be beyond that, as we live out our calling for God in the workplace, down our street, and in our family. God has wired you with certain skills and passions that can be harnessed for him.

Lord, take me and use me. I seek to pursue lasting satisfaction in you and lasting fruit for you. Amen!

RESPECTABLE OR REVOLUTIONARY?

Philippians 3:8

"I consider everything a loss compared to the surpassing greatness of knowing Christ Jesus my Lord, for whose sake I have lost all things."

Let me be honest with you: I think my biggest struggle is bridging the inconsistencies in my life between believing in a revolutionary message and seeking to behave in a respectable manner. The apostle Paul wrote the above verses from prison, having gone from total societal respectability to disapprobation. He was a revolutionary. During the Pope's visit to Cuba in 1998, someone daubed this graffiti on a public wall: "To be a Christian without being a revolutionary is a mortal sin." I don't quite agree, but I echo the heartbeat. Similarly my heart leaps at what Robert Capon describes:

> *What happened to the category-smashing, life-threatening, anti-institutional gospel that spread through the first century like wildfire and was considered (by those in power) dangerous? What happened to the kind of Christians whose hearts were on fire, who had no fear, who spoke the truth no matter what the consequence, who made the world uncomfortable, who were willing to follow Jesus wherever he went? I want to be "dangerous" to a dull and boring religion. I want a faith that is considered "dangerous" by our predictable and monotonous culture.*

Every decision we face in our respectable culture is sucking us into a mould of conformity and fitting in. I hate it. It's suffocating, it's domesticating, it's neutralizing. I see so little hope of breaking the mould of mediocrity, of liberating ourselves from the shackles of convention, apart from finding others who similarly ache for authenticity.

Do you echo the above? Or have you been taken out completely? Sometimes it's safer to settle for lower expectations and a smaller God, but no, for Christ's sake, we must not!

Those Christians still exist. God is calling you to be one of them. You can't do it alone. Seek them out. Get your hands dirty and do life together. Join the revolution!

Lord God Almighty, I ache for authenticity today. Enough with being respectable, help me join the revolution. Amen!

ACCOUNTABLE OR UNACCOUNTABLE?

James 5:16

"Therefore confess your sins to each other and pray for each other."

12

JUNE

My girlfriend was coming to visit me from the States. I knew back then that I didn't want to sleep with her until or if we were to get married, but based on my previous track record, I didn't fancy my chances of staying pure. So I told my friend Tom, and we agreed together that if I messed up in any way, he would take a big sum of money donated to Burundi and burn it in front of me! It sounds unorthodox, maybe even weird, but it worked. I didn't touch her, which is a good job because she wasn't my future wife and I wasn't her future husband. Without a relationship of accountability with Tom, I have no doubt it would have gone very differently.

Accountability involves a group of people engaged in intentional, open, ruthlessly honest relationships for mutual encouragement, strengthening, and challenge. Having people like that in my life has been crucial. At key times, when faced with marriage difficulties, sexual temptation, ethical issues, or whatever, I can call them in and lay myself bare.

Apparently only 15 per cent of evangelicals have any form of such accountability, and they are the branch within Christendom with the highest number. There's nothing the devil likes more than to keep us isolated. Are you? You are if you don't have any accountability relationships. And notice they have to be ruthlessly honest, otherwise they aren't fit for purpose. I remember at university getting up to no good for a year with a girlfriend. I chose not to tell my prayer partner about that area of my life and he didn't ask me. What a wasted opportunity!

A problem shared is a problem halved. We share with God, but need to share with others too, as our verse above states. If you don't, you're on dangerous ground. Make a good choice today!

Lord, help me identify the right person/people to be accountable with, and to follow through in making it happen today. Amen!

James 5:16

"Therefore confess your sins to each other and pray for each other."

MORE ACCOUNTABILITY OR UNACCOUNTABILITY?!

Did you follow through on yesterday? If not, here's a second day on the issue of accountability, in case you needed another prod to act on it. If you're still resistant, maybe you identify with George Barna's assessment below:

> *The postmodern insistence on tolerance is winning over the Christian church. Our biblical illiteracy and lack of spiritual confidence has caused us to avoid making discerning choices for fear of being labelled judgmental. The result is a Church that has become tolerant of a vast array of morally and spiritually dubious behaviors and philosophies. This increased leniency is made possible by the very limited accountability that occurs within the body of Christ. There are fewer and fewer issues that Christians believe churches should be dogmatic about. The idea of love has been redefined to mean the absence of conflict and confrontation, as if there are no moral absolutes that are worth fighting for.*

The choice is ours, and it requires honesty: do I want to fire on all cylinders, be as spiritually effective as possible, and live a disciplined life of fruitfulness, or will I settle for less than God's best for me? Please make a good choice. The stakes are high. And if you don't know how to go about it when you meet up with your key people, Richard Foster offers us five questions to ask each other in the group:

- What experiences of prayer and meditation have you had this week?
- What temptations did you face this week?
- What movements of the Holy Spirit did you experience this week?
- What opportunities to serve others have you had this week?
- In what ways have you encountered Christ in your study of the Bible this week?

Do that, and you'll be flying! Here's praying you commit to establishing and maintaining such a group of accountability.

Lord, in all honesty I can/can't be bothered to do this. Draw me closer to you and others today. Amen!

RESPOND TO OR IGNORE THE POOR?

Proverbs 17:19

"He who is kind to the poor lends to the Lord, and he will reward him for what he has done."

Authenticity is very attractive and compelling. James 1:27 tells us that "religion that our God and Father accepts as pure and faultless is this: to look after orphans and widows in their distress." Listen to Robert Murray McCheyne's challenge to his congregation in Scotland in 1848:

> *Now, dear Christians, some of you pray night and day to be branches of the true Vine; you pray to be made all over in the image of Christ. If so, you must be like him in giving… "Though he was rich, yet for our sakes he became poor"…*
>
> *Objection 1: "My money is my own." Answer: Christ might have said, "My blood is my own, my life is my own." Then where should we have been?*
>
> *Objection 2: "The poor are undeserving." Answer: Christ might have said, "They are wicked rebels, shall I lay down my life for these? I will give to the good angels." But no, he left the ninety-nine, and came after the lost. He gave his blood for the undeserving.*
>
> *Objection 3: "The poor may abuse it." Answer: Christ might have said the same; yea, with far greater truth. Christ knew that thousands would trample his blood under their feet; that most would despise it; that many would make it an excuse for sinning more; yet gave his own blood.*
>
> *Oh dear Christians! If you would be like Christ, give much more, give often, give freely, to the vile and the poor, the thankless and the undeserving. Christ is glorious and happy and so will you be. It is not your money I want, but your happiness. Remember his own words, "It is more blessed to give than to receive."*

Lord, help me to engage with and contribute positively to the plight of the poor on an ongoing meaningful and impactful basis. Amen!

CRACKED OR WHOLE?

2 Corinthians 4:7

"But we have this treasure in jars of clay to show that this all-surpassing power is from God, not from us."

A man in India had two large clay pots, which he carried at each end of a pole hung across his shoulders. One pot was new while the other was cracked, so at the end of each trip to fetch water and return to irrigate his field, the latter pot was only half-full. Day after day, the water-bearer continued, until the cracked pot could contain itself no longer, ashamed at its constant failure to accomplish what it was meant to. "I'm so sorry, please forgive me. I'm damaged and useless. You should dispose of me and get a new pot in my place. I'm not giving you value for your efforts," the pot said.

The water-bearer replied, "I've always known about your crack, and knew I could use you just as you are. Haven't you seen the beautiful flowers along the path to the stream? I planted those seeds because I knew you'd water them faithfully each day. All these months I've been able to pick these beautiful flowers to give away and bring joy to others. If you weren't just the way you are, all that beauty would not have come into being."

The devil has been a liar, deceiver, and accuser from the beginning. If you feel like an obsolete cracked pot, remember today that God wants to use you, that you still have a role to play. Just as the water spilled through the cracks to water the flowers, so God's light shines out through your cracks to bring hope to others. Everyone is cracked somewhere, whether they admit it or not. People can't relate to perfect beautiful jars, but with us as jars of clay, the glory goes to God, not to us. He wants to use you today.

Lord, take me as I am, cracks and all, and use me as you want, for your glory. Amen!

ANGELS OR FAIRIES?

Psalm 91:11

"For he will command his angels concerning you to guard you in all your ways."

16
JUNE

In 1858, John and Mary Ann Paton sailed for the cannibal island of Tanna. One fearful day, they were chased home by the tribe they were trying to reach out to. They shut the door, dropped to their knees, and cried out to God for protection. Expecting their house to be stormed at any time, they continued praying through the long night as they heard the chants of the cannibals outside. But the attack never came. A few months later, the tribal chief converted to Christ. He immediately wanted to talk about that memorable night, and he asked Paton, "Who were all those men with you?" Paton insisted it was just his family there that night. The chief got angry and argued back: "There were hundreds of tall men in shining garments with drawn swords circling about your house, so we could not attack you."

Angels are not fairies. Fairies are the stuff of children's stories, but angels are very real. I have no doubt angels watched over me during Burundi's long-running civil war. One day we got through a stretch of road in which there were four ambushes and forty people were killed. Some angelic visitations are very obvious, as with the above. In the Bible, where angels appeared, it usually similarly caused great fear in the person they appeared to, such was their shining countenance. Often they would say, "Do not be afraid!" At other times we might not even know that an angel is among us, as Hebrews 13:2 says: "Do not forget to entertain strangers, for by so doing some people have entertained angels without knowing it."

There's no need to become obsessed with angels, but neither should we discount them. There is certainly a whole lot more going on than meets the eye.

Lord, teach me to recognize the "super" in the midst of the "natural". Amen!

RITUAL OR REALITY?

Ephesians 6:12

"For our struggle is not against flesh and blood, but against the rulers, against the authorities, against the powers of this dark world and against the spiritual forces of evil in the heavenly realms."

Sometimes our prayer lives can become stale, dutiful, and dry. We can go through the motions without any sense of urgency, passion, or desperation. At such times we need a reminder of the reality of the battle going on in the heavenly realms.

Prayer and fasting play an important role as spiritual disciplines in my journey with Christ. When I discovered what Satanists were praying for, or rather against, it certainly added a realization of how critical it is to engage in spiritual warfare. Here are twelve things that Satanists are encouraged to pray for daily:

1. *That the Anti-Christ will come before the church is ready.*
2. *That ministries, leaders, and missionaries will fall.*
3. *That ministries and works of the Lord will be destroyed.*
4. *That Christians become complacent, want peace above all, seek churches that do not preach the full gospel and pastors who will seek peace at all costs.*
5. *That Christians stop fasting and praying.*
6. *That the gifts of the Spirit shall be ignored.*
7. *That families and marriages break up.*
8. *That pastors, ministers, and leaders of the body fall into dispute and turn on each other.*
9. *That there be no unity of pastors and churches within cities.*
10. *That pastors and leaders fall into illness and disability so they can no longer carry on.*
11. *That the next generation will be murdered and not come into their generational destiny.*
12. *That the church will not loose and equip people to come into their destiny.*

Does that make you think about prayer differently? Is it just a ritual, or do you recognize the reality of spiritual warfare?

Lord, I choose to put on the full armour of God today. Teach me to pray effectively. Amen!

PROUD OR HUMBLE?

Daniel 4:37

"Those who walk in pride God is able to humble."

18

JUNE

Remember King Nebuchadnezzar? He pronounced the words above having lived them out in his own experience. It was he who walked on the roof of the royal palace in Babylon, reeking with pride, and boasting: "Is not this the great Babylon I have built as the royal residence, by my mighty power and for the glory of my majesty." He'd been warned by a dream which Daniel interpreted, but still refused to give glory to God until the most humbling of humiliations rendered him mad for a season before he was restored. He found out the hard way that what the book of Proverbs says is true: God "hates pride and arrogance" (8:13), "when pride comes, then comes disgrace" (11:2), and "pride comes before destruction" (16:18).

Pride afflicts us all. It involves an over-inflated view of self and an under-inflated view of others. Muhammad Ali was a great boxer but perhaps he was an even greater exponent of pride. Once on a plane, an air stewardess said to him, "Sir, please fasten your seatbelt." He replied, "Superman don't need no seatbelt." Quick as a flash, she shot back, "Superman don't need no airplane, now fasten your seatbelt!"

As C.S. Lewis wrote, "A proud man is always looking down on things and people. And of course as long as you are looking down, you cannot see something that is above you." William Law said, "pride must die in us or Christ cannot live in us." The opposite of pride is humility. "God opposes the proud but gives grace to the humble" (James 4:6). He saves, guides, and crowns the humble (Psalm 18:27; 25:9; 149:4). James says in 4:10, "Humble yourselves before the Lord, and he will lift you up."

How are we doing today? Proud or humble? May we choose the path of humility.

Lord God, I confess my pride. Help me to walk in humility today. Amen!

KITCHEN OR COMMUNITY?

Matthew 5:23, 24

"Therefore, if you are offering your gift at the altar and there remember that your brother has something against you, leave your gift there in front of the altar. First go and be reconciled to your brother; then come and offer your gift."

Ugandan revivalist Bishop Festo Kivengere tells of arguing with his wife in the kitchen on one occasion, shortly before he was due to preach in the community. He then said goodbye and left the house, but God convicted him and told him to go back home. He relays the ensuing dialogue as follows:

> *"Festo," said the Lord, "you go back and apologise to your wife." "But Lord, I've got a very important sermon to preach." "You go and apologise to your wife." "But Lord, there are hundreds of people waiting for me and we're going to have a good time tonight." "You go and apologise to your wife." "But Lord, I'm almost late and someone's waiting to collect me." "All right," the Lord said, "you go and preach your sermon and I'm going to stay with your wife in the kitchen."*

Bishop Festo ended the story as follows: "I went back into the kitchen and apologised. So there was revival in the kitchen before there was revival in the community!"

I'm totally nailed by that story and the verse above, having just had the exact same scenario with my wife! I couldn't go on writing this without apologizing, in the kitchen, and reconciling over miscommunicated plans with visitors coming in a few hours!

We can all relate to having arguments, but Jesus' warning in our verse is one of the most sober challenges in the Bible. If we've got any unresolved issues with anyone that we can do anything about, he tells us to deal with them before expecting there to be blessing in our relationship with him.

Is there any relationship breakdown or situation you need to address? It's worth getting peace in the kitchen!

Lord, I resolve to pursue reconciliation with… today. Amen!

MOUNTAINS OR BEYOND?

Psalm 121:1, 2

"I lift my eyes up to the mountains – where does my help come from? My help comes from the Lord, the Maker of heaven and earth."

Dietrich Bonhoeffer's first ever sermon was on Psalm 121. It was so apt for a man who would become famous for staying faithful to Jesus through the toughest of circumstances and even to death. He was gripped by the reality of this Christ, who demanded his entire obedience, and who in turn gave him such a depth of meaning, purpose, and security that even death itself could not take away. He wrote, "Peace is the opposite of security. To demand guarantees is to want to protect oneself. Peace means giving oneself completely to God, wanting no security, but in faith and obedience, resting in the hand of Almighty God."

Psalm 121 is all about the choice we have when confronted with the mountains of our circumstances. Will we fix our eyes and attention on those obstacles – be they worries, problems, or even threats of physical danger – or will we fix our eyes on Jesus, the author and creator of our faith? I read once that "obstacles are those frightful things you see when you take your eyes off the goal". So let's keep our eyes on Jesus! He's where our help comes from. With a daily sacrifice of praise and thanksgiving that doesn't depend on the ups and downs of our immediate circumstances we can make the choice to lift our eyes up, not to the hills of our problems, but to the hill of Calvary, and to our Saviour Jesus Christ, who died that we might live, and offers to take our worries and replace them with the peace that passes all understanding.

A word of caution: our immediate circumstances don't always turn out well. They didn't with Bonhoeffer. But then he knew the real, eternal ending to his story. And I trust you do too.

Lord, I choose to hang in there today, to look beyond my problems to you, risen Christ. Amen!

Matthew 16:25

"Whoever wants to save his life will lose it, but whoever loses his life for me will find it."

FOLLOWER OR FAN?

21

JUNE

Jesus wants followers, not fans. Not so long after pronouncing the words above – and despite Peter's protestations that even if all the others left, he would keep following Jesus – Jesus was left to face the cross alone. His disciples had proved to be fair-weather fans, not followers.

A few centuries earlier, Alexander the Great had conquered most of the known world. In one confrontation, he approached a strongly fortified city with just a small company of soldiers. He came forward and demanded to see the king. The king approached to hear Alexander's demands. "Surrender to me immediately," commanded Alexander. The king laughed. "Why should I surrender to you? We have you far outnumbered. You are no threat to us!" Alexander responded by lining up his men and ordering them to march straight towards the nearby cliff. The defending soldiers and king watched incredulous as man after man marched off the edge of the cliff without hesitation. After ten of his men had thus died, Alexander ordered the rest to stop. The king realized that with such loyal enemy soldiers willing to die for the cause, his defeat was guaranteed. He surrendered on the spot to Alexander the Great.

Will we show that same dedication to the cause of Christ? Fans won't, but followers will. Thankfully, God is in no way capricious like Alexander, and by His grace the deserting disciples were restored and re-commissioned by the risen Jesus, and then empowered and equipped by the Holy Spirit to live and die for him. And indeed many of them did! Tertullian, in his great apology for the Christian faith, challenged the Roman authorities: "Kill us, torture us, condemn us, grind us to dust. The more you mow us down, the more we grow, for the seed of the Church is the blood of the martyrs."

Lord, I pray for those followers of yours who, even today, are dying for their faith. Help me choose to be a follower, not a fan. Amen!

IN THE BOAT OR ON THE WATER?

Matthew 14:29

"'Come,' said Jesus. Then Peter got down out of the boat, walked on the water and came towards Jesus."

Peter gets a bad press for his repeated blunders but he was the only one who had the courage in the first place to step out in faith and walk on water. Yes, he then took his eyes off Jesus and sank under the water, but nobody could ever take that glorious experience away from him. He took the plunge, and I'm sure he never regretted it.

How about you? The nature of the life of faith is that we are drawn out of our comfort zones and beyond areas of our own control. Otherwise faith isn't needed, and we can manage in our own strength. Be honest with God. I believe sometimes he speaks and challenges us to move with him, but we quash his voice for years and years out of fear. Be open to him afresh today to rattle your cage of self-sufficiency. Maybe this poem from John Ortberg's book *If You Want to Walk on Water, You've Got to Get out of the Boat* will resonate with you on some level:

To sinful patterns of behaviour that never get confronted and changed,
Abilities and gifts that never get cultivated and deployed –
Until weeks become months
And months turn into years,
And one day you're looking back on a life of
Deep intimate gut-wrenchingly honest conversations you never had;
Great bold prayers you never prayed,
Exhilarating risks you never took,
Sacrificial gifts you never offered
Lives you never touched,
And you're sitting in a recliner with a shriveled soul
And forgotten dreams,
And you realize there was a world of desperate need,
And a great God calling you to be part of something bigger than yourself –
You see the person you could have become but did not;
You never followed your calling.
You never got out of the boat.

Lord, may the above not be the case with me! I choose to get out of the boat and keep my eyes fixed on you today. Amen!

FEAR OR PLEASURE?

Zephaniah 3:17

"The Lord your God is with you, he is mighty to save. He will take great delight in you, he will quiet you with his love, he will rejoice over you with singing."

Read that verse again... What a glorious promise and picture of God's delight in his children! Do you feel God's pleasure in you?

In the film *Chariots of Fire*, we see the stark contrast of fear and pleasure in the two protagonists, Harold Abrahams and Eric Liddell. On one occasion, before a race, a friend says to Abrahams, "I hate losing. How about you?" Abrahams replies, "I don't know, I've never lost." Then later in the film, having already lost the 200m, he's now about to run the 100m, when he says to the friend, "I'm forever in pursuit and I don't even know what it is I'm chasing. You know, I used to be afraid to lose. Now I'm afraid to win, because I only have ten lonely seconds to justify my existence. And even then I'm not sure I will." He does win and in record time, but he goes away as the loneliest man on earth, and with a huge sense of despondency. He thought he'd accomplished what would bring meaning but it let him down.

Then we come to a scene in which Liddell is about to run the 400m, and there is a flashback to a conversation with his sister. She is worried that he is too caught up with his running, at the expense of his calling to China: "Eric, when are you going to stop?" He replies, "God has made me for a purpose – for China. But he's also made me fast, *and when I run I feel his pleasure*. To not run would be to hold him in contempt."

How about you? When do you feel his pleasure? Stop living someone else's life. Seek God, surrender to him, walk in obedience, and he'll delight in using you.

Lord, I want to feel your pleasure. Show me the way today. Amen!

REST OR DISTRESSED OR DEPRESSED OR...?

Matthew 11:28

"Come to me, all you who are weary and burdened, and I will give you rest."

During the war years in Burundi, it was a very stressful environment. There was the extreme poverty, the listening to bombs fall, the death threats, and more. It was in that context that my Great Aunt, who had also worked out here, sent me a note that read:

Look around, and be distressed;
Look within, and be depressed;
Look to Jesus, and be at rest.

There is so much to look around at and get distressed by; and then if you spend too much time looking within yourself at your own issues, you can easily end up depressed; but if we keep our eyes fixed on Jesus, however weary and burdened we are, he says, "I will give you rest."

How do you picture rest? Two painters were trying to depict their understanding of rest. The first chose a beautiful, picturesque lake scene, surrounded by elegant mountains. The second artist splashed his canvas with a thundering waterfall, in the middle of which a defiant birch tree reached upwards, bending over the foam. On one branch sat a robin, covered in spray, observing the cascading water either side and beneath it. The first artist's work more accurately depicted *stagnation*; the latter's work more authentically portrayed *rest*.

We can take brief escapes on holidays to peaceful lakes and mountains, but our lives feel much more like the thundering waterfall. We need to find a branch somehow, somewhere, in the midst of the stress and frenetic speed of life to be still, to centre ourselves in Jesus, to breathe deeply, and commune with him. Otherwise his voice will get drowned out, and we'll miss what he's saying. And then at the end of each day, let's follow Victor Hugo's advice: "When you have accomplished your daily task, go to sleep in peace; God is awake!"

Lord, teach me to look to you and find rest. Amen!

John 14:18

"I will not leave you as orphans; I will come to you."

ORPHAN OR CHILD?

We were all orphans once, separated and removed from the presence of our Father; but through the cross our identity as a child of God, a co-heir with Christ, was secured. Our Father, before the creation of the world, "destined us for adoption as his children through Jesus Christ" (Ephesians 1:5 NRSV). Yet we still often live like we're orphans.

Living in Burundi, I would estimate over 20 per cent of the young people I work with are orphans because of the war, disease, or poverty. What characterizes their lives is fear. Orphans don't live in peace. They experience crippling loneliness. They lie, cheat, steal, and manipulate because of deep insecurity driving them to provide for and protect themselves. They're desperate for approval and terrified of failure. They struggle with self-worth, have doubts about their God-given purpose, and feel overlooked, abandoned, and rejected.

If we're honest, we can see some of those characteristics in our own lives as well, as we strive to provide for and protect ourselves. We feel threatened, and get jealous and competitive, comparing ourselves to others because we're not secure in our God-given purpose. Like the orphan, we can easily fall into addictive behaviour by looking to other things for comfort, such as food, relationships, or even ministry – all of them to silence the fear and insecurity for a moment.

We can choose today to receive the love of the Father, and to trust and depend upon him for provision, protection, and purpose – *or* we can choose to remain as orphans, removed from our Father. Why not choose to live in peace, security, and grace? Why not receive the lavish love of the Father (1 John 3:1)? And then be generous with all he has provided for you, be assured of his protection, and be free and secure to live out your God-given calling for his glory.

Lord, I choose to live as your child today. Amen!

OBEDIENCE OR DISOBEDIENCE?

John 14:15, 21, 23–24

"If you love me, you will obey what I command... Whoever has my commands and obeys them, he is the one who loves me. He who loves me will be loved by my Father, and I too will love him and show myself to him... If anyone loves me, he will obey my teaching. My Father will love him, and we will come to him and make our home with him, He who does not love me will not obey my teaching."

Jesus preached on obedience (three mentions alone in John 14), and modelled the life of obedience: "Although he was a son, he learned *obedience* through what he suffered, and, once made perfect, he became the source of eternal salvation for all who obey him" (Hebrews 5:8–9).

So we know we're meant to obey, but will we? If we don't, Tozer gives us a strong warning:

> *Whenever you hear God's truth, God's Word, you will go either in the direction you are moved, or you will just wait. If you wait, you will find that the next time you hear the truth, it will not move you quite as much. The next time, it will move you less, and the time will come when that truth will not move you at all!*

Is there a block in my spiritual life? I want God to show himself to me, but he seems really distant. Could that be because of some disobedience? Dorothy Kerin wrote, "Obedience is the key that unlocks the door to every profound spiritual experience." Oswald Chambers said, "We learn more by five minutes' obedience than by ten years' study."

Have you been in a situation, or is there one coming up soon, where you will tone down and compromise your integrity and God's standards because of peer pressure and the longing for acceptance and approval? Remember Peter before the Sanhedrin as he declared, "We must *obey* God rather than men" (Acts 5:29).

Lord God, help me live a life of obedience to you for your glory. Amen!

POVERTY OR RICHES?

Luke 6:20

"Blessed are you who are poor, for yours is the kingdom of God."

There was huge persecution under Emperor Valerian in AD 250 because of the rampant growth of the church. It was said at the time that "all of Rome were becoming Christians", so Valerian's officials did their best to stamp it out. They began a ruthless campaign of stripping all Christians of their property, and they zealously carried out Valerian's edict to arrest and execute all bishops, priests, and deacons.

Brother Laurence was deacon and treasurer of one of the better-known churches. He encouraged his people to give all their belongings away to the poor rather than have them taken by the corrupt officials. He was then approached by the officials and offered amnesty if he would show where all the church's treasures were located. He agreed to do so, and asked for three days to collect all the church's riches into one central place. In the meantime he assembled the poor, disabled, blind, sick, widows, and orphans. When Valerian came to inspect the treasure trove, Laurence flung open the doors and declared emphatically, "These are the treasures of the church!"

Valerian was so enraged he ordered Laurence to face the most gruesome death possible – not just beheading but torture. Laurence was roasted on a gridiron and he died on 10 August AD 258. It's reported he even managed to joke with his executioners: "You may turn me over. I'm done on this side." Such courage had a profound impact on the observers at the execution, including several senators who gave their lives to Christ. Rather than suppress the growth of Christianity in Rome, his death only served to hasten its spread.

Brother Laurence had a deep grasp of what constitutes poverty and riches. Do we likewise understand that the poor are the treasures of the church? Our society tends to discard them, so will we buck or follow that trend?

Lord, I choose to be involved with your treasures. Show me what that might look like today. Amen!

MORE OR LESS?

Malachi 3:9, 10

"You are under a curse – the whole nation of you – because you are robbing me. Bring the whole tithe into the storehouse, that there may be food in my house. Test me in this, and see if I will not throw open the floodgates of heaven and pour out so much blessing that you will not have room enough for it."

A flagging rural church appointed a new treasurer, who was the manager of a grain elevator. He agreed to serve on two conditions: he wouldn't submit any report until the end of the first year, and no questions would be asked for that period. When he presented his report at the end of the first year, it blew everyone away. He'd paid off the church debt of $150,000. He'd renovated the meeting hall. He'd renewed overseas support to several missionaries, and there was even a healthy surplus in the bank. The congregation demanded to know how he'd done it. He quietly replied, "All you farmers bring your grain to my elevator. I simply withheld 10 per cent and gave it to the church. You never missed it."

Actually under the new covenant, we're not under obligation to tithe, thank God! But grace is never less than law. The point of the tithe is that it costs us. For some, 10 per cent is nothing, for others it's crippling. The cross is the standard for giving in the Bible. Thank God again that Jesus didn't tithe his blood! So is there a cross in your economic life? And remember, "God loves a cheerful giver" (2 Corinthians 9:7).

Mark Batterson has the right approach: "One of the turning points of my life came the day I stopped setting income goals and started setting giving goals. It was a paradigm shift. I finally came to terms with the fact that making money is the way you make a living and giving it away is the way you make a life."

Lord, I choose to be a cheerful generous giver in response to your lavish generosity towards me. Amen!

WORK OR WORSHIP?

Revelation 4:10, 11

"The twenty-four elders fall down before him who sits on the throne, and worship him who lives for ever and ever. They lay their crowns before the throne and say: 'You are worthy, our Lord and God, to receive glory and honour and power.'"

What a vision! When Handel was asked what inspired him to write *Messiah*, he said, "I saw the heavens opened and God upon his great white throne." Dear God, grant us similar glimpses of your glory!

Tozer highlights the primacy of worship and laments how quickly it gets displaced: "We take a convert and immediately make a worker out of him. God never meant it to be so. God meant that a convert should learn to be a worshipper, and after that he can learn to be a worker. The work done by a worshipper will have eternity in it." Oswald Chambers adds, "Beware of anything that compares with loyalty to Jesus Christ. The greatest competitor of devotion to Jesus is service for Him... The one aim of the call of God is the satisfaction of God, not a call to do something for Him."

I fear we get too busy to be good worshippers. How slow we are to learn that although we have direct access to God, we can't worship effectively if we only give him the dregs of our time. Worship needs to be intentional. All the deepest and most profound experiences of worship in my life have come when I've dedicated time, space, and energy to pursuing God. Do we have our priorities right? Chuck Swindoll has commented that we're guilty of playing at worship, worshipping work, and working at play. Acceptable worship involves the whole person in a humble attitude of dependence on God, acknowledging the "worth-ship" of our Creator and Sustainer.

Lord, I choose to make time to worship you today. You are worthy of all praise and adoration. Take me deeper. May all my work for you be done as a worshipper first and foremost. Amen!

1 Thessalonians 5:18

"Give thanks in all circumstances, for this is God's will for you in Christ Jesus."

COUNTING BLESSINGS OR WOES?

I find this verse a challenge to me today several months into a debilitating illness. It's a verse we've memorized with our little children, so I need to practise what I preach! And yet, as I list all the blessings in my life, they massively outnumber the woes. And it is humbling to live alongside others who have suffered so much more. My colleague Sarah's husband was murdered, so she is now a widow with four children and no social security, yet she beams and praises the Lord for his many blessings to her.

A short-term mission team went to the island of Tobago to serve in a leper colony. During a worship service, the team leader asked if anyone had a favourite song they wanted to sing. A woman's hand shot up. When he turned to her, he was horrified by her appearance. Her hand was a fingerless stump, her face was disfigured, her nose, lips, and ears were gone. But she beamed with joy, and asked him, "Could we sing 'Count Your Many Blessings'?" The missionary started the song but couldn't finish. Another team member later said to him, "I suppose you'll never be able to sing the song again." He answered, "No, I'll sing it again. Just never in the same way."

Sometimes, it's only in retrospect that we can thank God for blessings, which at the time we considered woes. I'm hoping that's the case with my illness. A by-product of enforced rest has been this book. On a much deeper level, Alexander Solzhenitsyn was able to reflect on his hideous suffering in the Soviet gulag: "It was only when I lay there on rotting prison straw that I sensed within myself the first stirrings of good. So, bless you, prison, for having been in my life."

Lord, I count my many blessings today and I choose to give thanks in all circumstances. Amen!

John 10:10

"I have come that they may have life, and life to the full."

LIVE OR EXIST?

Jack London wrote, "I would rather be ashes than dust! I would rather that my spark should burn out in a brilliant blaze than it should be stifled by dry rot. I would rather be a superb meteor, every atom of me in magnificent glow, than a sleepy and permanent planet. The proper function of man is to live, not to exist. I shall not waste my days in trying to prolong them. I shall use my time."

My granny spent forty years of her life in Rwanda. As a "retired" 83-year-old widow, when Grandpa died, she went back out here to work with widows. There were thousands in her area left by the genocide. She started a widows' meeting and hundreds came. The meetings became an incredible forum of self-help, as the widows began working together, building each other houses and lifting each other out of poverty. Three years later, after a huge celebration meeting with them, in which she preached for an hour and danced with them, she said "Adieu" – like she knew she was going to die – and wobbled home. She then ate, had a game of Scrabble, and graduated to glory. What a great life!

For the follower of Christ, there's no such thing as retirement and then coasting in self-indulgence to the grave; and for us younger ones, let's not settle for existing, for dull respectability, or for accumulating possessions. Granny left nothing much in terms of "stuff", but she left a living inheritance in the transformed lives of thousands of people. Jesus promises fullness of life. Be honest, have you settled for less? Circumstances might conspire against you, but keep a good attitude, and seek God for what he wants you to do.

Lord, I choose today to use my time well and to live, not just to exist. Amen!

COVETOUSNESS OR CONTENTMENT?

James 4:2

"You kill and covet, but you cannot have what you want. You quarrel and fight. You do not have, because you do not ask God. When you ask, you do not receive, because you ask with wrong motives, that you may spend what you get on your pleasures."

In the film *Wall Street*, a powerful financial tycoon named Gordon Gekko personifies the spirit of the age, which has captured our world and is likewise negatively influencing the church. At one point, while trying to inspire his minions, Gekko says, "Greed is good. Greed is right. Greed clarifies, cuts through, and captures the essence of the evolutionary spirit. Greed – mark my words – will save the USA."

Well it clearly hasn't, and won't! Rather it destroys relationships, friendships, and marriages. David Watson wrote:

> *Once we accept the biblical view of man, we should cease to be surprised by the covetousness which dominates our society today and the constant pursuit of money and possessions, even when this denies human values and destroys personal relationships. Politicians promise monotonously to "raise the standard of living", but the implicit assumption is that "living" is synonymous with "earning". It is what I get out of it, in terms of hard cash that determines the value of many a job. Money is seen to be the ultimate in self-fulfilment. Any analysis of today's moods which does not focus on the basic selfishness and covetousness of man misses the heart of it all.*

One of our weaknesses is our inability to distinguish needs from greeds. Covetousness involves getting what you want, while contentment results in wanting what you get. And the more you have to live for, the less you need to live on. Those who make possessions their ultimate goal never have enough. Let's rather seek to learn with Paul the secret of being content whatever the circumstances (Philippians 4:11, 12), remembering that "godliness with contentment is great gain" (1 Timothy 6:6).

Lord, I choose today to be governed by your Word, not by the lies of our culture. Amen!

EASY OR TOUGH?

2 Timothy 3:10–12

"You, however, know all about my… endurance, persecutions, sufferings… In fact, everyone who wants to live a godly life in Christ Jesus will be persecuted."

In a telling discussion, the spiritual leader of Islamic fundamentalist Hezbollah in Lebanon, Ayatollah Fadlallah, said to Brother Andrew, "You Christians have a problem." "What do you think our problem is?" "You're not following the life of Jesus Christ any more." "So what do you think we should do about that?" "You must go back to the Book."

Going "back to the Book" will involve re-reading the Scriptures and noticing they are filled with references to the reality of how tough and painful it is to follow Jesus all the way. If we consider just one of Paul's epistles, in 2 Timothy he writes (as well as the above verses), "Join with me in suffering for the gospel" (1:8); "That is why I am suffering as I am" (1:12); "Endure hardship with us like a good soldier of Christ Jesus" (2:3); "Therefore I endure everything for the sake of the elect" (2:10); "Endure hardship" (4:5). Only a highly selective and blinkered reading of Scripture can produce a working understanding that to come to Jesus is to be spared of any problems, to experience uninterrupted ease and prosperity. There are plenty of wonderful promises for us to take hold of, but only within the context of the Bible as a whole. So will we get back to the Book, delve deeply into its riches, and live out the message?

Salvation was a free gift for us, but bought at great cost by the Lord. Although grace was free, it wasn't cheap. God paid with the blood of his Son on the cross, and we in turn are called to follow. So although the entrance fee is nothing, the annual subscription is everything! Yet however hard it may be at times, we can be assured that after the pain comes the gain.

Lord, I want to live authentically for you. Help me to endure hardship for your name. Amen!

SUBMIT OR RESIST?

Malachi 3:3

"He will sit as a refiner and purifier of silver."

During a weekly Bible study group in Kentucky, the book of Malachi was being studied. In Malachi 3:3, they read, "He will sit as a refiner and purifier of silver." The group discussed this analogy to understand its significance. It seemed the Lord chooses to put his people in the furnace; the purpose is to burn off the impurities; God watches the refining process take place; it's a painful process.

One woman in the group was fascinated by the analogy and wanted to gain the full impact of it, so she went to see a silversmith in action the following day. She observed him at work for a while, and then asked him, "Do you have to sit the whole time the refining process is taking place?" "Yes," he replied, "it's crucial – because if the time of the refining process is exceeded by the slightest degree, the silver will be damaged." The woman was comforted by the thought that similarly the Lord was watching over her, and however difficult her current circumstances were, he was in control. God wouldn't let the refining process go on a minute longer than was required, because his purposes were good, and he didn't want her to be damaged. The silversmith carried on gazing intently into the furnace.

After a further while, the woman got up to leave, but as she was halfway out of the door, he called her back and told her he had forgotten one important detail: he only knew that the refining process was complete when he could see *his own image* reflected in the silver.

There's no doubt that if we submit to the Lord's refining process, it will involve embracing the pain. We can choose to resist and live on with the dross and impurities, but how short-sighted that would make us. Trust him today; he knows what he's doing.

Lord, I choose to trust you and submit to your refining process in my life. Amen!

Colossians 1:16, 17

"All things were created by him and for him. He is before all things, and in him all things hold together."

INCLUSIVE OR EXCLUSIVE?

Dallas Willard wrote, "The aim of God in history is the creation of an all-inclusive community of loving persons, with himself included in that community as its prime sustainer and most glorious inhabitant." Richard Foster commented on the above:

> *I believe that God is gathering just such a community in our day. It is a community that combines eschatology with social action, the transcendent Lordship of Jesus with the suffering servant Messiah. It is a community of cross and crown, of conflict and reconciliation, of courageous action and suffering love. It is a community empowered to attack evil in all its forms, overcoming it with good. It is a community of unselfish love, and witness without compromise. It is a community buoyed up by the vision of Christ's everlasting rule, not only imminent on the horizon but already coming to birth in our midst.*

In our disconnected age, such a vision of community is very attractive. Meaning is found in community, not individualism. Hope is nurtured in relationship, not isolation. Yet it also provides an antidote to thinking such a community can live a separatist disengagement from society at large. We need to hear the challenge of a professor of theology: "We want none of your talk of forgiveness, we want to see a community where forgiving, accepting love is happening and changing personal behaviour."

Are you part of such a community? It might be your church, but most churches are too big really to act as a committed community. Historically the spread of the church under persecution came when the "*oikos*" (extended family of aunties, uncles, cousins, servants) moved together and embodied kingdom values. So a life-group or network of ten to twenty people committed to intentional relationships was beautifully effective and attractive to outsiders. Would you consider it?

Lord, I choose today to become more rooted in intentional community and more welcoming to outsiders. Amen!

LIGHTHOUSE OR BATTLESHIP?

Isaiah 26:4

"Trust in the Lord for ever, for the Lord, the Lord, is the Rock eternal."

This story was recorded by an officer in a naval magazine:

> *Two battleships were assigned to the training squadron and had been at sea for several days in heavy weather. I was serving in the lead battleship and was on watch on the bridge when the night fell. The visibility was poor with patchy fog so the Captain remained on the bridge keeping an eye on all activities. Shortly after dark the lookout on the bridge reported: "Sir there's a light bearing on the starboard bow." The Captain asked: "Is it steady or is it moving about?" The lookout replied: "Steady, Captain." This meant that we were on a dangerous collision course with that ship. The Captain then called to his signalman: "Signal that ship – we're on a collision course – I advise you to change your course 20 degrees." Back came the signal: "It's advisable for you to change your course 20 degrees." The Captain said: "Send the message – "I'm a Captain. Change your course 20 degrees." The signal came back: "I'm a seaman second class – but you'd better change your course 20 degrees." By that time our Captain was furious. He spat out: "Send the message – I'm a battleship. Change your course 20 degrees." Back came the flashing light: "I'm a lighthouse." We changed course.*

It's a well-known story, and makes a powerful point. How easy it is to have an over-inflated view of ourselves, our abilities, our comprehension of the facts. Yet only "the Lord is the Rock eternal". Politicians, heads of corporations, and even ship captains speak and people listen. Sometimes it's right that we do, but they will invariably have a limited perspective, so we always need to remember the one ultimate, secure, unshakeable "lighthouse", the Word of God.

Lord, I choose to be strongly anchored in your Word today. Help me discern your voice amidst the many competing for my attention. Amen!

AVOID OR EMBRACE?

Romans 5:3, 4

"We also rejoice in our sufferings, because we know that suffering produces perseverance; perseverance, character; and character, hope."

Nineteenth-century British naturalist Alfred Russell Wallace was second only to Charles Darwin in contributions to his field. One of his most astute observations concerned the saving nature of struggle. He stumbled across it as he watched moths struggling to hatch out from their cocoons. One particular moth was having a hard time getting out because of its underdeveloped wings, so Wallace thought he'd help speed up the process. He took his penknife and made a tiny incision in the cocoon to facilitate the moth's exit. But he soon came to regret the intervention. The moth hadn't needed his help. The process of straining and stretching to get out unaided was an integral part of the strengthening of the moth's wings. The aborted process meant the moth wasn't equipped to last long. It did beat its wings, folding and unfolding them, but Wallace observed it had less colour, strength, and vitality than the other moths. Over the course of its brief life span the "helped out" moth flew poorly, fed inefficiently, and ultimately died long before it should have.

No doubt, like me, there've been times when you've asked God to short-circuit the painful ordeal you've been going through. Hopefully, again like me, you can look back in gratitude on at least some of those instances and see that what came out of the struggling could not have been gained any other way.

These lines from the old folk song capture it well:

Is the rain falling from the sky keeping you from singing? Is that tear falling from your eye because the wind is stinging?
Don't you know the seed could never grow if there weren't any showers? Though the rain might bring a little pain, just look at all the flowers.
Don't you fret now child, don't you worry. The rain's to help you grow, so don't try to hurry the storm along. The hard times make you strong."

Lord, today I choose to embrace rather than avoid… Amen!

TOLERANT OR INTOLERANT?

John 14:6

"I am the way, the truth and the life. No one comes to the Father, except through me."

Are you a tolerant person? It's a loaded question, isn't it?! The above pronouncement is one of many in the Bible that most people in our relativist postmodern age find totally outrageous and offensive.

A few generations ago, tolerance involved disagreeing with someone but insisting on their right to have and express an opinion contrary to one's own. I might not agree with Muslims, or communists or neoconservatives or whoever, but they had a right to express their own beliefs, which could be challenged in open debate. Tolerance was directed towards the individual, even if they were advocating something abhorrent, because under the modernist paradigm, it was assumed that the truth would come out from among whatever proliferation of competing ideas.

Under postmodernity, however, toleration itself has been redefined, such that you cannot say that *anyone* is wrong. How totally intolerant that would be! Now tolerance involves *all viewpoints and positions, not the individual's viewpoint*. We're no longer in a position to say that any viewpoint is wrong; indeed such thinking becomes the only thing that is not to be tolerated.

With such a pervasive redefining of what constitutes tolerance, followers of Jesus – indeed anyone who believes in absolute truth as they see it – cannot avoid being labelled intolerant. We come along and say this view of tolerance is wrong, but under this view of tolerance we are being intolerant and therefore should not be tolerated. We are thus labelled bigots.

When unpacked like this, we can see how flawed a foundation our culture now rests on. Everything is up for grabs, and can be redefined – indeed we can see this taking place under our very eyes. We can feel intimidated, cowed, or ashamed. But no! "Jesus Christ is the same yesterday, today and forever" (Hebrews 13:5). Stand firm on the Rock of Ages.

Unchanging God, help me be unashamed in speaking the truth in love today. Amen!

STAY ON OR JUMP OFF?

Ecclesiastes 12:13

"Now all has been heard; here is the conclusion of the matter: Fear God and keep his commandments, for this is the whole duty of man."

When I was seventeen, I was asked a question which many of us were faced with: "What university are you going to go to?" I never debated whether it was the right question to answer or not. I never questioned if university was even the right course of action for me to take. I was on a conveyor belt, and so I went to university as the next phase of my "manufacturing process". Years later, I wish I'd been asked, or been aware enough to know, that the question could instead have been: "Do you even want to go to university?"

I loved my time at university, and I'm glad I went. A degree helped me get where I am today, but do you get my point? We're all on a conveyor belt – it might even be a great conveyor belt for some of us– but we need to recognize that fact to see whether or when we should be staying on or jumping off.

One of the schools we used to play against was called Rugby School (where the sport allegedly originated). It hit the headlines a few years ago when one of their pupils questioned the conveyor belt in an unconventional manner. During term-time, he sold his stereo and CD collection, bought a plane ticket to the Bahamas, and disappeared. Journalists tried to track him down, and eventually succeeded. One asked him, "Fenn Chapman, 16-years-old, from Rugby School, why did you do it?" He replied, "I started thinking about my future: university, a job, buying a car, getting married, a mortgage, and then dying. I thought there had to be something more to life than this. So I had to get away and think things through."

I'm with Fenn. How about you: jump off, stay on, or what?

Lord, help me to live the life you have called me to live, for your glory. Amen!

VILE OR SILENT?

Romans 1:16

"I am not ashamed of the gospel, because it is the power of God for the salvation of everyone who believes."

10

JULY

Nobody likes being mocked or marginalized, slandered or scoffed at, be it by colleagues or friends or random people we come across. Well, God wants us to surrender our fear of people, our desire for popularity, and our longing for respect and reputation. He wants us to stand up and be counted, to face the music, to nail our colours to the mast.

Observing one of the pivotal decisions in John Wesley's life highlights the inner conflict that went on as God called him to radically surrender his reputation. His contemporary and friend, Whitefield, had already resorted to preaching in fields and marketplaces, due to the fact that evangelicals were being denied access to more and more pulpits countrywide. Wesley didn't want to preach in the open air, but there seemed little alternative. He went through a time of deep inner turmoil and wrestling. The idea of preaching in the fields was repugnant to him, as to just about everyone else in his day – except Whitefield, who was seeing astonishing results.

Gradually Wesley came round to the idea. When a friend remonstrated with him and appealed to him not to soil his good standing in society by stooping to such crude methods, Wesley replied, "When I gave my all to God I did not withhold my reputation." He began preaching in the open air, saying, "I consented to be more vile... I set myself on fire, and people came to see me burn."

When I see open air preachers, I always feel a mixture of embarrassment on their behalf and admiration that they believe enough in their Lord to face all that mockery. But the merits or demerits of street evangelism is not the issue. Are you/am I ashamed of our Lord? Will you/will I choose to make and take opportunities to share life with the lost? Come on!

Lord, use me today to speak unashamedly and effectively about you to someone who needs you. Amen!

SOFT OR HARD?

Philippians 2:17

"But even if I am being poured out like a drink offering on the sacrifice and service coming from your faith, I am glad and rejoice with all of you."

I'm sure you're probably like me in terms of feeling overwhelmed at times by the needs of this world. We see horrific pictures on the news of famines or wars and it touches us momentarily, but we change channels to watch something less disturbing and so quickly forget. We choose to harden our hearts. Every day, I battle with this. There are women and kids sitting in the dirt fifty yards from me as I write this. Will I embrace the pain of keeping my heart soft, or settle for a hardening of it?

Jackie Pullinger has led a remarkable life working among prostitutes, heroin addicts, and gang members for over four decades. In one sermon she exhorted us: "God wants us to have soft hearts and hard feet. The trouble with so many of us is that we have hard hearts and soft feet."

So may we keep our hearts soft – that's half of it – now how about the tough feet? Paul writes the above verse from prison. He's suffered for the cause. He knows that what he's exhorting others to won't be easy. His soft heart rejoices for how they've grown in their faith while his calloused feet endure enforced rest from the many miles of travelling and preaching the good news.

While exploring Central Africa, David Livingstone once received a letter from a missionary society down in South Africa: "Have you found a good road to where you are? If the answer's 'yes', we want to send other men to come and help you." Livingstone replied, "If you have men who will come *only* if they know there's a good road, I don't want them."

Are you laying down any conditions before offering your life to God?

Lord God, I choose to have a soft heart and tough feet, for Christ's sake. Amen!

CLEAN OR DIRTY?

Psalm 24:3, 4

"Who may ascend the mountain of the Lord? Who may stand in his holy place? The one who has clean hands and a pure heart."

In 1949, a great revival took place in the Hebrides. Seven men and two women had decided to pray and not stop until God visited them in a powerful way. One night, at a prayer meeting held in a barn, one of them read the above verse, shut his Bible, and said, "It seems to me just so much sentimental humbug to be praying as we are praying, to be waiting as we are waiting here, if we ourselves are not *rightly related* to God." He asked God to reveal if his own hands were clean and his own heart was pure. Suddenly God's awesome presence swept the barn. They came to see that there was a direct correlation between revival and *holiness*. A power was let loose that night that shook the island. A man arrived and felt compelled to go to church and get right with God. People had visions in their own homes. When Duncan Campbell arrived for the planned mission, all the services were packed out and people fell to the floor in repentance under the power of God.

As Tozer commented, "Prayer for revival will prevail when radical amendments to lifestyle are made, not before." If we're serious about meeting with God, we have to move beyond the "sentimental humbug" which the man above referred to, and embrace lifestyles of authentic obedience. We'd all love to see God move in power where we are, but at what cost? How much do you want of God? Because nobody has less of God than they want.

Think about that last line; I'll repeat it:

How much do you want of God? Because nobody has less of God than they want.

Lord, I mean business. I choose to become "rightly related" to you today. Amen!

GRACE OR JUDGMENT?

Hebrews 9:27, 28

"Just as man is destined to die once, and after that to face judgment, so Christ was sacrificed once to take away the sins of many people; and he will appear a second time, not to bear sin, but to bring salvation to those who are waiting for him."

Not many people enjoy talking about judgment, hell, or punishment. Jesus didn't shy away from such topics, but he didn't pit grace against judgment, and he spoke with grace and compassion.

Andrew Carnegie was born in Dunfermline in 1835. He went on to become one of the richest men in the world, and gave away vast sums of money to help the poor. His father initially attended the local Presbyterian church, but one Sunday was so horrified to hear the minister talk about infant damnation with such relish that he stormed out mid-service, declaring: "If that be your religion and that your God, I shall seek a better religion and a nobler God." That is how both William and Andrew Carnegie ended up living philanthropic lives as sceptics, never having found the "nobler God" that William had referred to.

Interestingly, it isn't sinners whom Jesus primarily addresses in his discourses on hell, but believers who were complacent about their places in heaven. If we're full of ourselves and our sense of "chosenness", like the Pharisees were, then we're not in a good place at all. But to those who knew they were "sinners", Jesus spoke of grace. He wasn't in the habit of "dangling people over the pit". Hence David Pawson suggests the need "to *see* sinners in this danger, but not necessarily to *tell* them". Similarly, it is better for the evangelist "to have hell more frequently in his heart than on his lips. This will fuel his fervency and increase the urgency of his appeal."

Lord, please fuel my sense of fervency and urgency to bring light and life to a dark and dying world. Amen!

COURAGE OR FEAR?

John 16:33

"In this world you will have troubles; but take heart, I have overcome the world."

Are you feeling courageous today? Winston Churchill said, "Success is never final; failure is never fatal. It is courage that counts."

In Harper Lee's *To Kill A Mockingbird*, Atticus says, "I wanted you to see what real courage is, instead of getting the idea that courage is a man with a gun in his hand. It's when you know you're licked before you begin but you begin anyway and you see it through no matter what. You rarely win, but sometimes you do."

The difference with Jesus is that he warns his disciples of troubles ahead, but assures them of victory despite them, so long as they persevere. His disciples certainly appeared to have been "licked" after his crucifixion, but with the Holy Spirit's empowering at Pentecost, they were equipped to face up to any trial sent their way. One young lady defined courage as "knowing the worst – and discovering that, in God's world, the very worst can't really hurt you".

Henri Nouwen takes us deeper into the meaning of the word:

> *"Have courage" we often say to one another. Courage is a spiritual virtue. The word courage comes from the Latin word "cor", which means "heart". A courageous act is an act coming from the heart. A courageous word is a word arising from the heart. The heart, however, is not just the place where our emotions are located. The heart is the centre of all thoughts, feelings, passions and decisions. A courageous life, therefore, is a life lived from the centre. It is a deeply rooted life, the opposite of a superficial life. "Have courage", therefore means: "Let your centre speak".*

Lord, I choose to take heart today, to live a courageous life. I praise you that you have overcome the world. Thank you that we likewise can be more than conquerors through you. Amen!

DESERVED OR UNDESERVED?

1 Corinthians 15:9, 10

"For I am the least of the apostles and do not even deserve to be called an apostle, because I persecuted the church of God. But by the grace of God I am what I am."

Echoing the apostle Paul's words above, the former slave trader, John Newton, similarly with plenty of blood on his hands, was able to declare: "I'm not what I ought to be, I'm not what I would like to be, I'm not what I hope to be, but I'm not what I was, and *by the grace of God I am what I am*."

The above two men knew how sinful they were. That's the first requirement to receiving God's undeserved grace. One of the most beautiful encounters in the Bible takes place when a prostitute appears at Simon the Pharisee's home. She breaks every rule in the book as she interrupts the respectable men's gathering, lets down her hair, and washes Jesus' feet. Jesus responds to the judgmental, flabbergasted men: "I tell you, her many sins have been forgiven – for she loved much. But he who has been forgiven little loves little" (Luke 7:47).

We might want to take credit for what we've done in our lives, but take a long hard look back. Whatever you did was a product of the time and place you were born into, your talents and health and opportunities – and none of this you earned! It's all grace.

Tullian Tchividjian wrote, "The operative power that makes you a Christian is the same operative power that keeps you a Christian: the unconditional, unqualified, undeserved, unrestrained grace of God in the completed work of Christ. The banner under which Christians live reads, 'It is finished'. So relax, and rejoice. Jesus plus nothing equals everything; everything minus Jesus equals nothing. You're free!"

Thank you, Lord, for this fabulously liberating truth. I choose to live in the freedom of your grace today. Amen!

TONED DOWN OR UNCOMPROMISING?

2 Timothy 2:8, 9

"Remember Jesus Christ, raised from the dead, descended from David. This is my gospel, for which I am suffering even to the point of being chained."

16

JULY

Paul always insisted on "speaking the truth in love" (Ephesians 4:15). Truth without love can damage people, while love without truth may placate but ultimately will deceive them. As we journey with Christ, we more likely face the temptation to tone down and compromise our message in the name of conflict avoidance or being "relevant".

"I love him. He's not a Christian but hopefully he'll come to faith through me." "I don't feel comfortable with this approach but I've got to go along with it or they'll reject me." "God isn't judgmental, he's a God of love." "Jesus wants to bless you and make you happy." There's some truth in the mix, but we just tone it down and it loses its cutting edge.

Peter Cartwright was an itinerant Methodist preacher in the nineteenth century. One Sunday morning, as he entered the church he was told that President Andrew Jackson was in the congregation, and was warned not to say anything offensive. When the time came, Cartwright stood in the pulpit and began: "I understand that Andrew Jackson is here. I have been requested to be guarded in my remarks. Andrew Jackson will go to hell if he doesn't repent." Everyone was shocked and wondered how the president would respond. After the service, President Jackson greeted Peter Cartwright warmly and said: "Sir, if I had a regiment of men like you, I could whip the world!"

Many of our brothers and sisters around the world are suffering because they are unwilling to tone down the gospel. Paul wrote the above in chains. Will you and I be ashamed today?

Lord, I confess that sometimes I am ashamed and fearful to speak up for you. Help me today to speak the truth in love, for your glory. Amen!

Psalm 24:1

"The earth is the Lord's, and everything in it."

STEWARDSHIP OR OWNERSHIP?

When someone brought news to John Wesley that his home had been destroyed by fire, he exclaimed, "The Lord's house burned? One less responsibility for me!" How could he react like that? Because he knew that, as the creed says, "All things come from you [God], and of your own do we give you."

We are stewards, not owners. When our children were born, the first thing we did was commit them to the Lord as his, not ours. Your house, your car, your treasured "whatever" – it's not yours, it's God's. As Abraham Kuyper wrote: "There is not one square inch in all of God's creation that Jesus does not cry out, 'Mine!'"

Stewardship is not ownership so much as the management or supervision of something entrusted to one's care by another. And to be a good steward for God, we need to (1) know his will (through the Scriptures primarily, but also through the revelation of the Holy Spirit and the discernment of others), (2) submit to his will (willingly, not through coercion or manipulation by others), and (3) do his will the right way (for example, King Saul did the right thing but in the wrong way when he offered a sacrifice to God rather than wait for Samuel the priest to arrive and do it, in 1 Samuel 13).

So today, do you feel like you're on track? Do you know God's will and submit to his will, and are you seeking to do his will his way? If yes, be encouraged. If no, what needs changing? Is there an idol that needs to be named and dealt with? Often people end up not so much owning but being owned by their possessions. Yet purpose in life is much more important than property or possessions. Having more to live with is no substitute for having more to live for.

Lord, help me to hold things loosely, to be ready to lay them down. I choose to use whatever you have loaned me for your glory today. Amen!

PREMISES OR PROMISES?

1 Timothy 6:12

"Fight the good fight of faith."

How aware are you there's a fight to be fought, and how engaged are you in it? John Piper wrote, "Life is a war. That is not all it is, but it is always that." Søren Kierkegaard talked of the many parade-ground Christians who wear the uniforms of Christianity, while only few are willing to do battle for Christ and his kingdom. Too many church members, oblivious to the battle going on, are just sitting on the premises instead of leaning on the promises of God.

One night in an area steeped in witchcraft, I woke up petrified with an oppressive spiritual presence in my room. I rebuked it in Jesus' name, and went back to sleep. In the morning, my hosts asked me if I'd slept well. "Nobody sleeps well on their first night. There's so much witchcraft directed at us that we have to be praying." My context is different from yours, but make no mistake, we're all in a battle. But are we playing our part?

The 82nd and 101st Airborne Divisions were dropped behind enemy lines before the Allies launched their D-Day offensive towards the end of the Second World War. Their job was to cut off Hitler's reinforcements, and what transpired among them included stories of incredible heroism, but also deep cowardice. All of them jumped, but while some fought heroically, others found places to hide out – and one group discovered a wine cellar and got totally drunk. All of them knew they were at war, but the latter refused to stand up and fight.

Which is your part – sitting on the premises or leaning on the promises? In dangerous denial, or fully engaged?

Lord, help me not to be complacent in how I live out my faith journey. I choose to be alert and fully engaged in the spiritual battle going on. Guide me today as I seek to serve you. Amen!

Matthew 6:24

"You cannot serve both God and Money."

GOD OR GOLD?

Sydney Harris wrote, "Money is a good servant but a poor master. The lure for gold is stronger than the human will, and with many a man it stands between his soul and his God. Someday it will be discovered that the bars that shut many out of the kingdom of heaven are forged of silver and gold."

Sixteen of Jesus' thirty-eight parables deal with money. The New Testament talks more about money than about heaven and hell combined, and five times more about money than prayer. So it's clear that from God's perspective our relationship to money is an important indicator of our level of maturity. The early church seemed to understand this. Emperor Hadrian once asked Aristides, "Just who exactly are those Christians?" Although Aristides wasn't one of them, he gave the following summary: "They love one another, they never fail to help widows, they save orphans from those who would hurt them. If they have something, they give freely to the one who has nothing. If they see a stranger, they take him home, and they're happy as if he's a real brother."

What a wonderful testimony to the saints of Aristides' day and what a challenge for us today! Money is important. We need it to live. But let's recognize its limits. It can buy a house but not a home; it can buy entertainment but not happiness; it can buy a good life but not eternal life. From my experience, the happiest people are those who are most generous with it. One friend said to me that the most exciting moment of his life was when he made us a six-figure donation.

So are your loyalties torn? Are you trying to bargain with God? You can't take anything with you when you leave this earth, so choose wisely now.

Lord, I choose to serve you alone. Help me grow in generosity to others. Amen!

SENSE OR NONSENSE?

Psalm 53:1

"The fool says in his heart, 'there is no God'."

20

JULY

Sir Isaac Newton, one of the great scientists of the seventeenth century, once built a model of the solar system as part of his ongoing studies. An atheist friend came to see him and asked him who had made the model. "Nobody!" Newton replied. When his friend accused him of being ridiculous, Newton explained that if he had a problem with accepting that a model needed a maker, why have a problem when confronted with the real universe?

George Bernard Shaw was a regretful atheist, and mourned the folly of his own belief system: "The science to which I pinned my faith is bankrupt. I believed it once. In its name I helped destroy the faith of millions of worshippers in the temples of a thousand creeds. And now they look at me and witness the tragedy of an atheist who has lost his faith."

It's rare that atheists can be persuaded by verbal argument to change their position. What is more compelling than mere words is a changed life.

In the nineteenth century, an atheist called Charles Bradlaugh challenged a Christian minister, Hugh Price Hughes, to a debate about faith. Hughes agreed on the condition that each of them brought to the debate 100 people whose lives had been positively changed by their commitment to their respective positions: either to Atheism or to Christianity. Hughes then lowered the requirement to fifty to appease Bradlaugh, and then to twenty, then to ten, and then to one. The debate never took place in the end, but the point was made…

Nobody can argue against your own story. Jesus has changed your life, so go on, share it with someone today. You know it makes sense!

Thank you, Lord, that my life has meaning and purpose in you. Give me an opportunity to share my story with someone today. Amen!

DEEP OR SHALLOW?

Colossians 2:6, 7

"Continue to live in him, rooted and built up in him, strengthened in the faith as you were taught."

In different parts of Burundi we often go through periods of drought. Farmers who plant corn can never rest on their laurels, even when there are good rains. Their crop is always vulnerable, because the plants don't push their roots deep down in search for water when there are abundant rains. The roots remain near the surface, so a sudden drought can kill them off very quickly.

It can be remarkably similar with us followers of Jesus. With the abundance of "rains" of freedom to worship, access to great teaching, peace, and prosperity, we could easily settle for shallow roots instead of becoming "rooted and built up in him", as the verse above says. If that's the case, then when droughts come, in the form of financial, relational, or health problems or whatever else, we're ill equipped to maintain faith in God. We suddenly doubt his faithfulness, power, and sovereignty. We just haven't gone deep enough.

As a teenager when I came to faith, I memorized promises in the Bible, verses like Jeremiah 29:11, "For I know the plans I have for you, plans to prosper you and not to harm you" and Philippians 4:13, "I can do all things through Christ who gives me strength". Now don't get me wrong, I wholeheartedly recommend learning Scriptures. Those are great promises, and I still stand on them and claim them for my life. But my shallow triumphalist interpretation of those verses needed challenging so as to push my roots deeper. It was only during the harder times, for example, that I embraced the promise that "everyone who wants to live a godly life in Christ Jesus will be persecuted" (2 Timothy 3:12).

You can't bear good fruits without deep roots. How are your fruits? How are your roots?

Lord, I choose to become deeply rooted in you today so that I will be able to weather all life's storms in the future. Amen!

BLINKERED OR BALANCED?

Romans 12:1

"Therefore, I urge you, in view of God's mercy, to offer your bodies as living sacrifices, holy and pleasing to God."

God wants living sacrifices, not suicide bombers. He wants balanced, not blinkered, commitment. A Latin American Marxist student broke off the engagement to his fiancée in a letter, giving the following reasons: "Marxism is the one thing about which I am in dead earnest. It is my life, my business, my hobby, my dream, my sweetheart. I work for it in the daytime and dream of it at night. I cannot carry on any friendship, or love affair or even conversation, without relating it to this force which drives and guides my life."

Well, that's way too extreme. You can't deny the depth of conviction and commitment to his cause, but Jesus isn't asking us to adopt such blinkered and imbalanced loyalty. We don't just want to replace a single-issue Marxist fanatic (or Islamist, or secularist, and so on) with a single-issue Christian fanatic. It's not the case that God matters more than everything else, so nothing else matters in the light of him. On the contrary, because God matters infinitely, everything else matters much more in the light of him.

So the environment matters immensely, because God is Creator of the world. He loves his world, is committed to it, died for it, and will ultimately re-create it. Art matters because we're made in God's image, and his creativity has been passed on to us. Justice matters, because it's an intrinsic component of God's character. That's why Christians are to be at the forefront of shaping and contributing to issues of the environment, the arts, justice, or whatever other sphere, as we seek to witness to our Creator and bring glory to him.

How are you choosing to offer yourself up as a living sacrifice today? He gave you all your gifts. Use them for his glory.

Lord, I choose to offer myself up to you as a living sacrifice. Use me as you will. Amen!

Philippians 4:13

"I can do all things through Christ who gives me strength."

DREAM OR FANTASY?

John O'Brian was the son of a horse trainer. Due to their peripatetic lifestyle, he'd attended dozens of schools sporadically over a number of years, and fallen far behind his peers in his education. After yet another move to a new area, he was given an end-of-year assignment. He was to write about his future dreams. In consultation with his dad, he designed a 600-acre ranch, complete with training track and training area. He poured himself into the assignment, even taking a mechanical design class to help him better design the property. He submitted the assignment and waited in anticipation of getting a good grade. But the next day, the teacher dismissively returned his paper, having given it an F. He made John stay behind and shouted at him, "I gave you an F because I asked for your dream." The boy replied that he understood and that was exactly what he had submitted. The teacher said, "I want something even remotely possible, not your fantasy. You've barely scraped through the academic year. I've checked your past records. You've got no chance to even make it to university. This is a ridiculous dream. Go back and write something a little more realistic." John returned home to his dad. In conclusion to their talk, his father said, "It's up to you, son." John went back to his teacher the next day, threw the paper at him, and said, "You can have your F, I'll keep my dream!" That paper assignment now hangs on the office wall on John O'Brian's 600-acre farm.

Can you remember any such dream you once had? Are you still dreaming now? Langston Hughes wrote, "Hold fast to your dreams, for if dreams die, life is a broken-winged bird that cannot fly." If God is for us, who can be against us? (Romans 8:31).

Father God, I choose to resist discouragement today and to be obedient to your call on my life. Amen!

HALF-TIME OR GAME OVER?

Philippians 1:6

"...being confident of this, that he who began a good work will carry it on to completion until the day of Christ Jesus."

24

JULY

Researchers tell us that most people maintain a learning attitude up until the age of forty, and from that point on they simply stop learning, content with settling to live the rest of their lives with the limited knowledge of those first four decades. How tragic! You can choose straightaway not to be like that!

Instead of having an attitude which essentially says "Game over!", we can embrace a reflective period more akin to half-time. No matter what stage of life we're at, there is so much more to learn, to grow into, and therefore to leverage in due course for God's glory. God has begun a good work in us, which we want to see come to completion, We don't want to mentally check out and sleepwalk our way into retirement. No, we can choose to make the rest of our years the best of our years.

As Søren Kierkegaard wrote, "The thing is to understand myself, to see what God really wishes me to do... to find the idea for which I can live and die." Augustine said that the beginning of adulthood was asking the question of your own legacy: what do I wish to be remembered for? Of course we don't know when we'll die, but we can shape our epitaph in how we choose to live life now. That means moving beyond narrow definitions of what constitutes success in life to broader definitions of what is truly significant and impacting for those around us.

So today, do take time to reflect on your journey – how far you've come, whether you're on the right track, where you want to be headed, what goals have been accomplished or remain unaccomplished, and what you want your epitaph to be.

Lord, help me to finish strong in your name, Amen!

2 Corinthians 5:7

"For we live [or walk] by faith, not by sight."

FAITH OR SIGHT?

If you've never experienced it, I recommend seeing a pack of impala in full flight. They can leap 10ft (3m) high and 30ft (9m) long with just one seemingly effortless jump. Power and beauty in motion. And yet, when caught and kept at zoos in enclosures, they will never jump out over the mere 3ft fence because they only jump if they can see where they will land. With no roof keeping them shut in, freedom is one simple leap away.

Are we like those impalas? If we live by sight – like them – it's easy to keep us caged. There are new vistas, new opportunities, new adventures to be had if we're prepared to launch out into God's purposes and live by faith. Note well we're not talking about a blind leap in the dark. No, our faith is rooted in the Truth, so we can have confidence that as we prayerfully seek and trust God, he will guide our leaps, our steps and our stops.

Maybe that begins with baby steps. Maybe we pray with George Whitefield: "Help me begin to begin!"

Hudson Taylor, the great missionary statesman who pioneered work in the Chinese hinterland in the nineteenth century, said that "unless there is an element of risk in our exploits for God, there's no need for faith." Ouch! Aren't I taking any risks in following Christ? Then I might have a faith, but I'm not living by faith. I'm living by sight.

How about you?

Lord, I want to be an authentic follower of Jesus. I'm risk-averse yet recognize if I always play it safe, then I'll condemn myself to a stunted faith experience. Help me begin to begin. Help me not to take stupid risks, but guide me to reach out beyond my comfort zones, so that those baby steps grow into majestic impala-style leaps for your glory. Amen!

THIRSTY OR SATISFIED?

Ephesians 5:18

"Be filled with the Spirit."

The Greek present tense is used in the above verse, meaning the infilling of the Holy Spirit in the life of a believer is not a once-for-all event but an ongoing need for refilling and refuelling. To those who do think it's a once-for-all experience, Martyn Lloyd-Jones issues this challenge: "Got it all? Well, if you have got it all, I simply ask in the name of God why are you as you are? If you have got it all, why are you so unlike New Testament Christians? Got it all! Got it at your conversion! Well where is it, I ask?"

Are you thirsty today, or satisfied? Abraham Heschel wrote, "He who is satisfied has never truly craved." I hope you haven't given up on the potential of a life saturated with God's presence. The cravings we feel, we were made to feel, and only God can satisfy. John Piper wrote in *A Hunger for God*, "If you don't feel strong desires for the manifestation of the glory of God, it is not because you have drunk deeply and are satisfied. It is because you have nibbled so long at the table of the world. Your soul is stuffed with small things, and there is no room for the great."

I remember several periods of my life of being so filled by the Holy Spirit that I didn't want to leave his presence. I wanted to live in that continued state of heightened reality. When I saw people, I couldn't help but share of God's goodness with them. Some converted immediately, others thought I was mad! But the point I want to make is, how easy it is for us to settle for a stunted satisfaction with spiritual inertia. We fear beginning to crave, lest we are left disappointed yet again.

"Come, all you who are thirsty… that your soul may live" (Isaiah 55:1–3).

Fill me afresh today, Lord, and every day, and keep me thirsting for more of you. Amen!

Acts 4:32

"All the believers were one in heart and mind. No one claimed that any of his possessions was his own, but they shared everything they had."

SHARING OR HOARDING?

The early church has much to teach us. What followed verse 32? "With great power the apostles continued to testify to the resurrection of the Lord Jesus, and *much grace was upon them all*. There were no needy persons among them" (verses 33, 34, emphasis mine).

The believers were so liberal with their possessions because they knew that their citizenship was in heaven, that Jesus was coming again in judgment, and that it was more important to store up lasting treasures in heaven than selfishly hoard on earth what would in any case ultimately rot and decay. But can you see the correlation between giving and grace? Was it because the believers were so liberal with their possessions that God was so liberal with his grace?

On many occasions I've been overwhelmed by the sacrificial sharing of destitute believers in Burundi. Some time ago, I drove with a colleague on my motorbike to a displacement camp. It was a very dangerous outing. The rebels had just sent down the chopped-off heads of the soldiers they had ambushed. There were 40,000 people in the camp, who had been forcibly regrouped several months earlier. They had no electricity, water, or sanitation. On average ten people were dying day after day, week after week. After the church service, I was taken into a tin shack, and fed beans and rice. I knew this was far beyond what they could afford. They were languishing in misery and starving to death, while I had a packed fridge back home. They were giving me so much out of their so little, as so often we give so little out of our so much.

Are you more inclined to share or hoard? Take an inventory of all you have. Any action needed?

Lord, I want to experience the liberality of your grace in my life, so I choose to express that same liberality to others today. Amen!

LONGEVITY OR FULLNESS?

John 10:10

"I have come that they may have life, and life to the full."

Jesus pronounced these words, and then modelled them for us, although he died in his early thirties. He clearly didn't have a long life, but he did have a full life. So don't confuse longevity with fullness – they are not the same thing. As Abraham Lincoln said, "In the end, it's not the years in your life that count. It's the life in your years." Many people reach their old age with deep regrets that they didn't really live the life they should have. May it not be the same with us! Ashley Montague was on to something when he said, "The idea is to die young, after living as long as possible!"

I never thought I'd reach thirty, let alone forty years old. The verse above became a life motto for me. Whether God was going to allow me to be a casualty of the war, or (as has thus far transpired) whether he would grant me longer on this earth, I resolved to have the fullest life possible – even if it ended up being cut short.

The war sharpened my senses and helped me identify what constituted a full life. It was one that prioritized people over possessions. It was one of strict discipline to maximize limited time, but one in which that strict discipline included guarding time for rest and fun. It involved investing in people or projects that would surpass and outlive me. It involved the willingness to embrace both tears and laughter, despair and hope, doubt and certainty, defeat and victory.

So are you shooting for longevity or fullness? For possessions or people? Are you committed to results or relationships? To success or significance? Jesus guides us in our answers by both warning and encouraging us that "whoever wants to save his life will lose it, but whoever loses his life for me and for the gospel will save it" (Mark 10:35).

Lord, I choose life to the full today. Amen!

1 Samuel 3:10

"Speak, for your servant is listening."

LISTEN OR IGNORE?

In 1908, a young Liberian called Jasper Toe cried out, "If there is a God in heaven, help me find you." He heard an unknown voice reply, "Go to Garraway Beach. You will see a box on the water with smoke coming out of it. And from that box on the water will come some people in a smaller box. These people in the small box will tell you how to find me." He duly walked seven days to the seaside. Meanwhile, John Perkins and his wife were rounding the coast of Liberia on a steamboat. They knew they had been called by God, but they didn't yet know where God wanted them exactly! Suddenly, they felt the Holy Spirit say to them, "This is where I want you. You need to disembark right now!" The ship's captain initially refused as it was cannibal country, but such was their insistence he eventually relented, and they rowed ashore in a canoe with all their meagre worldly belongings. Jasper Toe was waiting for them. He took them home, taught them the language, became their first convert, and in time planted hundreds of churches throughout Liberia!

Oh that we all received such extraordinary, obviously supernatural guidance! Yet maybe, just maybe, we do. Both Perkins and Toe could easily have ignored the Holy Spirit's prompting. Perkins could have played it safe and stayed on the ship. Toe could have ignored the crazy instructions he received. But through their obedience, God in his mercy engineered a beautiful breakthrough for the glory of his name.

God is speaking all the time. Are we still enough, quiet enough, attentive enough to listen? Could that person who springs to mind that we quickly dismiss be God's prompt for us to get in touch with them? Could that creative idea for a new initiative that we quash be an exciting opportunity for him to use us? Listen up!

Lord, I choose to listen to you today, and act on what you say. Amen!

PRISONER OR FREE?

Galatians 5:1

"It is for freedom that Christ has set us free. Stand firm, then, and do not let yourselves be burdened again by a yoke of slavery."

30

JULY

The context of the verse above is freedom from the yoke of the law, but it applies in the same way to the issue of forgiveness. Christ died to set us free. If we remain enslaved, it is because we have chosen to remain so and reject the freedom he offers.

When Bill Clinton first met Nelson Mandela, he said to him, "Mr Mandela, when you were released from prison, I woke up my daughter at 3 a.m. I wanted her to see this historic event. As you marched from the cell block across the yard to the prison gate, the camera focused in on your face. I have never seen such anger, and even hatred, in any man as was expressed on your face at that time. That's not the Nelson Mandela I see today. What was that all about?" Mr Mandela replied, "I'm surprised that you saw that, and I regret that the cameras caught my anger. As I walked across the courtyard that day I thought to myself, '*They've taken everything from you that matters. Your cause is dead. Your family is gone. Your friends have been killed. Now they're releasing you, but there's nothing left for you out there.*' And I hated them for what they had taken from me. Then, I sensed an inner voice saying to me, 'Nelson! For twenty-seven years you were their prisoner, but you were always a free man! Don't allow them to make you into a free man, only to turn you into their prisoner!'"

Is there any person or situation in your life that is keeping you unnecessarily imprisoned, be it to fear, or bitterness, or hatred? Jesus came to set you free – and if the Son sets you free, then you will be free indeed! (John 8:36)

Lord God Almighty, I choose to walk free today, and show others the way to freedom in you. Amen!

Galatians 6:9, 10

"Let us not become weary in doing good, for at the proper time we will reap a harvest if we do not give up. Therefore, as we have opportunity, let us do good to all people..."

HOLD BACK OR DO IT ANYWAY?

Mother Teresa had a hand-written note hanging on her bedroom wall which said:

People are often unreasonable, illogical, and self-centred;
forgive them anyway.
If you are kind, people may accuse you of selfish, ulterior motives;
be kind anyway.
If you are successful, you will win some false friends and some true
enemies; be successful anyway.
If you are honest and frank, people may cheat you;
be honest and frank anyway.
What you spend years building, someone could destroy overnight;
build anyway.
If you find serenity and happiness, they may be jealous; be happy anyway.
The good you do today, people will often forget tomorrow;
do good anyway.
Give the world the best you have, and it may never be enough;
give the world the best you've got anyway.
You see, in the final analysis, it is between you and God;
it never was between you and them anyway.

She in her time and we in ours are faced with opportunities to choose well or badly every day. Most people make such choices reactively, based on how those around them might think or respond. But, in the final analysis, it is indeed "between you and God". Os Guinness wrote about Winston Churchill's experiences at the hand of a vitriolic Member of Parliament. Churchill was asked whether he was hurt by the blistering attack. He replied, "If I respected him, I would care about his opinion. But I don't, so I don't." While, of course, we should hold the world in respect, we who live before the Audience of One can say to the world, "I have only one audience. Before you I have nothing to prove, nothing to gain, nothing to lose."

We all get weary, but don't give up. The above verse promises us we will reap a harvest. So keep focusing on your Master's business!

Lord, help me choose well today. Amen!

PURSUE OR ENSUE?

1 Corinthians 15:58

"Always give yourselves fully to the work of the Lord, because you know that your labour in the Lord is not in vain."

A reflective Sting said in an interview, "Getting what I had desired for so long – success – and finding it didn't equate with actual happiness, made me even more unhappy. What is happiness? It's not in being famous or desired by all these people. It must be somewhere else." Queen's Freddie Mercury said shortly before his death, "You can have everything in the world and still be the loneliest man, and that is the most bitter type of loneliness. Success has brought me world idolization and millions of pounds, but it's prevented me from having the one thing we all need – a loving, ongoing relationship."

Victor Frankl provides a solution with regards the pursuit of success:

> *Don't aim at success – the more you aim at it and make it a target, the more you are going to miss it. For success, like happiness, cannot be pursued; it must ensue, and it only does so as the unintended side effect of one's personal dedication to a cause greater than oneself or as the by-product of one's surrender to a person other than oneself.*

I hope that ultimately you can say that the "cause greater than oneself", the "person other than oneself" in your life is Jesus. If that is the case, then success need not be measured by how you do compared to how somebody else does, but by how you do compared to what you could have done with what God gave you. It follows from your commitment to obeying Jesus in your daily life. It touches on your working life, but also your family life, and your community life. How am I doing as a brother, a husband, a son, a father? How am I doing as a friend, a colleague, a neighbour?

Lord, help me to surrender to you today – to put seeking your will above my pursuit of success and happiness. Amen!

CHEAP OR COSTLY GRACE?

Romans 6:15, 23

"What then? Shall we sin because we are not under the law but under grace? By no means!... For the wages of sin is death, but the gift of God is eternal life in Christ Jesus our Lord."

2

AUGUST

A church sign once read, "Welcome to our church where salvation is free, but discipleship will cost you everything!" Dietrich Bonhoeffer, who was willing to die for his faith, wrote the following:

> *Cheap grace is the preaching of forgiveness without requiring repentance, baptism without church discipline, Communion without confession, absolution without personal confession. Cheap grace is grace without discipleship, grace without the cross, grace without Jesus Christ, living and incarnate.*
>
> *Costly grace is the treasure hidden in the field; for the sake of it a man will gladly go and sell all that he has. It is the pearl of great price to buy which the merchant will sell all his goods. It is the call of Jesus Christ at which the disciple leaves his nets and follows him.*
>
> *Costly grace is the gospel which must be sought again and again, the gift which must be asked for, the door at which a man must knock.*
>
> *Such grace is costly because it calls us to follow, and it is grace because it calls us to follow Jesus Christ. It is costly because it costs a man his life, and it is grace because it gives a man the only true life. It is costly because it condemns sin, and grace because it justifies the sinner. Above all, it is costly because it cost God the life of his Son: "ye were bought at a price", and what has cost God much cannot be cheap for us. Above all, it is grace because God did not reckon his Son too dear a price to pay for our life, but delivered him up for us. Costly grace is the Incarnation of God.*

Those words are worth re-reading slowly and digesting...

I praise you, Lord, for your amazingly costly grace. Help me to live a fragrant grace-filled life today. Amen!

SIGH OF SADNESS OR BREATHLESS EXPECTATION?

Job 19:25–27

"I know that my redeemer lives, and that in the end he will stand on the earth. And after my skin has been destroyed, yet in my flesh I will see God; I myself will see him with my own eyes – I, and not another. How my heart yearns within me!"

We know how Job was stripped of everything – loved ones, wealth, and health – and yet he was somehow still able to declare the above hope-filled statement, despite the utterly bleak circumstances he found himself in.

Our faith in Christ involves a constant wrestling between assurance and doubt, confidence and questioning, certainty and uncertainty, and these not only conflict with but also sometimes complement each other. Oswald Chambers observed:

> *The nature of the spiritual life is that we are certain in our uncertainties, consequently we do not make our nests anywhere. Certainty is the mark of the common-sense life; gracious uncertainty is the mark of the spiritual life. To be certain of God means that we are uncertain in all our ways, and we do not know what a day will bring forth. This is generally said with a sigh of sadness; it should rather be an expression of breathless expectation.*

I like that. Most of us are naturally wired to want all our ducks in a row, to keep everything under our control, to master the unpredictable. But the fact is, we cannot control all circumstances. Life is unpredictable. But what we *can* be confident of, is that God is over all. He ultimately calls the shots. I'd rather he did than I! And so I'm going to choose a sense of breathless expectation over a sigh of sadness any day. And in faith I'll join the apostle Paul as he writes to the Philippians that he is "confident in this, that he who began a good work in you will carry it on to completion until the day of Christ Jesus" (1:6).

You know what lies ahead of me today, Lord. I choose to live certain in my uncertainties. Amen!

WAIT IN HATE OR RESOLVE IN LOVE?

1 Corinthians 13:4, 5

"Love is patient, love is kind. It does not envy, it does not boast, it is not proud... it is not easily angered, it keeps no record of wrongs."

There have been a few people in my life I've hated, and sometimes I felt it was plain impossible to improve the relationship. I found the following exchange between Annette and her Grandmother in Patricia St John's *Treasures of the Snow* very helpful:

> *"If you hated someone, you couldn't ask Jesus to come into your life, could you?"*
>
> *"If you hate someone, it just shows how badly you need to ask Him to come in. The darker the room, the more it needs the light to come in."*
>
> *"But I couldn't stop hating Lucien."*
>
> *"No, you're quite right. None of us can stop ourselves thinking wrong thoughts, and it isn't much good trying. But Annette, when you come down in the morning and find this room dark with the shutters down, do you say to yourself, I must chase away the darkness and the shadows first, and* then *I will open the shutters and let in the sun? Do you waste time trying to get rid of the dark?"*
>
> *"Of course not!"*
>
> *"Then how do you get rid of the dark?"*
>
> *"I pull back the shutters, of course, and then the light just comes in!"*
>
> *"But what happens to the dark?"*
>
> *"I don't know; it just goes when the light comes!"*
>
> *"That is exactly what happens when you ask Jesus to come in. He is love, and when love comes in, hatred and selfishness and unkindness will give way to it, just as the darkness gives way when you let in the sunshine. But to try to chase it out alone would be like trying to chase the shadows out of a dark room. It would be a waste of time."*

Is there anyone you need to forgive? Don't stay in the dark. Pull back the shutters and let Jesus in today!

Lord, I choose to address the situation with... today. Amen!

1 Thessalonians 4:11, 12

"Make it your ambition to lead a quiet life… so that your quiet life may win the respect of others."

PREACH IT OR LIVE IT?

Now I'm an evangelist, so the words above don't come naturally to me! Paul certainly wasn't saying don't seize opportunities to share your faith, but sometimes, we need to just zip our mouths shut, live a quiet attractive life, and win people over that way so that they then want to find out why we live as we do.

When American journalist Stanley discovered Livingstone in Central Africa, he spent four months with the doctor. Stanley later wrote:

> *I went to Africa as prejudiced as the biggest atheist in London. But there came a long time for reflection. I saw this solitary old man there and asked myself, "How on earth does he stay here? What is it that inspires him?" For months I found myself wondering at the old man carrying out all that was said in the Bible… But little by little my sympathy was aroused. Seeing his piety, his gentleness, his zeal, his earnestness, I was converted by him although he had not tried to do it! It was not Livingstone's preaching which converted me. It was Livingstone's living!*

Malcolm Muggeridge wrote of Mother Teresa, while he was searching for spiritual answers to life: "To me she represents essentially love in action, which is surely what Christianity is all about." Calling for radical discipleship at the Lausanne Congress, some of the church leaders from Latin America affirmed that "there is no biblical dichotomy between the word spoken and the word made visible in the lives of God's people. Men *look* as they *listen*, and what they *see* must be one with what they *hear*."

It's the inconsistencies between words and deeds expressed in Jesus' name by his followers which have so often nullified our intended positive impact. As St Francis is reputed to have said, "Preach all the time, and if necessary, use words!"

Lord, I choose today to live a life that attracts people to you. Use me, with or without words being spoken. Amen!

CRISIS OR OPPORTUNITY?

Romans 9:17

"For the Scripture says to Pharaoh: I raised you up for this very purpose, that I might display my power in you and that my name might be proclaimed in all the earth."

However bad our circumstances might be today, they are unlikely to be worse than those of the poor Israelites languishing in despair as slaves in Egypt. Yet as Albert Einstein observed, "In the midst of difficulty lies opportunity." Through their neglect of God, they'd ended up in a mess. Their crisis made them increasingly desperate, aware that they couldn't make it on their own. And in that state of brokenness, they were ripe for God's intervention.

We're all at times confronted by seemingly impossible situations, but with a shift in perspective they are potentially wonderful opportunities in disguise. In the Chinese picture-letter alphabet, the symbol for "crisis" is a combination of two characters, one meaning "danger" and the other "opportunity". So we can choose our own attitude and look at it either way. As Winston Churchill said, "The pessimist sees difficulty in every opportunity. The optimist sees the opportunity in every difficulty."

Normal people don't actively seek out crises in their lives. I personally want to avoid them wherever I can, which I think is right, unless a dysfunctional situation needs addressing proactively. But crises come our way regardless of how hard we try to avoid them. And with the benefit of hindsight, I am mostly grateful for the crises the Lord has allowed me to go through. When the Israelites turned back to the Lord, he rescued them. Repeatedly. They had a story of his faithfulness. The crises were opportunities to grow, to learn, to become more like him. As the Chinese proverb says, "The gem cannot be polished without friction, nor man perfected without trials."

So as you review your circumstances today, can you see any bright ray of hope in the midst of a dark challenging situation? You may or may not, but God does. Hold on to that!

Lord, would you turn each crisis into an opportunity in my life. Amen!

Matthew 6:4, 6, 18

"Your Father, who sees what is done in secret, will reward you."

PRIVATE OR PUBLIC?

Whether it's giving, praying, or fasting, three times in Matthew 6 we read the same refrain. Whereas others with wrong motives may give/pray/fast in public to impress those around them, it is those disciplines carried out in private before the Audience of One that the Lord promises to reward.

Character is what we are in the dark, when nobody's there to impress. That's the real you. We can fake it and impress others, and sometimes even manage to deceive ourselves, but ultimately we'll show our true colours. As Jesus said to the Pharisees, "You brood of vipers, how can you who are evil say anything good? For out of the overflow of the heart the mouth speaks" (Matthew 12:34).

Private victories precede public ones – not the other way round – just as you can't harvest a crop before you plant it. Gethsemane preceded Golgotha, just as the cross we bear precedes the crown we will wear.

As Rick Warren has pointed out, "In ministry, private *purity* is the source of public *power*." William Wilberforce knew how costly it would be to give his whole life over to seeking the abolition of slavery. He fought a fierce internal battle in secret with the Lord before accepting that his calling was to champion the liberty of the oppressed as a Parliamentarian. He wrote in his journal in 1788, "My walk is a public one. My business is in the world; and I must mix in the assemblies of men, or quit the post which Providence seems to have assigned me."

Most of us have a thick mask on for the public sphere. How far removed is the public from the private you? Don't be tempted to concentrate on improving the public; work first on the private – then the public will take care of itself.

Lord, I choose to seek your approval alone today. Amen!

GIVE UP OR TRY AGAIN?

2 Corinthians 4:8–10

"We are hard pressed on every side, but not crushed; perplexed, but not in despair; persecuted, but not abandoned; struck down, but not destroyed."

In 2013, 64-year-old US endurance swimmer Diana Nyad became the first person to swim the 110 miles from Cuba to the US without a shark cage. She took fifty-three hours non-stop, escorted by boats and her team of thirty-five people. The rules of the swim meant she wasn't allowed to hold on to the support boat at any time. Her team helped her maintain the right course and gave her food and water. As well as a bodysuit and gloves, she wore a special silicone mask to protect her face from the jellyfish stings that had plagued her last attempt. Her team also had equipment that generated a faint electrical field around her designed to keep sharks at bay. During the last stretch, they guided her through the best route into Key West to avoid dangerous eddies, currents, shipping lanes, reefs, and swarms of jellyfish.

Amazing! But further, it turns out she'd tried four other times: in 1978 (i.e. several decades earlier), twice in 2011, and once again in 2012. Each time she'd failed. During her previous attempt in August 2012, Nyad had had to be pulled out of the water after forty-one hours when a squall and repeated jellyfish stings had made it impossible for her to continue.

Struggling to breathe on completing the feat, she told the waiting TV crews, "I have three messages: one is we should never ever give up; two is you are never too old to chase your dreams; and three is it looks like a solitary sport but it is a team."

Preach it, sister! Paul and Nyad, in very different ways, just wouldn't give up. They were both big dreamers. And they acted out those dreams with others on their team. God help us to do the same.

Lord, I choose to hang in there, not to give up, and to cling to you, whatever comes at me. Show me also today who constitutes my team. Amen!

Colossians 4:18

"I, Paul, write this greeting in my own hand. Remember my chains."

REMEMBER OR FORGET?

Elsewhere, Paul writes that "you are the body of Christ" and "if one part suffers, every part suffers with it" (1 Corinthians 12:26, 27). Most of us don't live in parts of the world where persecution is institutionalized, which is a real blessing; but let's not forget our brothers and sisters, maybe 250 million of them, who are suffering in very real ways day by day because of their faith in Jesus.

North Korea regularly tops the list as the worst country to live in as a Christian. Thousands upon thousands are locked away in prison camps right now because of their faith. Many North Koreans recite daily the Lord's Prayer and the five principles of faith. The expectations of suffering within their faith life are evident in these principles:

- Our persecution and suffering are our joy and honour.
- We want to accept ridicule, scorn, and disadvantages with joy in Jesus' name.
- As Christians, we want to wipe others' tears away and comfort the suffering.
- We want to be ready to risk our lives because of our love for our neighbour, so that they also become Christians.
- We want to live our lives according to the standards set in God's Word.

Do re-read those and dwell on them for a while.

Open Doors, Release International, IJM, Voice of the Martyrs, and Barnabas Fund are some of the groups who send out regular updates so that we can pray strategic informed prayers, and get involved in campaigns for imprisoned and persecuted believers. Why not contact one of them today and subscribe?

It's easy to get wrapped up in our own affairs, so the above is a healthy antidote if we're tempted to slip into self-pity regarding our own problems.

Lord, I choose to remember the persecuted church today. Forgive me when I've forgotten them. Intervene for them. And all the more help me use the freedoms I have for your glory. Amen!

ONE OR MANY?

Philippians 3:10

"I want to know Christ."

Sometimes Hollywood scripts are inspired. In *City Slickers*, Jack Palance plays a wily old cowboy and Billy Crystal is the younger businessman on a ranch holiday. They're riding along on horseback and have a memorable and frank exchange which culminates with the following:

> PALANCE: Yeah. You all come out here about the same age. Same problems. Spend fifty weeks a year getting knots in your rope then… then you think two weeks up here will untie them for you. None of you get it. (Long pause) Do you know what the secret of life is?
>
> CRYSTAL: No, what?
>
> PALANCE: This. (Holds up his index finger)
>
> CRYSTAL: Your finger?
>
> PALANCE: One thing. Just one thing. You stick to that and everything else don't mean s——.
>
> CRYSTAL: That's great, but what's the one thing?
>
> PALANCE: That's what you've got to figure out.

Have you figured it out yet?

What's your life purpose? What really gets you excited? What do you want to give your life to? Obviously as a follower of Christ in its broadest sense we'd want to echo Paul's "one thing" in the verse above, but more specifically and individually, what is your "one thing"? We're all created unique, with different gifts, passions, and opportunities. As Søren Kierkegaard wrote, "The thing is to understand myself, to see what God really wishes me to do… to find the idea for which I can live and die."

To answer these crucial life-defining questions takes time and space. They can't be solved in a three-minute hurried "quiet time" inconveniently squeezed somewhere in the midst of a busy day. But one thing's for sure: if we don't make time to wrestle with them, we'll simply continue to be ineffectual as we spin plates and crisis manage, victims of our own hectic decisions and bad choices.

Lord, I don't want to live constantly spinning too many plates. Help me to discover what that "one thing" is. Amen!

STIRRED OR INDIFFERENT?

Romans 9:2, 3

"I have great sorrow and unceasing anguish in my heart. For I could wish that I myself were cursed and cut off from Christ for the sake of my brothers."

Paul was so desperate for the lost to be found that he was willing to make himself a curse in their place. Do I have anything like the same compassion for those around me? I fear not, but I aspire to it. As Spurgeon wrote:

> *When a man's heart is so stirred that he weeps over the sins of others, he is elect to usefulness. Winners for souls are first weepers for souls. As there is no birth without travail, so is there no spiritual harvest without pain and tears. When our hearts are broken with grief at man's transgressions, we shall break other men's hearts. Tears of earnestness beget tears of repentance: "Deep calleth unto deep".*

Many of us watched in horror as the twin towers of the World Trade Center crumbled to pieces, killing many innocent people. Yet every day, as John Zumwalt notes, the equivalent of fourteen towers collapse as approximately 50,000 people die among the unreached of our world without ever having heard of Jesus; and Jesus watches them with the same horror that we felt on 11 September 2001. He pleads with us to wake up from our own slumber and wake others up so that we address these issues with urgency instead of casual indifference.

Does the above stir you, or leave you indifferent? Zumwalt's comments relate to the whole wide world, but how about the neighbours down your street, the colleagues you work with, guys at the club, family members? All of those we interact with who are lost – some happily so but others aching for meaning and purpose – they need us to get over our own apathy, indifference or fear, and take Jesus to them. Let's do it!

Lord, forgive us for looking at the world with dry eyes. Use us today, for your glory. Amen!

INCARNATE OR ABSTRACT?

Matthew 25:40

"The King will reply, 'I tell you the truth, whatever you did for one of the least of these brothers of mine, you did for me.'"

We know God more fully as Emmanuel – God with us – because he became incarnate as Jesus, "God with flesh on". He calls us both to incarnate the message and to see his imprint in the lives of those we come into contact with, which is what Matthew 25 is addressing. God is not meant to be an abstract concept to us, and neither is our following of him meant to remain an abstract mental adherence to a set of propositional statements.

A little street urchin was standing barefoot in front of a shoe shop, peering through the window, and shivering with cold. A lady approached him and said, "Little man, what are you looking at?" "I was asking God to give me a pair of shoes," was the boy's reply. She took him by the hand into the store and asked the clerk to get some socks for the boy. She then asked if he could give her a basin of water and a towel. She then took the little guy to the back part of the store, removed her gloves, knelt down, washed his little feet, and dried them with a towel. By this time the clerk returned with the socks. Placing a pair upon the boy's feet, she bought him a pair of shoes. She patted him on the head and said, "No doubt, my little fellow, you feel more comfortable now?" As she turned to go, the astonished boy caught her by the hand and, looking up in her face, said, "Are you God's wife?"

It's a simple illustration, but a profound concept. Will you and I embody the message we profess to believe today? It'll definitely cost us, but authentic living is more compelling than the most coherent verbal argument in the world.

Lord, help me to see Jesus in everyone and be Jesus to everyone today. Amen!

Romans 8:31

"If God is for us, who can be against us?"

SIXTY-NINE ELEPHANTS OR ONE ANT?

The legendary Michael Jordan was no deity, but on the basketball court in one particular game he was as close to perfection as anyone has ever got. On 28 March 1990, he scored a staggering sixty-nine points against the Cavaliers at the Richfield Coliseum. He himself always considered it his greatest ever performance. On his team that day was a relatively unknown benchwarmer called Stacey King. King hardly got any playing time, but in the few minutes he was on court, he scored one free throw. Years later, when King retired after a somewhat less distinguished career than Jordan, he was asked what his career highlight was. He replied, "My highlight was the night Michael Jordan and I scored 70 points!"

An ant was nestled behind the ear of an elephant as they approached a rickety rope bridge. They gingerly made their way across it, fearing plunging into the ravine below. It creaked and swayed, but thankfully they made it safely across, at which point the ant whispered into the elephant's ear, "Wow, did you see how *we* really shook that bridge?!"

Isn't the above verse a comforting thought? I mean, God is on our team – or rather we are on his. He doesn't need us, but he chooses to use us. He's the real points-scorer and bridge-shaker. Sometimes we delude ourselves and try to take all the credit, but hopefully both Stacey King and the ant (and us in turn) recognize deep down that the positive result wasn't principally down to them or us. God is the one who really makes things happen. We get to partner with him. He takes ultimate responsibility and gets ultimate glory. In the best sense of the word, we're hangers-on!

So let's enjoy the privilege, give it our best shot, play our part, and give him the glory today.

Thank you, Lord, that I get to be on your team. I choose to embrace my role and give it 100 per cent today. Amen!

SULK OR SALK?

Philippians 4:13

"I can do all things through Christ who gives me strength."

The context of Paul's "all things" was his experiences of being in need and living in plenty, of being hungry and well fed, and things going badly or well. He had innumerable setbacks in his journey of discipleship, but ultimately he kept on fighting for his King. He wasn't saying he could do anything, but he was convinced that nothing was impossible if it was God's will, and if it was being done "through Christ who gives me strength".

Jonas Salk was the great doctor who pioneered polio research and eventually developed the Salk polio vaccine. Before he developed a vaccine for polio that finally worked, he tried 200 unsuccessful ones. Somebody once asked him: "How did it feel to fail 200 times?" "I never failed 200 times," Salk replied. "I was taught not to use the word 'failure'. I just discovered 200 ways how not to vaccinate for polio!"

From his experiences came the Salk Theory. He'd had to deal with a legion of critics over the years. On one occasion he made an interesting observation about the nature of criticism, which seems to hold true for any person who is attempting anything of any worth: "First, people will tell you that you are wrong. Then they will tell you that you are right, but what you're doing really isn't important. Finally, they will admit that you are right and that what you are doing is very important; but after all, they knew it all the time."

If you're trying to get something significant done in your life and are deeply discouraged today, take some encouragement from both Paul and Jonas Salk. They both had ample reasons to give up and settle for less, but they were driven to keep going. As the verse above says, it is not our strength but Christ's. Salk didn't sulk, and neither should we!

Lord, I choose to persevere today, to live and work and do all things "through Christ who gives me strength". Amen!

John 10:27

"My sheep listen to my voice; I know them and they follow me."

HEAR OR LISTEN?

We all hear similar sounds... but what do we listen to?

A Masai community leader was invited to New York for a symposium. In Times Square, amidst all the blaring of horns and bustle of humanity, he grabbed his host and said, "I hear a cricket!" He then slowly crossed the street to where some shrubs were growing. He looked into the bushes, beneath the branches, and to his friend's great amazement, there was a small cricket.

"That's impossible!" exclaimed his friend. "You must have super-human hearing!"

"Not quite," said the Masai. "My ears are no different from yours. It just depends on what you're listening for."

"Maybe – but there's no way I would have heard a little cricket in the middle of New York City," said the friend.

"That's because you don't care about crickets," said the Masai. "But I bet you would be amazed at what your ears can pick up when it's a priority. Here, let me show you."

He then reached into his pocket, pulled out a few coins, and discreetly dropped them on the pavement. Amazingly enough, with the noise of the crowded street still blaring in their ears, the friends noticed every head within twenty feet turn and look to see if the money that jingled on the pavement was theirs.

"Get the point?" asked the Masai. "It all depends on what's important to you."

God is speaking the whole time. But maybe listening to his voice is like picking up the sound of a cricket during commuter rush hour. What are your ears attuned to?

Why do I find it so easy to check the latest developments on Facebook but so hard to open my Bible? Why is time with God the first thing that I pass up on if an unexpected distraction comes my way?

Lord, I choose to hear and listen to you today. Help me prioritize time with you, and recognize distractions for what they are. Amen!

FULLY OR PARTLY?

Leviticus 20:7

"Consecrate yourselves and be holy, because I am the Lord your God."

D.L. Moody was an evangelist from Chicago. He wasn't highly educated, but he had a passion for souls. Before he came to England, in the summer of 1872, he knew that he would have to shake London in order to have a fruitful time throughout the rest of the land. This was of course before the age of easy mass communication. I used to cycle across London Bridge each day on my way to Bible college and wonder how on earth you could shake London with the gospel.

In a similar vein, his contemporary, Charles Spurgeon, had written, "Give me twelve men – importunate men, lovers of souls, who fear nothing but sin and love nothing but God – and I will shake London from end to end." At any rate, Moody did shake London, or rather, God did through Moody and the whole of England on the back of it.

It is estimated that he led a million people to Christ throughout several decades of relentless preaching on both sides of the Atlantic. On one occasion, earlier on in his life, he was talking to a man named Henry Varley. Varley said, "You know, D.L. (as he was known to his friends), the world has yet to see what God will do with one man fully consecrated to Him." Moody thought about it. "The world has yet to see what God *will do* with one man. *Any* man? Doesn't have to have a great education? Any man… *fully* consecrated to Him." That was the condition – full consecration to the Lord. He continued to mull it over, and finally he concluded: "By the grace of God, *I'll be that man*!"

There's so much holding us back from full consecration. What comes to mind in your life? Wrestle with it. What's it worth, really? And then hopefully, having counted the cost, choose to join Moody in saying: "By the grace of God, *I'll be that man*!"

I choose to consecrate myself fully to you today, O Lord, Amen!

RESPOND OR RESIST?

Isaiah 6:8

"Here I am. Send me!"

One of my heroes is Robert Jermain Thomas. In 1866, he felt God's call to penetrate Korea with the gospel following a massacre of about 8,000 local believers by the antagonistic regime. In human eyes it was foolish to respond. However, despite the nagging temptation to resist God's call, Thomas boarded a US trading vessel and sailed up to Pyongyang. Despite repeated warnings to turn back they kept going until they were stranded on a sandbank. The Koreans set fire to their ship, at which point all the other men on board tried to escape but were killed by soldiers on the riverbank. Thomas alone remained on board and he threw all the Bibles he'd brought with him to those watching on the banks of the river. Eventually he jumped into the river with his clothes ablaze. Reaching the bank he begged a soldier to receive his last Bible as a gift. The soldier hesitated but then fulfilled his duty by thrusting his lance through the 27-year-old Welshman. Those present were deeply impacted by the scene. Some of the Bibles were rescued and the pages used as wallpaper in people's houses. Within a short period though, curiosity grabbed them and they began reading the Scriptures and became Christians despite the massive personal cost that conversion brought them. One young man's life, lived and laid down with such urgency, had led to the expansion of God's fledgling kingdom in that land.

No doubt Thomas's experience is one far removed from most of us, and a little extreme. But God is still calling his people to be involved in his mission to redeem a lost humanity. Where do you think you fit in the grand puzzle? The Holy Spirit indwelling each one of us is constantly prompting us to come alongside folk we meet, to take the initiative, to step out of our comfort zones. With God's help, let's not resist his invitation to witness to him today.

Lord, I choose to respond to whatever your Spirit prompts me to do today. Amen!

ENGAGED OR DISENGAGED?

1 Peter 2:9

"But you are a chosen people… that you may declare the praises of him who called you out of darkness into his wonderful light."

18

AUGUST

The needs are everywhere, and sometimes overwhelming. The call is to everyone, but sometimes I choose to disengage. After all, I can't do everything, so why set myself up for failure by trying to do anything? Engaging is painful, so rather disengage and protect myself. I've got enough issues of my own to deal with as it is…

I think many of us reason like that, but then we miss God's call on our life. And yes, we are all most definitely called! As William Booth, founder of the Salvation Army declared:

> *"Not called!" did you say? "Not heard the call", I think you should say. Put your ear down to the Bible and hear Him bid you go and pull sinners out of the fire of sin. Put your ear down to the burdened, agonized heart of humanity and listen to its pitiful wail for help. Go stand by the gates of hell and hear the damned entreat you to go to their father's house and bid their brothers and sisters and servants and masters not to come there. Then look Christ in the face – whose mercy you have professed to obey – and tell him whether you will join heart and soul and body and circumstances in the march to publish his mercy to the world.*

That's a rallying cry I want to respond to! As Paul exhorts the Ephesians, "Live as children of light (for the fruit of the light consists in all goodness, righteousness and truth) and find out what pleases the Lord. Have nothing to do with the fruitless deeds of darkness, but rather expose them" (5:8–11).

As you go about your life today, ask God to show you what he wants you to get involved in, who he wants you to encourage, where he might use you to bring righteousness, goodness and truth.

Lord, I choose to live fully engaged today. Amen!

NOW OR NEVER?

2 Corinthians 6:1, 2

"As God's fellow-workers, we urge you not to receive God's grace in vain. For he says, "In the time of my favour I heard you, and in the day of salvation I helped you". I tell you, now is the time of God's favour, now is the day of salvation."

On 19 February 1944, one of the most costly battles in the Second World War was fought at Iwo Jima, 600 miles south of Tokyo. Its two strategic airstrips were needed by the Allies as launch pads for attacks on Japan. Twenty-two thousand Japanese soldiers knew they were there to defend to the death. About 26,000 US troops died to take it. There were numerous examples of heroism amidst the bloody carnage. Thousands upon thousands of men sacrificed themselves for the greater cause. If you were to visit there today there is a message etched outside the cemetery, which reads:

When you go home
Tell them for us and say
For your tomorrow
We gave our today

Paul urges us not to receive God's grace in vain. He says now is the time, today is the day. Now, or maybe never, if we leave it too late. The choice is ours. So will you, will I, give our today for others' tomorrows?

Living in a warzone in Burundi for many years (at the time of writing it's peaceful again) made me very aware of the value and urgency of each day. We used to listen to shells landing and know that a few yards away some people had just had their last today. It became so clear that each day was a gift. Today could be enjoyed, shared, and maximized, or it could be misused, misspent, and wasted.

Think about Paul's words, "Now is the time of God's favour, now is the day of salvation." In the light of God's favour today, how will you live your life?

Lord, I choose to give my today for you and for all those I come into contact with. Amen!

HARDSHIP OR PRIVILEGE?

Romans 8:17

"Now if we are children, then we are heirs – heirs of God and co-heirs with Christ, if indeed we share in his sufferings in order that we may also share in his glory."

Paul talks of our incredibly privileged position as children of God, and therefore co-heirs with Christ – but keep reading what the rest of the verse says. We can be under no illusions that it will all be sweetness and light.

Oswald Chambers died of a ruptured appendix, aged forty-three, while serving the Lord in Egypt as a chaplain in the First World War. He said, "If you have to calculate what you are willing to give up for Jesus Christ never say that you love Him. Jesus Christ asks us to give up the best we have got to Him, our right to ourselves." So often we seek a more comfortable cross; we settle for respectable religion; we embrace a pale diluted distortion of true authentic discipleship; and in what has become an entrenched entitlement culture, giving up the right to ourselves is about as countercultural and counterintuitive as you can get.

Yet what a privilege that any of us, in any capacity, at any time, in any place, can serve the King of Kings! When you're tempted to think of God's work as a hardship, remember David Livingstone's words: "If a commission by an earthly king is considered an honour, how can a commission by a Heavenly King be considered a sacrifice?"

Lord, I'll be honest and say I like the idea of being a co-heir with Christ and sharing in his glory, but I'm not so keen on sharing in his sufferings. Help me to keep my eyes fixed on you today, to maintain a good attitude, to embrace the challenges and difficulties, and to live out my faith with a sense of privileged humility and joy. For Christ's sake, Amen!

PART TIME OR ALL IN?

Psalm 139:23, 24

"Search me, O God, and know my heart. Test me, and know my anxious thoughts. See if there is any offensive way in me, and lead me in the way everlasting."

In all honesty, are you part time or all in for Jesus? Every once in a while, I read A.W. Tozer's prayer of commitment below. It's not something that can be skimmed over and easily dismissed. It challenges me to the depths of my being as I search my heart with integrity and commit afresh to follow Jesus without conditions or caveats. How about copying it and carrying it around with you, or sticking it in your Bible to re-read regularly. Here it goes:

I come to you today, O Lord,
To give up my rights,
To lay down my life,
To offer my future,
To give my devotion, my skills, my energies.
I shall not waste time
Deploring my weaknesses
Nor my unfittedness for the work.
I acknowledge your choice with my life
To make your Christ attractive and intelligible
To those around me.
I come to you for spiritual preparation.
Put your hand upon me,
Anoint me with the oil of the One with Good News.
Save me from compromise,
Heal my soul from small ambitions,
Deliver me from the itch to always be right,
Save me from wasting time.
I accept hard work, I ask for no easy place,
Help me not to judge others who walk a smoother path.
Show me those things that diminish spiritual power in a soul.
I now consecrate my days to you,
Make your will more precious than anybody or anything.
Fill me with your power
And when at the end of life's journey
I see you face to face
May I hear those undeserving words:
"Well done my good and faithful servant".
I ask this not for myself
But for the glory of the name of your Son.
Amen!

KEEP HOPE OR LOSE COURAGE?

James 1:2–4

"Consider it pure joy, my brothers, whenever you face trials of many kinds, because you know that the testing of your faith develops perseverance. Perseverance must finish its work so that you may be mature and complete, not lacking anything."

One of the church's most popular old hymns is "Now Thank We All Our God". It was written by Martin Rinkart in the early 1600s. He was a Lutheran pastor in the town of Eilenburg in Saxony during Germany's Thirty Years War. Eilenburg was a walled city, so it became a haven for refugees seeking safety from the fighting. Tragically, with overcrowding and food scarcity, a plague and famine decimated those gathered, such that Eilenburg became a giant morgue. In one year alone, Pastor Rinkart conducted funerals for 4,500 people, including that of his own wife. The war dragged on and on. Yet through it all, he never lost courage or faith, and it was during the darkest days of Eilenburg's agony that he was able to write this hymn:

Now thank we all our God,
with hearts and hands and voices,
Who wondrous things hath done,
In whom the world rejoices
keep us in His grace,
and guide us when perplexed,
and free us from all ills,
in this world and the next.

Remarkable! Rinkart kept focused on God's promises of heaven even while going through a living hell. He kept pouring out God's love in a world filled with hate. He kept lifting his sights to a higher plane although buried deep in destruction. He was able to cling to hope in the pits of despair. So can we try to do the same?

Trials are never pleasurable at the time, but as the above verse tells us, "the testing of your faith develops perseverance. Perseverance must finish its work so that you may be mature and complete, not lacking anything."

Lord, I choose to embrace the path to maturity and completion, however painful. Fill me with joy, hope, and the ability to persevere today through all circumstances, for your glory. Amen!

Romans 11:36

"For from him and through him and to him are all things. To him be the glory forever. Amen!"

ALL ABOUT ME OR ALL ABOUT HIM?

There's a beautiful worship song by Paul Oakley called "It's all about you". The words go on: "And all this is for you, for your glory and your fame..." In a lively worship service, a friend of mine was sitting next to a young man who had his hands raised and eyes shut and was belting out the song which he obviously knew off by heart – well almost – he just mixed up the personal pronouns, so his passionate rendition included: "It's all about meeeeee (long note), and all this is for meeeeee, for my glory and my fame!" Ironically, he was probably the most honest person in the house, because it's hard to displace the meeeee and really keep it all about Jesus. I know I've been guilty, if not literally of singing it, of living like it's all about me.

Elyse Fitzpatrick wrote:

> *Whenever the gospel slips from our conscious thought, our religion becomes all about our performance, and then we think everything that happens or will ever happen is about us. When I forget the incarnation, sinless life, death, resurrection, and ascension, I quickly believe that I'm supposed to be the unrivaled, supreme, and matchless one. It's at this point that I'm particularly in need of an intravenous dose of gospel truth. He is preeminent.*

So here's a dose of gospel truth: there is a God, and it's not me. It's all about Jesus, not all about me. While we matter, we're not the point. I am blessed to be a blessing. His death brings me life, and life to the full. He is the bread of life, the light of the world, the gate, the good shepherd, the resurrection and the life, the way, the truth and the life, and the vine. Those are Jesus seven "I AM's from John's gospel. He is, I'm not.

Thank God for that! Here's to living in the light of those truths.

Lord, help me to live like it's all about you today, Amen!

KNEES BUCKLING OR STANDING FIRM?

Matthew 11:28

"Come to me, all you who are weary and burdened, and I will give you rest".

The Flying Wallendas were a family of tightrope walkers, among the greatest in all of circus history. One of their acts was walking a tightrope in the formation of a four-level pyramid. Four or five men formed the first level, two or three men made up the second level, two more were on the third, and finally a little girl topped the pyramid. They would proceed in formation across the tightrope from one side of the arena to the other. It was a stunning feat, which they repeated weekly around the world.

One evening in Detroit, as the show came to its climax, the spotlights picked the Wallendas out of the air as they started moving across the wire. About two-thirds of the way across, one of the men on the first level, young Dede Wallenda, began to tremble in his knees. He cried out in German, "I cannot hold on any longer!" With that, he crumpled, and the entire pyramid collapsed. Many of the Wallendas fell to the floor fifty feet below. One died, and several were crippled for life.

I don't know if you've ever felt like Dede Wallenda? We often face crushing pressures that make our knees buckle. Many of us are only hanging on in there by the skin of our teeth. The danger is to wait until it's too late to cry: "Help! I can't hold on any longer, I'm going to fall off!" Choose to be proactive today. The consequences of not doing so could be disastrous. Jesus calls us to himself. He wants to take our weariness and burdens and give us rest.

God calls us to be Jesus to those around us, and them to us. So reach out to others – be it *for* help if you're near breaking point, or *to* help if you're doing well and have something to offer.

Lord, I choose to accept your offer of rest in you today. Amen!

PRAIRIE CHICKEN OR BALD EAGLE?

Psalm 8:4, 5

"What is man that you are mindful of him, the son of man that you care for him? You made him a little lower than the heavenly angels and crowned him with glory and honour."

Each one of us is of immeasurable value to God. We are "fearfully and wonderfully made" (Psalm 139:14). However, there is a danger for each of us of having either an over- or under-inflated view of ourselves in Christ. Many struggle with the latter, and the consequences are far-reaching.

The story is told of a baby eagle being born into a family of prairie chickens, because the abandoned egg was hatched by a mother hen. Eagles were made to soar gracefully above the heights while prairie chickens are so lowly that they eat rubbish. So the eagle grew up thinking he was a prairie chicken, conditioned to cluck and scavenge just like his adopted siblings. One day he looked up to see a majestic bald eagle soar through the air, swooping down and then scaling the heights again. When he asked his family what it was, they responded: "It's an eagle. But you could never be like that because you're just a prairie chicken." Then they returned to pecking in the dirt. The eagle spent his whole lifetime thinking he was just a prairie chicken, but looking up enviously at the circling eagles high up in the clouds. There were occasional pangs of longing, but it never occurred to him to lift his wings and try to fly.

Like the eagle, we were born to fly. Sometimes we're told we're not worth much, so we end up living like those prairie chickens. But today, re-read the above verses, know that you have God's divine imprint in you, believe what he says about you. Then look up, spread your wings, and fly! God wants you to be all that you were created to be.

Lord, I choose to fly. Teach me what that looks like today. In your Name, Amen!

DYNAMITE OR PEACE?

26

AUGUST

1 Timothy 1:15, 16

"Here is a trustworthy saying that deserves full acceptance: Christ Jesus came into the world to save sinners – of whom I am the worst. But for that very reason I was shown mercy so that in me, the worst of sinners, Christ Jesus might display his unlimited patience as an example for those who would believe on him and receive eternal life."

Paul, by God's grace, was given a second chance to reinvent himself so that his life counted for good as a church leader and planter instead of for bad as a church destroyer. Seeing how people will view us once we're gone can be very helpful in determining how we take decisions and choose to live today.

In 1898, Swedish chemist Alfred Nobel woke up one morning and read his own obituary in the local newspaper. It went as follows: "Alfred Nobel, the inventor of dynamite who died yesterday, devised a way for more people to be killed in a war than ever before, and he died a very rich man." It transpired that it was in fact Alfred's older brother who had died – the newspaper reporter had got his facts wrong. But for Alfred, it was a blessing in disguise and a wake-up call. It had a profound effect on him. He hated the idea of being remembered for developing the means to kill people efficiently and for amassing lots of money. So he initiated the Nobel Prize, the award for scientists and writers who foster peace. Nobel said, "Every man ought to have the chance to correct his epitaph in midstream and write a new one."

It's easy to take decisions that make us deviate ever so slightly from our core purpose and values, and not notice at first. Today could be an opportunity to make some changes so that we, like Alfred Nobel and the apostle Paul, indeed live out the epitaph we want to be ours by the time we graduate to glory.

Lord, I choose today to be true to who you're calling me to be. Amen!

Nehemiah 8:10

"The joy of the Lord is your strength."

FORCE OF NATURE OR CLOD OF AILMENTS?

Circumstances in our lives often dictate that we lose our joy. I feel it myself today as I write this. Protracted problems with no apparent end in sight suffocate my soul. Yet I recognize that half the issue is focusing on myself and my problems rather than on God and his multiple grace gifts in my life. He is our strength and our shield, and *his* joy is *my* strength.

George Bernard Shaw had a taste of joy in his life. He described it as follows:

> *This is the true joy in life — the being used for a purpose recognized by yourself as a mighty one, the being a force of nature instead of a feverish, selfish little clod of ailments and grievances, complaining that the world will not devote itself to making you happy. I am of the opinion that my life belongs to the whole community, and as long as I live, it is my privilege to do for it whatever I can. I want to be thoroughly used up when I die, for the harder I work, the more I live. I rejoice in life for its own sake. Life is no brief candle to me. It is a sort of splendid torch which I've got ahold of for the moment, and I want to make it burn as brightly as possible before handing it on to future generations.*

That certainly stirs me out of any temptation towards self-pity! Only in the last few decades has it become commonplace for people to live with a sense of entitlement to happiness, the result of which is a large number of people behaving like "feverish, selfish little clods of ailments and grievances, complaining that the world will not devote itself to making them happy". Rather may we be a "force of nature" bearing "a splendid torch", and making it "burn as brightly as possible before handing it on to future generations"!

Lord, I choose an attitude of gratitude and joy today. Amen!

FLESH AND BLOOD OR RULERS AND AUTHORITIES?

Ephesians 6:12

"For our struggle is not against flesh and blood, but against the rulers, against the authorities… in the heavenly realms."

Living and working in Africa where witchcraft is commonplace, where almost everyone knows that both God and Satan are real, gives one a very different perspective on life to those with a largely Western secular worldview. Without seeing demons under every stone or attributing every problem encountered to demonic activity, spiritual warfare is undoubtedly taken seriously. We ignore it at our peril.

In C.S. Lewis's book *The Screwtape Letters*, a devil briefs his demon nephew, Wormwood, in a series of letters, on the subtleties and techniques of tempting people. In one missive, the devil says that the objective is not to make people wicked but to make them indifferent. This senior devil cautions Wormwood that he must keep the patient comfortable at all costs. If the patient should start thinking about anything of significance, encourage him to think about his luncheon plans and not to worry so much because it could cause indigestion. And then the devil gives this instruction to his nephew: "I, the devil, will always see to it that there are bad people. Your job, my dear Wormwood, is to provide me with people who do not care."

In a similar vein, British witch Gerald Broussay Gardner said, "The witch wants quiet, regular, ordinary good government with everyone happy, plenty of fun and games, and all fear of death being taken away."

There is a spiritual battle going on. In a culture where apathy and indifference pervade, will you fully engage or not? The outward manifestations are clear. We now have the "Slacktivist Generation": they want to change the world but can't really be bothered!

It's time to pray – to really pray; and to do something – to really do something! What does that look like for you today?

Lord, I refuse to be numbered among the apathetic and indifferent. Teach me to pray, to see what is really going on in the unseen realm, and to live out my calling. Amen!

1 Peter 5:8

"Be self-controlled and alert. Your enemy the devil prowls around like a roaring lion looking for someone to devour."

LUXURY LINER OR TROOP CARRIER?

In the aftermath of the Second World War, William Francis Gibbs was commissioned by the US government to construct a state-of-the-art troop carrier for the navy. His brief was to design a ship capable of carrying 15,000 troops across the seas at high speed during wartime. The SS *America* was duly completed by 1952. She was a stunningly impressive ship, built at massive cost, capable of travelling at over 50mph and completing 10,000 miles without needing to refuel. Within ten days she could reach anywhere on the planet by sea, and she had no competitor to the title of fastest, most impressive and most reliable troop carrier in the world. It seemed that exciting days lay ahead...

... but ironically, she never carried any troops to war. Apart from during the Cuban missile crisis a decade later, during which she was put on standby, she lay completely redundant, her capacity and potential untapped. And in the end, she was decommissioned and turned into a luxury liner – impressive in a different way – but far from the grandiose goals of defending her nation. Now she entertained wealthy patrons as she gently wended her way across the oceans. Instead of carrying 15,000 troops to do battle, she catered for 2,000 indulgent pleasure-seekers who enjoyed the 695 staterooms, 4 dining saloons, 3 bars, 2 theatres, 5 acres of open deck with a heated pool, and more.

Which incarnation of the SS *America* more closely resembles your church, or your idea of church? And which attitude more closely resembles yours – that of the crack troops or of the carefree holidaymakers? Things look radically different on a luxury liner than they do on a troop carrier. Of course troops need R&R – time out to have fun and replenish their energy – but in general, as followers of Jesus, we need to remain alert and on guard, as our verse above tells us.

Lord, I choose to be alert and self-controlled today. Amen!

HOPELESS OR HOPEFUL?

Romans 15:13

"May the God of hope fill you with all joy and peace as you trust in him, so that you may overflow with hope by the power of the Holy Spirit."

Fiorello LaGuardia was the maverick mayor of New York City during the Depression. His ways of doing business were unorthodox, but usually appreciated. On one dark winter's night in 1935, he arrived unannounced at court and dismissed the presiding judge for the evening session. One case he dealt with concerned a destitute grandmother accused of stealing a loaf of bread. She told LaGuardia of all her woes – how her daughter's husband had deserted her, her daughter was sick and her grandchildren were at home hungry. But the storekeeper that she'd stolen from maintained a hard line, "Your Honour, you need to punish her to teach other people a lesson. Otherwise it'll happen again in this bad neighborhood."

Reluctantly, the mayor sighed, delivered his verdict, and addressed the old lady, "I've got to punish you. The law makes no exception – ten dollars or ten days in jail." But as soon as he'd made his pronouncement, he pulled a $10 bill out of his pocket and said, "Here is the woman's fine... and furthermore, I'm going to fine everyone in this court room fifty cents for living in a city where a person has to steal bread so that her grandchildren can eat. Mr Bailiff, collect the fines and give them to the defendant."

The New York Times ran an article the following day on how $47.50 was turned over to the bewildered old woman. Among the contributors were the red-faced storeowner, some seventy petty criminals, people with traffic violations, and city policemen – and a standing ovation accompanied the handover of the money!

Thank God that's how he treats us! "Mercy triumphs over judgment" (James 2:13). There is always hope, whatever our circumstances. May we live hopeful lives today. And, as Jesus said, "Freely you have received, freely give" (Matthew 10:8).

Lord, I choose to live a hope-filled life of extravagant grace and mercy today. Amen!

INTACT OR LOVED OFF?

1 John 3:1

"How great is the love the Father has lavished on us, that we should be called children of God! And that is what we are!"

31

AUGUST

In the touching old children's story of the Velveteen Rabbit, there is a conversation between Skin Horse and Rabbit as they lie side by side one day in the nursery before Nana comes to tidy up. Skin Horse is telling Rabbit about life. Rabbit asks him, "What is real? Does it mean having things buzz inside you and a stick-out handle?" "Real isn't how you're made," says Skin Horse. "It's a thing that happens to you. When a child loves you for a long, long time – not just to play with but really loves you, then you become real." "Does it hurt?" asks Rabbit. "Well, sometimes," says Skin Horse, for he's always truthful. "For when you're real, you don't mind being hurt." "Does it happen all at once, like being wound up, or bit by bit?" asks Rabbit. "It doesn't happen all at once," says Skin Horse, "you become, it takes a long time. That's why it doesn't happen often to people who break easily apart or have sharp edges or have to be carefully kept. Gradually, by the time you are real, most of you has been loved off and your eyes drop out and you get loose in the joints and very shabby, but those things don't matter at all because once you're real you can't be ugly except to people who don't understand."

Being real, choosing to love and be loved, can be messy and painful. C.S. Lewis wrote, "To love at all is to be vulnerable. Love anything and your heart will be wrung and possibly broken." He goes on to say that if you keep your heart intact, it will become "unbreakable, impenetrable, irredeemable". When his wife died of cancer, he questioned, "Why love if losing hurts so much? I have no answers, only the life I have lived. The pain now is part of the happiness. That's the deal."

Lord, I choose to love and be loved today. Amen!

2 Corinthians 4:9

"We are struck down, but not destroyed."

DOWN AND OUT OR ONWARDS AND UPWARDS?

In the 1992 Barcelona Olympic Games, British athlete Derek Redmond was running in the 400m. This was the culmination of months and even years of gruelling training and preparation, with his dad as trainer and coach. In the semi-final heat, he was out in front when his hamstring suddenly went, and he pulled up in agony. The race continued and finished while he was writhing in pain. But although he was down, he wasn't out. He dragged himself to his feet, and hobbled forward, lifting his injured leg step by step. The crowd rose to its feet and cheered him onwards. The pain was so excruciating that it didn't look like he'd be able to finish the race. But then a grey-haired plump man jumped over the railings, evaded security officials, and ran towards him. Many people wept as they watched him put his arms around Derek's waist and whisper encouragements in his ear. Together they made it to the finishing line. That other man was his father. During post-race interviewing, Redmond told the assembled press: "My father was the only one who could have helped me, because he was the only one who knew what I'd been through."

Similarly with us, the Holy Spirit comes alongside each of us wounded athletes (in the original New Testament Greek, the word "*parakletos*" is used of the Holy Spirit, and it literally means "called to one's side"). He helps carry us the rest of the way. And he is the only one who can do it, because he is the only one who knows what we've been through, and what lies ahead.

The apostle Paul, like Derek Redmond, was "struck down but not destroyed" (verse 9). May we be the same through the toughest of times. In verse 7, we read: "But we have this treasure in jars of clay to show that this all-surpassing power is from God and not from us."

Lord, I resolve to get back up whenever I take a hit and to live in the power of your Spirit today. Amen!

REAL OR FAKE?

1 Thessalonians 5:19–21

"Do not put out the Spirit's fire; do not treat prophecies with contempt. Test everything. Hold on to the good."

2

SEPTEMBER

In the mid 1990s, I paid my first ever visit to the famous London church, Holy Trinity Brompton, for their winter carol service, which was held in the dark with atmospheric candles lending great intimacy and ambience. The Holy Spirit was doing extraordinary things apparently, and even the secular press was reporting on it. Not one prone to manifestations of the Spirit, I went there nevertheless open to the Lord doing whatever he might choose to do in me. I hadn't been there long when I felt a warm glow on the back of my head. I kept my eyes shut and continued worshipping. But the warmth of the glow was undeniable – in fact it increased, and I thought I could feel a gentle pitter-patter all over my back. "God, what's happening?" It got hotter and hotter. "God! If this is you, have your way in my life. Oh, I love you. I surrender all. Make me holy, and more useful, I'll do anything, go anywhere for you!" After about a minute of such praying, the heat became unbearable – it was positively burning me. I opened my eyes and looked up, and there three feet above me was a chandelier gushing forth wax from a weeping candle!!!

I think God was having a good-natured chuckle at my expense back then. But joking aside, we all know that the Holy Spirit – *His* nature, role, and influence – are understood and expressed in radically different ways. Wherever you're coming from on the theological spectrum, Paul's words above are instructive to us. God is much bigger than we often allow him to be. Let's not limit him, but be open to whatever he might want to do, however he might want to do it – without losing our sense of discernment.

Lord, I choose to be open and obedient to you today. Amen!

CASE-FULL OF AMMUNITION OR ONE ROUND?

1 Peter 2:12

"Live such good lives among the pagans that, though they accuse you of doing wrong, they may see your good deeds and glorify God on the day he visits us."

Successful businessman Jerry Singleton grew attached to a little boy who was his regular shoe shiner at the train station. The boy was always meticulous in his work, which impressed Jerry. One day, Jerry asked him why he was so conscientious about his work. The boy replied, "Sir, I'm a follower of Jesus, and I try to shine every pair of shoes as if he himself were wearing them." Years later, Jerry reflected on how he'd seen something so deeply genuine in that shoeshine boy that it proved to be the catalyst to his decision to begin reading his Bible, and then deciding to become a follower of Christ himself. He credited his salvation to the little boy who shined every pair of shoes "as if Jesus Christ were wearing them". Charles Spurgeon once asked a cleaner who was a recent convert what difference choosing to follow Jesus had made in her life. Rather timidly she replied, "Well Sir, I now sweep under the doormats."

Choosing to follow Jesus totally changes how we live our lives. Or at least it should do. When many years ago my missionary grandfather was arguing over the original meaning of a text with an African believer, Yosiya put his head in his hands for a moment and then sighed, "You missionaries can defeat me with theological argument, but it is sterile, unless your lives show the truth of what you teach. You are like a soldier with a whole case-full of ammunition but no gun to fire it from. I have only one round of ammunition, my testimony, but it is effective when I fire it."

Today's verse shows the purpose and power of living an attractively different good life. May we too choose the one effective round over much ammunition without a gun!

Lord, I choose to live a good life for your glory today. Amen!

SPITTING OR SPAT AT?

Matthew 27:30

"The soldiers spat on him."

4

SEPTEMBER

During the dark years of communist rule in Romania, a large part of the church submitted to the authorities and compromised their faith. As far as the Romanian Government was able, it systematically undermined and destroyed the church. Richard Wurmbrand was at a pastors' congress in which all his ministry colleagues were being coerced into endorsing and submitting to the party line by forsaking their primary allegiance to Christ. What happened next was the catalyst for thirteen years of torture and imprisonment, much of it in solitary confinement. Wurmbrand wrote in *Tortured for Christ*, "My wife [Sabine] and I were present at this congress. She told me, 'Richard, stand up and wash away this shame from the face of Christ! They [the cowed church leaders] are spitting in His face.' I said to her: 'If I do so, you will lose your husband.' She replied: 'I don't wish to have a coward as a husband.'"

I worked in Hamburg's red light district for six months with the Salvation Army. We used to do street outreach with tramps, alcoholics, druggies, and prostitutes. Several times seemingly affable people suddenly turned violent, enraged, almost psychopathic towards me when I brought up the name of Jesus, to the point of spitting on and punching me. You might have experienced sudden deep anger from a more respectable colleague or acquaintance at the mention of Jesus. Somehow following the Prince of Peace can lead to violent situations or vitriolic attacks. If it does, stand firm, and read John 15 and 16: "No servant is greater than his master… if the world hates you, keep in mind that it hated me first… in this world you will have trouble, but take heart, I have overcome the world."

Wurmbrand experienced those truths in the extreme, as have many others before and after him. We will also, no doubt to a lesser extent. But let's not shy away as cowards; instead let's boldly and lovingly speak up for him.

Lord, forgive my times of cowardice. I choose to speak up for you today. Amen!

HALFWAY OR ALL THE WAY?

Luke 22:33–34

"Peter replied, 'Lord, I am ready to go with you to prison and to death.' Jesus answered, 'I tell you, Peter, before the cock crows today, you will deny three times that you know me.'"

We can take somewhat perverse comfort from Peter's fickle following of Jesus – the fact that he reneged on his bold commitment just hours later at the first opportunity to really test it – and yet Jesus chose him to lead despite knowing his weaknesses and failings to come, reinstating him graciously in John 21 to "feed my sheep".

Suffering for our faith in the Western world will become more mainstream in the coming years if we refuse to bow to the dictates of a vehemently secularist agenda from on high. And that is not something to be feared. The wheat must be sorted from the chaff. A number of years ago in the former Soviet Union during a wave of concerted persecution of Christians, a number of professing Christians were holding a clandestine prayer meeting. Suddenly, the doors burst open, and two fully armed Russian guards burst in. They shouted, "Get out of this place if you're not willing to die for your faith." Half of the professing Christians got up and left. They just ran. And then when the doors closed, the guards put down their guns, took off their hats, sat down, and said: "Praise the Lord! We were just sorting out the sheep from the goats before we'd risk fellowship!"

Fifteenth-century mystic Meister Eckhart wrote, "There are plenty of Christians to follow the Lord halfway, but not the other half. They will give up possessions, friends, and honours, but it touches them too closely to disown themselves." Peter started badly: according to the above, he just went halfway, and it was all talk with him; but praise God that he, and we too, can make a fresh start and vow to go all the way with Jesus. Let's do it!

Lord, I'm in, all the way with you today. Amen!

HUMILITY OR PRIDE?

James 4:6, 7

"But he gives us more grace. That is why the Scripture says: 'God opposes the proud but gives grace to the humble.' Submit yourselves, then, to God."

The idea that God stands in concerted opposition to the proud is a powerful and sobering one. I might fancy my chances against many or even most opponents, but if I choose pride then I'm choosing God as my opponent and my chances are bleak. Pascal warned us: "Know then, proud man, what a paradox you are to yourself. Be humble, impotent reason! Be silent, feeble nature! Hear from your master your true condition, which is unknown to you. Listen to God."

Humility, on the other hand, is the genuine conviction of one's unworthiness of the grace of God. It literally means a low estimate of self, which is not the same as self-deprecation. When you hear someone deprecating himself, usually you can put it down to some sort of insecurity or counterfeit humility. Philip Brooks said, "The true way to be humble is not to stoop until you are smaller than yourself, but to stand at your full height before some higher nature that will show you how small your greatness is. Stand at your very highest, and then look at Christ; then go away and be forever humble." Seeing how little we are alongside his greatness is the first step towards being what he wants us to be.

Each one of us has a lifelong battle to wrestle with pride. Helen Keller wrote, "I long to accomplish a great and noble task, but it is my chief duty to accomplish humble tasks as though they were great and noble. The world is moved along, not only by the mighty shoves of its heroes, but also by the aggregate of the tiny pushes of each honest worker." So may we choose humility, while paying heed to this warning: "If you pray for humility, be careful. Humility is learned through humiliations!"

Lord, give me grace to be a humble honest worker today. Amen!

Ephesians 5:15, 16

"Be very careful how you live... making the most of every opportunity."

ACTIVITY OR PRODUCTIVITY?

I'm sure you can relate to the feeling of getting to the end of a hectic day full of business and activity and yet not having got done the things you really wanted to. That's because it's easy to confuse activity and productivity. Many people, and you could be one of them, are busy without a purpose, allowing "urgent" matters (like answering a phone call when you're in the middle a deep conversation with someone) to displace important matters (like that very conversation). Sometimes we actually need to do less so as to focus on what matters most.

Living life on purpose produces passion. As Rick Warren writes, "Without a purpose, life is motion without meaning, activity without directions, and events without reason. Without a purpose, life is trivial, petty, and pointless... Without God, life has no purpose, and without purpose, life has no meaning. Without meaning, life has no significance or hope."

Beth Clark wrote:

> *I've noticed something about people who make a difference in the world: they hold to the unshakeable conviction that individuals are extremely important, that every life matters. They are willing to feed one stomach, educate one mind, and treat one wound. They aren't determined to revolutionize the world all at once; they're satisfied with small changes. Over time though, the small changes add up. Sometimes they even transform cities and nations, and yes, the world.*

I'm confident you want to make a difference in the world, you want to choose productivity over activity. So how will that change the way you go about today? In this season of writing, I am tempted every morning to answer all my emails and go on Facebook and Twitter first – but living life on purpose means disciplining myself to say no to those distractions and instead use the time when my brain is freshest to work on this. How about you?

Lord, help me today not just to be active but to be productive, for your glory, Amen!

BOILED TO DEATH OR ON YOUR GUARD?

Proverbs 4:23

"Above all else, guard your heart, for it is the wellspring of life."

One of the advantages of living in a developing country like Burundi is that out here we're not bombarded relentlessly with the same number of scantily clad women selling whatever product has nothing to do with their beautiful bodies. But wherever we are, adverts constantly seek to sow a sense of inadequacy, lust, and greed in us for whatever the advertisers want us to buy. I know a married couple who regularly pause the television with their kids to discuss the advert they've just seen. They ask the question: "What was the lie in that advert?" They're trying to get their kids to think, to discern, and to guard their hearts.

John Eldredge wrote:

> *We are at war, and the bloody battle is over our hearts. I am astounded how few Christians see this, how little they protect their hearts. We act as though we live in a sleepy little town during peacetime. We don't. We live in the spiritual equivalent of Bosnia or Beirut. Act like it. Watch over your heart. Don't let just anything in; don't let it go just anywhere. What's this going to do to my heart? is a question that I ask in every situation.*

You know the experiment with the frog in a pan of water? If you put a frog in a pan of boiling water, it obviously jumps out immediately, because the water burns it. However, if you put that same frog in a pan of cool water and just raise the temperature slowly, it will sit there until it is boiled to death. It just doesn't notice the heat rising. Amazing! And that is how many of us are getting taken out today. What we would have been shocked at just five or ten years ago no longer gets us jumping out of the pan, we just sit there… In what ways am I like that frog today? Please, please, feel the heat!

Lord, I choose to guard my heart today, Amen!

Philippians 1:6

"... being confident of this, that he who began a good work in you will carry it on to completion until the day of Christ Jesus."

PROBLEM-SOLVER OR ADVENTURE-LIVER?

Is life a problem to be solved or an adventure to be lived?

One of my cycling adventures took me all the way around Burundi with nine other men. We knew the end point, and were always working towards it, but the purpose of the trip was so much bigger than the final destination: it was to raise money for a school, to share Christ along the way, to spend time together, to observe the stunning scenery, to experience both laughs and tears in the highs and the lows, to battle through injury, sickness, tiredness, and bad winds. How absurd it would have been to ignore the other team members, ignore the beauty, and just keep our heads down in gritty concentration until we crossed the finishing line!

And yet, sometimes we live life that way.

It's easy to set up camp and call it home. But that stops the flow of the journey. Life is a process, with completion further down the road. We do want completion at the journey's end, but in the meantime ambiguity and uncertainty are part of the adventure to be embraced.

As we journey with Jesus, the above verse assures us he "will carry it on to completion". Don't push ahead of him. Enjoy the moment. Today. With others. Don't rush, always looking ahead. Enjoy your children at this stage of their development, not looking forward to another. Enjoy your friends, your health, your job, your current challenges. Ditch the problem solving and choose to live the adventure fully today!

Lord, I choose to embrace life as an adventure today. Thank you that you accompany me every step of the journey, and that you promise to bring it all to completion. Amen!

LIVE ROUNDS OR BLANKS?

Proverbs 12:18

"Reckless words pierce like a sword, but the tongue of the wise brings healing."

Towards the end of the Second World War, the Allies were bombing Berlin. Heavy and relatively cumbersome bombers would be accompanied by smaller more agile fighter planes to protect them from enemy fire so that they could unleash their heavy artillery. After what had been a devastating and ultimately successful bombing campaign, a number of fighter planes were flying on their way home, separated from the bomber. Suddenly a German plane appeared out of nowhere and attacked the bomber. Tracer bullets flew all around them, and then five pierced the plane, including the fuel tank. The pilot waited for an explosion and his imminent death, but neither came. He duly made it back to safety across the Channel. A few hours later, a mechanic knocked on the pilot's door and presented five crumpled but unexploded bullets to him – and to his amazement he discovered that all the bullets were empty of gunpowder, and in one was a folded note: "We are Polish POWs. We are forced to make bullets in factory. When guards do not look we do not fill with powder. Is not much but is best we can do. Please tell family we are alive." The scribbled note was signed by four Polish prisoners-of-war. Out of millions of bullets, those few made the difference and saved the lives of the pilot and his crew.

We're constantly firing off rounds at people, in terms of what we say, how we act, our general attitudes. And they can either be live rounds or blanks in terms of bringing life or death. So will we use our words today to tear down or build up? Will we do acts of service or disservice? Will our attitudes and interactions with others draw them towards or away from Jesus?

Lord, I choose to think, act and speak words of life today. Amen!

Matthew 6:33

"Seek first the kingdom of God and his righteousness."

BIG ROCKS FIRST OR NOT AT ALL?

The consultant pulled out a one-gallon, wide-mouthed mason jar and set it on a table in front of the executives. Then he produced a number of fist-sized rocks and put each of them into the jar. When the jar was filled to the top and no more rocks would fit inside, he asked, "Is this jar full?" Everyone said, "Yes." "Really?" He then produced some gravel and shook the jar as he poured it in to get it down into all the spaces between the big rocks. He asked them again, "Is the jar full?" Now they weren't so sure. "Probably not." "Correct!" He pulled out a bag of sand and poured it gently into the jar, filling the gaps left between the rocks and the gravel. Once more he asked, "Is this jar full?" "No!" they shouted. "You're catching on!" he said. Next he grabbed a pitcher of water and began to pour it in until the jar was filled to the brim. Then he looked up at the group and asked, "What is the point of this illustration?" One enthusiastic younger executive piped up, "The point is, no matter how full your schedule is, if you try really hard, you can always fit some more things into it!" The consultant replied, "Sorry, you're wrong, that's not the point. The truth this illustration teaches us is: *If you don't put the big rocks in first, you'll never get them in at all."*

I hope that the Big Rock in your life is Jesus, but what are the other "big rocks"? How about time with your loved ones, your education, dreams, investing in others? Spend some time today identifying those big rocks and resolving to put them in the jar first, or you'll never get them in the jar at all.

Lord, I choose today to seek first your kingdom and righteousness. Guide me in identifying and prioritizing the other "big rocks" in my life and putting them in the jar. Amen!

HE LOVES ME OR HE LOVES ME NOT?

John 1:12

"Yet to those who received him, to those who believed in his name, he gave the right to become children of God."

12

SEPTEMBER

I'm convinced that the single big enormous truth that we find so hard to grasp and so often skip over is essentially quite simple.

God loves you. Completely. And it doesn't depend on your performance, your holiness, your circumstances.

You know that thing girls do with a daisy? He loves me; he loves me not. He loves me; he loves me not. To what extent does your concept of God's love for you depend on your circumstances? You get a parking space: He loves me. You get ill: He loves me not. The sun shines for a picnic: He loves me. It rains on your walk to work and you get soaked: He loves me not. And what about your actions? To what extent does your performance as a follower of Christ affect your concept of God's love for you? You share your faith: He loves me. You lose your temper: He loves me not. You give money away: He loves me. You break your diet: He loves me not.

Saints, God loves you and his love doesn't change according to circumstances or personal holiness. With God there is only one thing to say with each pluck of a daisy petal: He loves me, He loves me, He loves me.

Often believing this truth and receiving this love is a choice we can make or ignore, and that choice will make or break our quality of life, our witness to Jesus, and our freedom in him. Will you believe him and receive his love today?

And I pray that you, being rooted and established in love, may have power, together with all the saints, to grasp how wide and long and high and deep is the love of Christ, and to know this love that surpasses knowledge – that you may be filled to the measure of all the fullness of God. (Ephesians 3:17–19)

1 Corinthians 16:13

"Be on your guard; stand firm in the faith; be men of courage; be strong."

HELP OR HINDER?

Sometimes when I've been fixing a bicycle or packing the car for a journey, my kids have asked to "help". But after a few minutes they've got distracted and lost interest, while still being there; and so in the end they've got in the way and their "help" has proved to be more of a hindrance.

A metaphor that is often used in the Scriptures for our Christian lives is that we are at war and called to fight the kingdom battle as part of God's army. It's natural that such militaristic metaphors were used in a country like Israel at the time, under brutal military occupation by the Romans. However, the army metaphor has stayed relevant even in peace times. We are at war. War against evil, against the powers and principalities of this world, against injustice. We know the result – the Lamb conquers – but we are called to be part of that victory.

William Booth knew that well when he named his organization the "Salvation Army". It was originally going to be called the "Volunteer Army", but he and his close friends realized that Christians aren't volunteer members of the army – rather they lay down their rights for Jesus' cause. So they swapped the word "Volunteer" with "Salvation" and the rest is history.

Once we get our heads around being part of God's army, the motivation for helping rather than hindering the cause becomes clear. In an army if you are not playing an active role you will get in the way of those who are, and become a risk not just to yourself but to those around you. So it is that by being spectators in the kingdom battle we put our brothers and sisters at risk as much as ourselves. That thought alone is enough to get me off my backside and back into the fray.

Lord, I choose to be an active member of your salvation army today. Amen!

PURE OR DIRTY?

Isaiah 55:1

"Come, all you who are thirsty, come to the waters."

14

SEPTEMBER

I've visited a number of friends' lavatories in the UK and found a plaque on the wall announcing that it has been twinned with a loo in Rutana Province, Burundi! It's an innovative and fun way of raising money for a sanitation project, but beyond that it provides a constant reminder to the hundreds of generous people who have twinned their loos, not to take for granted clean water and good sanitation.

Jesus spoke of another type of water: spiritual water. He talked about it welling up inside of us, and that it quenches our thirst. This water is seriously good for you – refreshing, cleansing, renewing, and life-giving. We all have it available to us through Jesus – we just have to come, we just have to drink.

So why is it, then, that we so often turn from it and drink out of puddles of dirty water that the world offers? Jeremiah prophesied long ago: "My people have committed two sins: They have forsaken me, the spring of living water, and have dug their own cisterns, broken cisterns that cannot hold water" (Jeremiah 2:13).

Ouch! I'm guilty as charged – but why do I do it, when the living water is so much better?

What constitutes a dirty puddle? Anything you turn to rather than God to meet your deep need isn't going to be good for you. It could be anything from shopping, booze, and food to trashy TV, the wrong sorts of websites, or an unhealthy fantasy life. Some things are obviously poisonous and damaging, while others won't seem so bad to us, but we all know when we're going elsewhere than to God to quench our thirst.

So let's choose daily to turn to the spring of living water and drink deeply, and regularly, as though our life depended on it. Because it does.

Lord, I choose to quench my thirst in you today. And in so doing may streams of living water flow out from me to bless others too. Amen!

INTO THE SKID OR INTO THE HEDGE?

1 Corinthians 15:58

"Therefore, my dear brothers, stand firm. Let nothing move you. Always give yourselves fully to the work of the Lord, because you know that your labour in the Lord is not in vain."

Whether it be driving on ice, snow, or silt, the natural response when entering a skid is to slam on the brakes and try to steer *out* of the skid. But that's usually the worst thing to do, and you often end up losing control and crashing. Similarly in difficult times we often react like that. However counterintuitive it might seem, the best thing to do is to steer *into* the skid, and by so doing to regain control of the wheel and be able to avoid an accident.

As we go about our daily lives, at various points we will hit a skid. This isn't a question of "if" but "when". And the hard times often come as we're making progress in our walk with Jesus. Satan likes to scare us off and intimidate us, so we back down and retreat to our safe worlds of low risk and high comfort. The intuitive thing to do at such times is to back off until it all calms down again – to steer *away* from the skid – but do that and spiritually you will end up in the hedge. Have the courage and the sense to steer *into* the skid!

How often are we told in the Bible not to be afraid? Paul was a supreme example of overcoming adversity and not being put off by rapidly deteriorating circumstances. He did it by strengthening himself in the Lord with thanksgiving and praise, and then by not giving up as he pursued what he knew was the right thing to do. And when things went badly for him he dug in even deeper! He increased the prayers and was determined not to be intimidated by life's circumstances.

Lord, help me to discern whether to steer into the skid or not when the next one comes my way. Either way may I live by faith, not fear. Amen!

STUDY THE MENU OR EAT THE MEAL?

James 1:22

"Do not merely listen to the word, and so deceive yourselves. Do what it says."

16 SEPTEMBER

A man once approached John Wimber, the founder of the Vineyard group of churches, complaining about the depth of teaching on a Sunday. "When are we going to get to the meat?" he asked. Wimber replied, "The meat is on the street." He meant that if you want the Word of God to "dwell in you richly" (Colossians 3:16), it wasn't enough just to be hearers of the word – you need to be doers of the word.

And here is the challenge. Why is it that our focus seems to be on learning more at the expense of doing what we already know? I love the access we have in this generation to so much excellent teaching, writing, and biblical resources – both new and old. At the click of a mouse I can access Christian classics by saints past and present. Yet as the volume of resources increases, the effective activity of the church seems to decrease – or am I just speaking from my personal battle to come out of hiding in my study books and engage with a lost and broken world? To stop reading about prayer and get on my knees and pray? To put down my treatise on love, cross the street and demonstrate love by my actions rather than my intentions?

Today you have a choice. You can spend your time studying the menu, reading it, researching it, admiring it, discussing it. Or you can eat the meal.

Let us try to put into practice what we know. Because at the end of the day, most of us are educated way beyond the level of our obedience already – and when we meet Jesus he isn't going to sit us down and test us on our biblical knowledge. He is going to ask, "When I was naked did you clothe me, when I was hungry did you feed me?"

And you don't need a theology degree or a certificate in food science to do that...

Lord, I choose to follow you in word and deed today. Amen!

Matthew 10:16

"I am sending you out like sheep among wolves. Therefore be as shrewd as snakes and as innocent as doves."

SNAKISH SHEEP OR WOLFISH DOVE?

An Indian farmer had crippling debts to the unscrupulous old village moneylender. The latter agreed to forgo all debts if he was allowed to marry the farmer's beautiful young daughter. She and her father were horrified at the prospect, but they seemed to have no options left. The moneylender suggested they let providence decide the matter. He would put two pebbles in a bag – one black and one white – and whichever she picked out would decide her fate. The white one would mean debt released unconditionally, the black one would mean marriage. Or, if she refused to pick a pebble at all, her father would be thrown into jail until the debt was paid.

The moneylender picked up two pebbles off the path, but the daughter noticed they were both black. She was stuck: if she refused to take a pebble, her father would be thrown in jail. If she picked a pebble, it meant sacrificing herself for her father's debt and imprisonment. If she pulled both out and exposed the man as a cheat, she and her father would be victim to his spiteful vengeance. What could she possibly do?

She had her head firmly screwed on the right way: she took a pebble out of the bag but "accidentally" fumbled it and let it fall onto the pebble-strewn path, where it immediately became lost among all the other pebbles. Then, she apologized, "Oh, how clumsy of me! But never mind, if you look into the bag for the one that is left, you will be able to tell which pebble I picked." Since the remaining pebble was black, it would have to be assumed that she had picked the white one. The moneylender couldn't admit his dishonesty. Thanks to her shrewdness, she and her father were free!

Shrewdness is a quality we don't always aspire to, but Jesus endorses it fully. Coupled with innocence, it makes the perfect combination!

Lord, I choose to be as shrewd as a snake and as innocent as a dove in all my dealings. Amen!

CORPSE OR FANATIC?

2 Timothy 1:6, 7

"I remind you to fan into flame the gift of God... for God did not give us a spirit of timidity, but a spirit of power, of love, and of self-discipline."

On a spectrum with "corpse" at one end and "fanatic" at the other, where do you think you are in terms of zeal for serving Christ? It's an interesting question. I suspect if we then substitute "sharing" for "serving", many of us will modify our positioning further towards the corpse end, because we are so reticent actually to speak about him. God certainly doesn't want fanatics, but as one of my mentors told me in my younger days, "Fanatics are better than corpses, because you can cool the former down, but you can't warm up corpses."

Paul urged Timothy to fan into flame the gift of God in him – not to be timid, not to feel inadequate, but to blaze brightly for Jesus. That's what he wants for us too. Ross Patterson wrote, "God wants to set his people on fire by his Holy Spirit, not just so that we can arrange church firework displays to entertain the saints, however spectacular they may be. He wants us to share the warmth of that fire with a dying world."

William Lloyd Garrison was a great abolitionist. He was the publisher of an anti-slavery newspaper called *The Liberator*. He was an angry man, burning with indignation towards the wicked institution of trafficking human lives. He hated slavery with every fibre of his being. On one occasion his best friend, Samuel May, tried to calm him down, "Oh, my friend, try to moderate your indignation and keep more cool. Why, you are all on fire." Garrison replied, "Brother May, I have need to be all on fire, for I have mountains of ice around me to melt."

Well, there's plenty of indifference and apathy around us that needs melting. Maybe you feel a sense of shame at where you are on the above spectrum – or maybe indifference? Speak to God about it.

Lord, rekindle my fire today. Amen!

Romans 8:28

"In all things God works for the good..."!

FOR BETTER OR FOR WORSE?

Have you had a bad day recently? "Enjoy" this one, as written up by Rebecca Dudley, editor of *News Tribune*:

> *Paul Johnson, 37, a mechanic from Maitland, had a day to forget last Tuesday. During the morning, he pushed his motorcycle from the patio into his living room, where he began to clean the engine with some rags and a bowel of petrol. When he finished, he sat on the motorcycle and decided to start it to make sure everything was still OK. Unfortunately, the bike started in gear, and crashed through the glass patio door with him still clinging to the handlebars. His wife had been working in the kitchen. She came running at the noise, and found him crumpled on the patio, badly cut from the shards of broken glass. She called the emergency services, and the paramedics transported Paul to the emergency room. Later that afternoon, after many stitches had pulled her husband back together, the wife brought him home and put him to bed. She cleaned up the mess in the living room, and dumped the bowl of petrol in the toilet. Shortly thereafter, her husband woke up, lit a cigarette, and went into the bathroom. He sat down and tossed the cigarette into the toilet, which promptly exploded because the wife had not flushed the petrol away. The explosion blew Mr. Johnson through the bathroom door. The wife heard the explosion and her husband's screams. She ran into the hall and found him lying on the floor with his trousers blown away and burns on his buttocks. She again ran to the phone and called for an ambulance. The same two paramedics were dispatched to the scene. They loaded Paul on the stretcher and began carrying him to the street. One of them asked the wife how the injury had occurred. When she told them, they began laughing so hard that they dropped the stretcher, and broke Mr. Johnson's collarbone.*

Nothing profound today – maybe just some perspective! Thank God he's with you "for better or for worse"!

Lord, I choose to laugh today. Amen!

OURS OR HIS?

Romans 14:8

"If we live, we live to the Lord; and if we die, we die to the Lord. So, whether we live or die, we belong to the Lord."

20

SEPTEMBER

If we, and all we have, belong to God, then actually we own nothing and owe everything.

Medical missionary Alexander Clarke was hunting in the Congo when he heard fearful shrieks. He ran through the bush to find a lion mauling an unfortunate man. He shot the lion, rescued the man, patched him up, and took him to the nearest hospital. Months later, as he sat on his veranda one Sunday afternoon, he heard lots of noise outside his compound. He opened the gate to find a line of animals – chicken, goats, sheep, and cows – followed by children and lastly the man he had rescued and his wife. The man came forward, knelt before the doctor, and said, "Sir, according to the law of our tribe, a man rescued from the jaws of a wild animal no longer belongs to himself but to his rescuer."

As our verse above states, we belong to the Lord. And it's not a lion's jaws we've been rescued from; rather we've been rescued from the jaws of hell and bondage to Satan. The man Clarke rescued understood the enormity of what had happened to him. May we likewise recognize that "whether we live or die, we belong to the Lord."

As Erwin McManus writes:

> *To belong to God is to belong to his heart. If we respond to the call of Jesus to leave everything and follow him, then there is a voice within us crying out. "Fight for the heart of your King!" Yet Christianity over the past two thousand years has moved from a tribe of renegades to a religion of conformists. Those who choose to follow Jesus become participants in an insurrection. To claim we believe is simply not enough. The call of Jesus is one that demands action.*

Lord, I choose willingly to be fully yours today. Amen!

1 John 3:14

"Anyone who does not love remains in death."

CONNECTED OR DISCONNECTED?

John Ortberg wrote: "I have never known anyone who failed at love yet succeeded at life. I have never known anyone who succeeded at love and failed at life. We need love to live." He's not limiting failed or successful love to marriage, by the way. This applies to all of us, whether married, divorced, or never married. We need love to live.

We were made to be connected to others. We will stagnate if we are disconnected but thrive and flourish if we are connected with God and people. It is all too easy to become isolated and disconnected in our society. But this is dangerous. It leads to self-absorption and giving in more easily to temptation and discouragement. Disconnected people are between two and five times more likely to die from any cause than people who are rooted in their community or family.

The life-giving power of being connected is seen in Winston Churchill. He had a long-lasting strong marriage with his wife, was deeply engaged with his offspring, had a close network of friendships, and he loved his work and his country. His lifestyle, however, was far from a healthy one: He smoked cigars constantly, drank too much, ate to excess, slept sporadically, and took no physical exercise – and yet he lived to be nearly ninety. When somebody once asked him, "Mr Churchill, do you ever take any exercise?" He replied, "The only exercise I get is serving as a pallbearer for my friends who died whilst they were exercising!"

We're not endorsing his lifestyle – far from it, see the entry for 2nd January – but the point being made here is that we are hardwired for connectivity. Meaning is found in community, not individualism. Are you plugged in at church, or just a passive spectator each week? Are you living life connected at the moment? If not, choose to do something about it today.

Lord, I choose to live my life connected with others. Amen!

SHARP OR BLUNT?

Hebrews 4:12

"For the word of God is living and active. Sharper than any double-edged sword, it penetrates even to dividing soul and spirit, joints and marrow; it judges the thoughts and attitudes of the heart."

If the Bible is such a sharp sword, why doesn't anyone seem to get struck with it these days? At most, it seems the biggest risk is of getting a paper-cut. The Bible is left as a sword rusting in a scabbard, blunt, and ineffective.

A student was looking for holiday work to help pay his tuition fees. He approached the foreman of a logging crew and asked him for a job. The foreman told him to grab an axe and show him what he was made off. The young man promptly felled the nearest tree, and was awarded a provisional contract. Come Wednesday evening, however, the young man was called in by the foreman, "Today's your last day, here's your pay cheque for the last three days." The student was distraught, "Why are you firing me? I'm the first one to arrive, the last one to leave, and I work hard all day." The foreman said, "We're letting you go because you've slipped far behind the others. On Monday you were the fastest but our charts show that today you were the slowest." Then, sensing there was real integrity in the young man, the foreman suddenly thought of something, "Have you been sharpening your axe?" The student replied, "Well, no Sir. I have been working too hard to take the time."

How about us? Are we too busy to sharpen our blade? God's Word is a powerful weapon. And so is prayer. Prayer hones the sharp edge of the blade. Without it, the more work we do, the duller we will get. To stay sharp we need to take time with him in prayer and his Word before going about his work.

Lord, help me recognize this truth today. I choose to be sharp. Therefore, I choose to spend quality time with you. Amen!

John 16:13

"But when he, the Spirit of truth, comes, he will guide you into all truth."

ROAD MAP OR TOUR GUIDE?

Sometimes in Christian circles we're given false choices: the Bible or the Spirit, conservative or charismatic, Word-driven or Spirit-led. They constitute a false dichotomy, but let's explore them a little. All analogies break down at some point, but try this one: the Bible can be likened to a road map, and the Holy Spirit can be likened to a tour guide. The guide knows the map (indeed wrote it!) and follows the map, and so I need to pay close attention to him. I can kid myself that I can get around fine by knowing the road map, but actually I need the tour guide to direct, reveal and empower me to get where I need to go and do what I need to do. The Pharisees ultimately made the mistake of seeing knowledge of the Word as an end in itself, rather than leading them to an encounter with the person of Jesus through the Spirit of God.

Bill Johnson wrote, "Those who feel safe because of their intellectual grasp of the Scriptures enjoy a false security. None of us has a full grasp of Scripture, but we all have the Holy Spirit. He is our common denominator who will always lead us into truth. But to follow Him, we must be willing… to go beyond our current understanding of what we know." That sounds scary, and almost dangerous. But the Spirit's highest goal is to bring glory to Jesus (verse 14), so he must lead us towards truth and not away from it.

Scary? Almost dangerous? Catherine Fox wrote, "The Biblical images to describe the work of the Spirit – fire, mighty rushing wind, and flood – are exactly the sorts of things we pay to insure ourselves against!" Has keeping things tidy become our great commission? The difference between graveyards and nurseries is that one has perfect order while the other has life. If we live like we've got God figured out, we've missed him.

Lord, I desperately need both Map and Guide. Lead me into all truth today, even if it gets messy. Amen!

BITTER OR BETTER?

Habakkuk 3:17, 18

"Though the fig-tree does not bud and there are no grapes on the vines, though the olive crop fails and the fields produce no food, though there are no sheep in the pen and no cattle in the stalls, yet I will rejoice in the Lord, I will be joyful in God my Saviour."

By the end of the book of Habakkuk, the prophet has learned to rest in God's appointments and await his working in a spirit of worship, however painful and hopeless Judah's situation seemed. How often we or our loved ones face circumstances beyond our control, comprehension, or capacity to withstand. There are seldom easy answers to offer up.

H.G. Spafford was a successful lawyer from Chicago endowed with huge wealth. He had a strong Christian faith, and was blessed with a beautiful wife and four daughters. One summer, Mrs Spafford and all four daughters boarded a ship to travel to Europe and do a grand tour of the cities, the art galleries, and the theatre. Tragically, disaster struck mid-Atlantic as their ship collided with another vessel and quickly sank. Very few people were rescued, but Mrs Spafford was one of them. She was able to send a cable to her husband: "All lost! I alone remain. What shall I do?" But that was not all – there had been a sudden bank crash in Chicago, and Mr Spafford had lost all his wealth. He had suddenly gone from being a very wealthy man to a very poor one.

So, what did he do? Did he give up, become bitter, and blame God? No, he sat down and wrote these moving words:

When peace like a river attendeth my way,
When sorrows like sea billows roll;
Whatever my lot, thou hast taught me to say,
It is well, it is well, with my soul!

How the words of that hymn have ministered to millions over the ensuing generations!

God, grant me the same faith to cling to you and not get bitter when things go wrong in my life. Amen!

Romans 1:16

"I am not ashamed of the gospel, because it is the power of God for the salvation of everyone who believes."

COURAGEOUS OR COOL?

A friend of mine in his mid-twenties wrote the following to me:

> *In your book "Dangerously Alive", you talk about a brief moment of despair when you thought of going back to England where it was safe and sanitized but "spiritually bankrupt" and where many people seemingly have "everything to live with and nothing to live for". As I read your stories, and got to these words, I found myself crying out in despair because I realised what a coward I've become and how much time and money I've wasted on sedating myself with cigarettes, alcohol, drugs, TV, clothes, pornography, Facebook and anything else which helps me ignore the fact my life has become about existing rather than living. I'm a complete product of my generation and my main concern is to be cool rather than be courageous for Christ.*

Will we choose to be cool for Christ, or courageous for Christ? Confession time: I used to think I was the coolest Christian on campus! I had long wavy matted hair, wore funky ethnic clothing, didn't bother with shoes much of the time, even in lectures, and I hit my pinnacle as the King of Christian Cool when I wore a T-shirt of a pig saying "Jesus saved my bacon"!

The fact is, coolness is overrated. Courage isn't. Coolness will pass (it's long gone for me). Courage stands firm. Coolness seeks to mask deficiencies and insecurities. Courage presses forward despite them. As Thucydides said at Pericles' funeral in 431 BC: "The secret of happiness is freedom, and the secret of freedom is courage."

May we model authentic faith in our lives, not bowing to fickle fads but resting secure in our status in Christ. May we be people of substance rather than flaky. May we be rightfully proud to be children of the King, and unashamedly invite others to be adopted into the family.

God, help me to be courageous for you, today and always. Amen!

PURPOSEFUL OR AIMLESS?

Philippians 3:14

"I press on towards the goal to win the prize, for which God has called me heavenward in Christ Jesus."

26

SEPTEMBER

Paul knew exactly what he was aiming at in life, living every day with a focus and sense of purpose that motivated and guided his every action. How about us?

In greyhound racing, the dogs are trained to chase after a mechanical rabbit, which is controlled by a man in the press box. He keeps the rabbit just in front of the dogs so that they keep chasing it as fast as they can. During one race at a Florida track, as the dogs hurtled after the rabbit, there was an electrical short circuit in the system. The rabbit came to a halt, exploded, and its few remains lay there in flames attached to the wire. This totally confused the dogs. Two of them broke several ribs as they careered into a wall. One began chasing his tail. Others howled at the spectators in the stand; and the rest just stopped running, lay down on the track, and rested.

Not one of them finished the race.

So many people are chasing an illusion – a mechanical rabbit of some sort – which they think is real. It seems to provide a sense of purpose, a goal to strive for, a reason to live. Sometimes it takes the wake-up call of our mechanical rabbit going up in smoke to recognize we were chasing after the wrong thing all that time. Many of our friends continue in their frenzied pursuit of their own illusion of choice. May we model to them another way.

I want to finish my race. Do you? What is your focus? Is it a mechanical rabbit that is going to go up in smoke? As Paul writes elsewhere in 1 Corinthians 9:24–26, "Run in such a way as to get the prize. Everyone who competes in the games goes into strict training… Therefore I do not run like a man running aimlessly." Let's join him in the race!

Lord, I choose to fix my eyes on you and run with a sense of focus, discipline and purpose today. Amen!

ALONGSIDE OR APART?

1 Corinthians 12:26, 27

"If one part suffers, every part suffers with it; if one part is honoured, every part is honoured with it. Now you are the body of Christ, and each one of you is a part of it."

A teenage boy in Milwaukee underwent extensive radiation treatments and chemotherapy to kill off the cancer that had been diagnosed in his body. After many weeks in hospital, he was discharged. He was skinnier than before and totally bald as a result of the treatment. As his parents drove him home from the hospital, fear began to rise in him as to how he would get treated back at school. He'd been offered a wig but had decided to just go as he was. He opened the front door and turned on the lights. Suddenly dozens of people shouted "Welcome Home!" He looked around in amazement at all his school friends who had gathered to celebrate his return. All of them had shaved their heads and were totally bald like him!

Going through tough times is hard enough even when you have people around who love and care for you. How much more for those who are completely isolated and unsupported! As the body of Christ, we need to support, love, affirm, and encourage each other. We suffer together and are honoured together, as the verse says.

Jesus' love for us was so extreme that he went way beyond head-shaving: he went all the way to the cross. As John 15:13 says, "Greater love has no one than this: that he lay down his life for his friends." Are you suffering alongside anyone today? Are you rejoicing alongside anyone today? Or are you living for yourself, isolated and alone, doing your own thing? Authentic Christian living means being adopted into an extended family in which we share the highs and lows, the pain and the joy. So have your antenna out today to see who God might like you to come alongside.

Lord, I don't want to suffer or rejoice alone. I choose to be part of something bigger today. Amen!

THERMOMETERS OR THERMOSTATS?

Matthew 5:13–16

"You are the salt of the earth. But if the salt loses its saltiness, how can it be made salty again? It is no longer good for anything except to be thrown out and trampled by men.

You are the light of the world. A city on a hill cannot be hidden. Neither do people light a lamp and put it under a bowl. Instead they put it on its stand, and it gives light to everyone in the house. In the same way, let your light shine before men, that they may see your good deeds and praise your Father in heaven.

The difference between thermostats and thermometers is very significant. A thermometer merely takes a reading of the environment it is in, reflecting the reality as is. It gives the temperature of a given area. If it's cold, the reading will reflect that. If it becomes warmer, the mercury in the gauge will expand and move upwards. Thermometers always adjust to their environment. Thermostats, on the other hand, change the temperature in the room. You can set the temperature higher or lower, and the whole environment will be adjusted and adapted to your chosen reading.

I fear more often than not I behave like a thermometer, even though I know I'm called to act like a thermostat. Thermostats didn't exist in Jesus' day, so he couldn't ask us to be one of them. His equivalent metaphors were that we should be salt and light, influencing and changing our environments rather than being influenced and changed by them.

Most days we'll be tempted to go along with negative humour, back-stabbing, grumbling, criticizing, and more. Without appearing superior, smug, or judgmental, let's try today to be the encourager amidst the moaners, the clean amidst the smutty, the hopeful amidst the naysayers – the salt, the light, the thermostat.

Lord, in your strength, I choose to be a positive influence and agent of change today, raising the bar rather than being dragged down to the lower common denominator. Amen!

MY WAY OR THE HIGH WAY?

1 Kings 18:21

"Elijah went before the people and said, 'How long will you waver between two opinions? If the Lord is God, follow him; but if Baal is God, follow him.' But the people said nothing."

More than 500 people died on 3 January 1944, in a tragic incident, which proved to be one of the worst train disasters in history. It happened in the El Toro Tunnel in Leon, Spain. The train in question was a long passenger train with engines on both ends. On a routine journey, the front engine stalled as the train entered the tunnel. The engineer at the front immediately started it again in order to proceed all the way through the tunnel. But in the meantime the rear engineer had started up his engine to lead the train backwards out of the tunnel. Both engines were pulling in opposite directions, with neither engineer knowing what the other was doing, and without means of communicating with each other. Each one simply thought they needed more power. In the meantime, the hundreds of passengers on the train in the tunnel died of carbon monoxide poisoning because the train couldn't make up its mind which way to go.

The most uncomfortable position to be in is to want to follow Jesus just a little; to give him just a bit of my life; to know what is right and the direction he's calling me in but to choose the guilt-ridden path that goes in the opposite direction. It's the worst of both worlds because you can't fully enjoy all the pleasures of sin and at the same time you know a journey on track with Jesus offers so much more.

Are you wavering today? Which areas of your life are marred by indecision, by holding back, by compromise? Jesus was very clear: "No one can serve two masters" (Matthew 6:24). And within the big spiritual battle that constitutes our lives, there are many mini-battles taking place in the areas of finance, relationships, motivation, and more.

Lord, I choose your high way, not my way, today. Amen!

LIFE OR DEATH?

1 Thessalonians 5:10

"He died for us so that, whether we live or die, we may live together with him."

30

SEPTEMBER

The Johnston family was involved in a serious car crash. The two boys in the rear took the brunt of the damage as a truck piled into the back of them. The eldest, Harry, was in a critical condition and urgently needed a blood transfusion. The logical donor was his younger brother, Peter, who shared the same blood type as Harry. Peter was badly injured himself but not in intensive care like his brother. Dad sat down next to Peter and asked him if he was willing to give some of his blood to help Harry. He explained that they had the same blood type and a transfusion was needed to save his brother's life. Peter was visibly scared but bravely said, "Yes, Dad, I'll give my blood to Mike so he can get well." The nurse gently stuck a needle in his arm, drew out a pint of blood from his vein, and then removed the needle again. As she did so, Peter turned and asked his father with tears rolling down his cheeks, "Daddy, when do I die?" Only then did it dawn on his father that Peter had misunderstood what the process involved, and that he was willing to die to save his brother.

As Paul wrote in Romans 5:7, 8, "Very rarely will anyone die for a righteous man, though for a good man someone might possibly dare to die. But God demonstrates his love for us in this: while we were still sinners, Christ died for us."

The spirit of Christ is sacrifice, of pouring out of ourselves for others. For the majority of us, it most probably won't mean dying, but it will be costly. Could you give a "blood transfusion" of whatever kind to help someone else today?

Lord, use me to bring life to someone today. Amen!

Deuteronomy 3:22

"Do not be afraid of them; the Lord your God himself will fight for you."

FIGHT OR FLIGHT?

Telemachus was a fourth-century monk who felt God calling him to Rome. In obedience, he went there and arrived to find crowds surging through the streets and into the Colosseum. When the gladiators came in and saluted the Emperor, it suddenly dawned on him that they were going to kill each other for sport. He left his seat, jumped over the rail and ran towards the warriors, shouting: "In the name of Christ, stop!" The crowd laughed along until they realized it wasn't part of the show. A gladiator slapped him with his sword, sending Telemachus flying to the ground. He got back up between the two fighters and again declared, "In the name of Christ, stop!" The crowd grew hostile and shouted at the gladiators to finish him off. The same fighter ran him through with his sword, and Telemachus lay down in a pool of blood on the sand. His last feeble dying words were the same again, "In the name of Christ, stop!" Something strange then happened. A hush came over the crowd. One man towards the back stood up and left, and then slowly everyone else did too. The year was AD 391, and that proved to be the last gladiatorial fight to the death in the Colosseum.

Saint Telemachus changed the course of history. And so can we. Never again in that great stadium did men kill each other for the entertainment of the crowd – and it was all because of one tiny voice that could hardly be heard above the tumult. One voice – one life – that spoke the truth in God's name. God is still looking for people willing to move beyond their fears to stand for him and cry out: "In the name of Christ, stop!" Or maybe "Start!"

Spend some time asking the Lord, and then listening, to see what he might want you to stand up for today.

Lord, I choose to fight with and for you today. Amen!

LONG WAY OR SHORT CUT?

1 Samuel 13:8–11

"Then [Saul] waited seven days, according to the time set by Samuel. But Samuel did not come… So Saul… offered the burnt offering. Now it happened, as soon as he had finished presenting the burnt offering, that Samuel came… And Samuel said, 'What have you done?'"

One of the commonest obstacles to success is the desire to cut corners. But short cuts never pay off in the long run. If we find that we continually give in to our moods or impulses, then we need to change our approach to doing things. Cutting corners is really a sign of impatience, laziness, and poor self-discipline. King Saul had no boundaries and didn't stick to God's standards. His lesson to us, learned the hard way, is that we need to apply God's standards of accountability and be accountable to them. This approach will protect us. As Mabel Newcombe wrote, "It's more important to know where you are going than to get there quickly. Do not mistake activity for achievement."

Self-discipline is a quality that is won through practice. So we need to be patient and be sure that the next step fits in with the ultimate goal. As Brian Tracy wrote, "There is never enough time to do everything, but there is always enough time to do the most important thing." Sometimes we're in such a hurry, wanting to climb the ladder of success, without realizing that the ladder's leaning against the wrong wall; and if it's leaning against the wrong wall, every step we take simply moves us further away from where we should be going.

So trust in the Lord and commit your ways to him. And here are some questions for reflection:

- Do you know where you're going today?
- Do you know what the "most important thing" is?
- Is your ladder leaning against the right wall?

Lord, help me choose and live the right answers to the above questions. Amen!

1 John 3:18

"Dear children, let us not love with words or speech but with actions and in truth."

WORDS OR DEEDS?

Every Christian knows, in theory, how to follow Jesus, but actually putting his teachings into practice – well, that's a bit more difficult. Saying that we ought to forgive our enemies is one thing; actually forgiving them is harder. Preaching about evangelism is easy; actually sharing your faith with your neighbour is not. The world knows this full well: actions speak louder than words but, as Mark Twain said, not nearly as often.

One overloaded pastor turned away a homeless lady seeking help, telling her he was too busy, but he assured her he would pray for her. She wrote the following poem and gave it to a local Shelter officer:

I was hungry, and you formed a humanities group to discuss my hunger.
I was imprisoned, and you crept off quietly to your chapel and prayed for my release.
I was naked, and in your mind you debated the morality of my appearance.
I was sick, and you knelt and thanked God for your health.
I was homeless, and you preached a sermon on the spiritual shelter of the love of God.
I was lonely, and you left me alone to pray for me.
You seem so holy, so close to God
But I am still very hungry, and lonely, and cold.

I relate to the pastor in that situation, because I've been in his shoes many times. But sometimes we get too busy, and sometimes BUSY means "Being Under Satan's Yoke". Our world grows weary of armchair prophets who only advise, and talk, and do nothing. But a body of people willing to serve, to give themselves, to forgive, to love – that group of people is enough to change the world.

How about you? Are you ready to "walk your talk"? Jesus did, and he calls us to join him. What might that look like today?

Lord, I choose to walk the walk and not just talk a good game. Amen!

SAFETY OR RISK?

Matthew 16:24, 25

Then Jesus said to his disciples, "If anyone wishes to come after me, he must deny himself, and take up his cross and follow me. For whoever wishes to save his life will lose it; but whoever loses his life for my sake will find it."

Our world loves safety. Our newspapers are full of reports warning us about risks – this food will increase your cholesterol, that country is too dangerous to visit, this new car is safer than that one. We are told what to eat, what to wear, how often to exercise, where to go on holiday – and all with the aim of reducing risk. Avoid bacon. Eat goji berries. Don't go to Afghanistan. Wear goggles before playing conkers. Maybe we should simply never leave the house at all.

The problem for us Christians is that authentic discipleship flies in the face of safety. Following God means that we follow in the footsteps of men who risked everything in his name: Joseph, who ended up in jail; Gideon, who took on an army of thousands with just a few hundred soldiers; John the Baptist, who got his head cut off; the apostle Paul, who suffered repeatedly. Tradition tells us that only one apostle, John, died peacefully. As the German theologian Dietrich Bonhoeffer said, "When Christ calls a man he bids him come and die." And he should know: Bonhoeffer was executed by the Nazis.

When we play it safe we leave little room for God to act. Without risk we don't need to have faith, and without faith then what is our relationship with God? But when we step out in faith, trusting that God is worthy of any sacrifice we might make, then God has a habit of showing up. Following Jesus means putting everything – absolutely everything – on the line.

Our world loves safety. Following Jesus calls for risk. What will it be?

Lord, I choose to take a risk for you today. Amen!

TRUTH OR GRACE?

John 1:14

"The Word became flesh and made his dwelling among us... The one and only Son... came from the Father, full of grace and truth."

Why is it so easy for us humans to lean towards extremes? We easily allow ourselves to get polarized into left or right wing, conservative or liberal, principled or pastoral, and so on. We see it all the time with people or even entire groups being labelled as "harsh" or "soft" on the issues of the day.

Yet when it comes to the Master, John states clearly that Jesus was full of both grace and truth – not one *or* the other but both one *and* the other – not so "gracious" as to avoid the difficult issue, nor so "truthful" as to kick people when they were down. Jesus rebuked a Samaritan woman for her many relationships and yet he did it in such a gracious way that she invited the whole village out to "come and meet the man who told me everything I ever did" (John 4:29). What a strange reaction to someone who spoke the truth! Except that she saw that he spoke the truth with love (Ephesians 4:15).

A few chapters later, a woman caught in the act of adultery was brought to Jesus. He said to those intent on killing her, "If any of you is without sin, let him be the first to throw a stone at her" (John 8:7). It's a phrase loved and quoted out of context by many, but when they do so they often miss the bit that follows, when Jesus turned again to the woman, and said, "Now go and leave your life of sin" (8:11).

Jesus grasped and modelled to us how grace can open the door for truth to then come in. He was full of grace *and* truth. Can you think of a situation in which you erred too far one way or the other that needs rectifying? Go and make amends, and be full of both today!

Lord, I choose to live with lashings of grace and truth. Amen!

WHOLE OR BROKEN?

Psalm 51:17

"My sacrifice, O God, is a broken spirit; a broken and contrite heart you, God, will not despise."

I like being whole. Being broken doesn't appeal to me at all. Yet when everything's going along wonderfully in my life, I often end up ignoring God for long periods. Then it seems to take something getting broken for me to come back to him. It's a pattern the Israelites modelled for us, and in particular David, who wrote the above verse.

I was deeply struck several years ago when I read the following words by John Eldredge: "Until we are broken, our life will be self-centered, self-reliant; our strength will be our own. So long as you think you are really something in and of yourself, what will you need God for? I don't trust a man who hasn't suffered."

Do re-read that last quote.

That doesn't mean we're to go looking for suffering, to want things to go wrong. Life sends enough brokenness our way without seeking it out. And the comforting thing is, as Vance Havner says, "God uses broken things. It takes broken soil to produce a crop, broken clouds to give rain, broken grain to give bread, broken bread to give strength. It is the broken alabaster box that gives forth perfume. It is Peter, weeping bitterly, who returns to greater power than ever."

So brokenness is to be accepted – not fatalistically or with resignation – but with anticipation that the Lord will use it for his purposes. On the subject, Yancey muses, "It seems to me Christians are too busy trying to stuff up the cracks and correct those imperfections. It's all right to try to fix our defects, but if it keeps us away from grace, it's not good. Light only gets in through the cracks." And shines out, we might add.

True wholeness will come eventually and ultimately – but not yet. In the meantime, be encouraged, and allow God to shine his light through your cracks.

Lord, I choose to be used in my brokenness today. Amen!

PHONY FARCE OR CONSISTENT CREED?

1 Thessalonians 2:8

"We loved you so much that we were delighted to share with you not only the gospel of God but our lives as well, because you had become so dear to us."

Graham Cyster was a South African evangelical Christian who was smuggled one night several decades ago into an underground communist cell of young people fighting apartheid. The leader spoke, "Tell us about the gospel of Jesus Christ." At this critical stage of their spiritual development, they seemed to be half hoping for an alternative to the violent communist strategy they were about to embrace. Cyster gave a clear, powerful presentation of the gospel. He showed how personal faith in Christ wonderfully transforms people and creates one new body of believers where there is neither Jew nor Greek, male nor female, rich nor poor, black nor white.

The group listened avidly until he finished his talk. Then one seventeen-year-old exclaimed, "That is wonderful! Show me where I can see that happening." Graham's face fell as he sadly responded that he couldn't think of anywhere in the whole of South Africa where Christians were truly living out the message of the gospel. "Then the whole thing is a piece of sh—!" the young man spat out angrily. Within a month he had left the country to join the armed struggle against apartheid – and eventually paid for it with his life.

That young man was right. How can we claim our faith is alive if we fail to live in a way consistent with our creed? As George Barna reflects, "Christianity has largely failed since the middle of the twentieth century because Jesus' modern-day disciples do not act like Jesus."

Ouch! Well what might we do? Instead of always hanging out with people similar to ourselves, how about actively seeking to befriend a Muslim, someone from a different race, or from a different socio-economic background? And then – and this is an even bigger challenge – invite them into your life such that the above verse is true for you. Now we're talking!

Lord, help me live out what I profess to believe today. Amen!

GEM OR JUNK?

Matthew 13:45, 46

"The kingdom of heaven is like a merchant looking for fine pearls. When he found one of great value, he went away and sold everything he had and bought it."

Mrs Shirley Martin went to the local Salvation Army thrift store in Vancouver and bought a box of buttons for one dollar. Her husband, a postman, was fast asleep one evening as she rummaged through the box. Among the many buttons, something sparkled. It looked like a diamond. She rushed through to the bedroom and woke her husband. "Darling, I think I've found a diamond!" "Oh, come on, dear, you're always having these crazy ideas," he replied, and nodded off again. Mrs Martin took the gem to twelve different jewellers. Some dismissed it as junk (one said it was worth forty-nine cents!), but others shook with excitement when they held it. Hans Reymer gave the gem a valuation of $19,300. Mrs Martin had accidentally come across a precious stone for just one dollar!

What's it worth to follow Jesus all the way? In the above verse, Jesus is showing it makes complete sense to give up everything in order to purchase the fine pearl. The merchant realizes the incredible value of the discovery he has made, and urgently tries to buy it as soon as possible at whatever the cost. Clearly he's not agonizing over the price – no, he knows that what he's discovered is of such immeasurable value that, however long it takes, whatever the effort, whatever the cost, it will be worth it. Consequently his worry isn't the sacrifice he'll have to make to get it, but rather whether someone else will get there first and he'll miss out on such a life-transforming and life-enhancing gift. He does it joyfully, knowing he has more than hit the jackpot. What's it worth? Anything and everything.

Take stock today of the pearl you've found, and your priorities as a result.

Lord, there's so much to be grateful for. I choose to give my all to you today. Amen!

Romans 4:20

"Yet Abraham did not waver through unbelief regarding the promise of God, but was strengthened in his faith."

ACT OR WAVER?

Wrinkly old childless Abraham received an amazing promise in Genesis 12 about leaving his comfort zone and in due time becoming a blessing to all nations through his progeny. He obeyed immediately, not procrastinating, dithering, or wavering. He acted on what God had told him.

In 1964, a 28-year-old woman called Kitty Genovece was attacked in a residential area of New York. She screamed for help for a full thirty minutes before dying from multiple stab wounds. Thirty-eight people heard her cries for help, some even looking out of the window and watched the attack take place, but none of them did anything to intervene, presuming someone else would. The term "bystander apathy" was born from this event.

I wonder what bystander apathy there is in my life. What horrific injustice am I standing by, passively observing, expecting someone else to intervene and rectify? Action must trump apathy or else our faith is deeply flawed. Something needs to be done. William Barclay wrote, "The more often you experience the emotion of doing something without the action of doing something, the less likely that something will ever happen for you." We can meet in groups to discuss doing something, and that experience in itself can be so stimulating that it creates the emotions that we have done something – but we haven't, and it's very likely that we won't do anything. It's like we're waiting for God to do something while *he's waiting for us to do something.*

As in Kitty's case, lives are at stake and we can't afford the luxury of being held back by past hurt, pride, apathy, or embarrassment. I don't think I've ever regretted responding to that sudden inner prompting of the Spirit to intervene in a given situation, even when the outcome wasn't dramatic or extraordinary. But plenty of times I've regretted dithering and disobeying his voice. How about you?

Lord, today I resolve to be alert to your voice and to act on what you say. Amen!

ME OR WE?

Romans 12:5

"So in Christ we who are many form one body and each member belongs to all the others."

An anthropologist proposed a game to a group of children in rural Botswana. He put a basket full of fruit near a tree, and then got them to line up. When he gave the signal, they could all run and see who got to the basket first. The fastest would win all the sweet fruits. When he told them to run, he was shocked by what happened: they all took each other's hands and ran together. They then sat down together sharing and enjoying their treats. When he asked them why they had run like that as one could have had all the fruits for himself, they said in unison, "Ubuntu! How can one of us be happy if all the other ones are sad?"

"Ubuntu" is a word used throughout Southern Africa in slightly different ways, but the most accepted understanding of the term is "I am because we are". It's not a biblical term but it is a biblical value. In Western culture we tend to think as individuals first before we consider our group identity, but in this regard we're in danger of deviating from God's blueprint for humanity. The culture of heaven is a collective one: all of us equal in the eyes of our Father. Heaven's culture says "we" not "me". Interestingly, the most popular version of the open-source computer operating system Linux is called "Ubuntu"!

As a younger sportsman I won trophies in both individual and team sports. You might think that there'd be more joy in the individual triumphs because all the glory and attention is focused on you; in fact, shared team triumphs were always more enjoyable. "We" triumphs over "me". Meaning, purpose, fulfilment, and joy are ultimately found in community rather than individualism.

Take a reality check on your own life. Is it too much about me? How can it become more we?

Lord, help "me" join up with others so that "we" can do life together beautifully. Amen!

Psalm 46:10

"Be still, and know that I am God."

PAUSE OR RUSH?

On a cold winter's morning in January 2008, an experiment was carried out in a Washington metro station to assess the behaviour of commuters. The idea was to analyse people's reactions to a busker playing the violin. Variables such as the beauty of the music and commuter time constraints were focused on to assess levels of musical appreciation. The big deal with this particular experiment was the person playing the violin. It was the famous violin virtuoso Joshua Bell, who only three days before had sold out the Boston Symphony Hall, playing to more than 10,000 people. Now sitting on the floor in the lobby of the metro, he used his 1713 Stradivarius, valued at several million dollars, and played six of his most beautiful pieces of music.

When preparing for the experiment, the metro management thought they might have to draft in extra security to cope with the crowds but a strange thing happened. Out of context, Bell became invisible. A few commuters and a couple of children paused, but the majority of people rushed ahead into their morning, unaware of the treasure in their midst.

It's so easy to get caught up in the busyness of life that we miss the beauty and the blessings of God. We can be so overwhelmed by all the noise bombarding us that we miss his gentle whisper. So Erwin McManus asks, "Will you refuse to be nothing more than an echo in a world full of meaningless noise?" Instead of "Thank God It's Friday", the new TGIF is Twitter, Google, iPhone, Facebook – and it's a culture that enables us to stay in touch, stay on top, stay informed, stay current 24/7 but also makes it almost impossible to encounter deep peace and quiet.

God is speaking all the time. He's a whole lot better and more worth listening to than Joshua Bell on his Stradivarius. Will you just rush on by today?

Lord, help me pause, wait, slow down, and listen attentively to you today. Amen!

INNOVATE OR STAGNATE?

2 Corinthians 3:14–18

"But their minds were made dull, for to this day the same veil remains when the old covenant is read… But whenever anyone turns to the Lord, the veil is taken away… And we, who with unveiled faces all reflect the Lord's glory, are being transformed into his likeness with ever-increasing glory, which comes from the Lord, who is the Spirit."

There is always the part that God does, and then there is the part that we have to do. It's a glorious partnership as we are transformed into his likeness.

On 8 July 2011, NASA launched the space shuttle for the last time. This programme was incredibly innovative and impactful, so why shut it down? The answer was that the cost of maintaining the programme was inhibiting new innovative ideas. We very easily become comfortable with successes and what we are good at, but these are the very things that can cause us to stagnate. As Kevin Kelly said, "Success flows directly from innovation, not optimization. It is not gained by perfecting the known, but by imperfectly seizing the unknown."

Life is a mixture of continuity and change. Too much of the former is stultifying; too much of the latter is overwhelming. Keeping in step with the Spirit means being open to both – not running ahead nor lagging behind. So a good question for us to ask is, "What's next, Lord?" And then more importantly, we need to decide to trust him and either keep on doing what we are already doing, or step into the "unknown" as he directs us. He is faithful and dependable. It's as if a veil covers over our vision when we become too comfortable with where we are in the transformation process. But if we keep our eyes on Jesus, we'll see that we have a long way to go to perfection. Then, as we turn to the Lord (the bit we do), he will take us to the next step, as we follow his lead.

Lord, I choose to keep in step with you today. Amen!

RESPONSIBLE OR POWERLESS?

Deuteronomy 30:19

"This day I call heaven and earth as witnesses against you that I have set before you life and death, blessings and curses. Now choose life!"

From 1933 to 1937, Viktor Frankl completed his residency in neurology and psychiatry at the Steinhof Psychiatric Hospital in Vienna. But it was during the war when he ended up in a Nazi concentration camp that his new found specialism developed. It was a freedom that his aggressors could not take away from him. He discovered that he could always find meaning in any situation, however sordid, and therefore a reason for living. He wrote, "Between stimulus and response there is a space. In that space is our power to choose our response. In our response lies our growth and our freedom." Now, when someone has been through what he has been through and has walked the talk in such horrific circumstances, I'm inclined to believe him. It was clear to him that life is full of choices. We're making choices every day and we often don't know it. Something happens to us and we react. In that split second, we've chosen, albeit instinctively, to react that way.

Another man who suffered years of imprisonment was Alexander Solzhenitsyn. He made a similar point, "I discovered I always have choices and sometimes it's only a choice of attitude… A man is happy so long as he chooses to be happy and nothing can stop him." These are challenging words forged in the crucible of suffering.

So if the last of our human freedoms is the ability to choose one's attitude in a given set of circumstances, will we take responsibility (note we are "response-able") for our attitudes, actions and choices today?

Our wonderful source of life instruction is the word of God – the Bible. Whether we choose to take these instructions seriously or not, we're actually making a choice either way. We can't get away from it. Freedom was high on Victor Frankl's agenda, but responsibility was even higher. He believed it is our responsibility to choose our reaction. How about you?

Lord, I choose love, joy, peace, patience, kindness, goodness, faithfulness, gentleness and self-control today. Amen!

DESTINY OR DESPAIR?

Esther 4:14

"Who knows but that you have come to your royal position for such a time as this?"

14

OCTOBER

God plucked Esther from obscurity and placed her in a unique position, as queen in a foreign land, to save her people from annihilation. That was her destiny and calling, which she stepped into and lived out for his glory and the liberation of the Jews. The prospective outcome didn't look promising, but the Sovereign Lord orchestrated events to accomplish his purposes in his time.

Without a belief that God has plans for us – a destiny (which he does, see Jeremiah 29:11) – we can easily give way to despair. The circumstances we face can either help or hinder us depending on how we respond to them. But, as the saying goes, whatever doesn't kill you makes you stronger. Despair stems from a lack of hope and expectation of breakthrough. What is it that keeps us trudging through the mud of despair and how can we make sure we don't get sucked down into it? Hope is the answer. Napoleon said that "a leader is a dealer in hope". He understood the need for a team to be encouraged and uplifted with the antidote to despair.

In Tolkien's *Lord of the Rings* trilogy, a small hobbit called Frodo Baggins becomes an unlikely hero in a tale of destiny, adventure, and good versus evil. He has many dark days in his quest to destroy the evil ring but is supported and encouraged throughout by his companions. As "the darkest hour is before dawn", Legolas the elf at one stage says as much: "Oft hope is born when all is forlorn".

Do you feel hopeless or hopeful about your destiny, about your longings, aspirations, and dreams? Don't despair! Ask the Lord for someone to come alongside you on your journey, to bring hope and encouragement when you need it. He hears your prayers, reads your thoughts, knows your needs, and answers in his time and in his wisdom. Trust him!

Lord, I choose to maintain my trust in you today. Amen!

INFLUENCED OR INFLUENCER?

Matthew 5:14, 15

"You are the light of the world. A town built on a hill cannot be hidden. Neither do people light a lamp and put it under a bowl. Instead they put it on its stand, and it gives light to everyone in the house."

One of the lists on the toptens.com website is the world's top ten most influential people of all time. The list includes the apostle Paul, Buddha, Gandhi, Confucius, and Einstein. Jesus Christ is at number one. How is it that a carpenter from Galilee, who only spent three years teaching those around him, is still being cited as the number one most influential person of all time?

Influence is the ability to alter or sway an individual or a group's thoughts, beliefs, and actions. How did Jesus do it? Did he fit in with the movers and shakers and try to influence from within? Did he suck up to those in authority to gain leverage for his cause? Did he preach a message that made his listeners feel good about themselves? Was he so attractive and charismatic that people just wanted to follow him to bask in his reflected glory? No, he preached and embodied a countercultural, simple message of repentance, humility, hope, and healing. His authentic demonstration of costly love was so attractive to the sick, the marginalized, and the disenfranchised that the news spread far and wide to the nations through the centuries.

So, what about us? Are we blinded by the bling, convinced by the crowds, followers of fads, and tuned in to trouble? Do we bring a message of hope and healing or of drudgery and despair? Do our friends seek us out for encouragement or to share gossip? Do we give off a fragrant aroma or a putrid stench? Do we raise the bar or slip to the lowest common denominator?

Lord, I choose with your help to shine brightly for you today, to radiate hope, to influence those I come into contact with positively for your glory. Amen!

CELEBRITY OR SERVANT?

Philippians 2:7

"He made himself nothing by taking the very nature of a servant."

Have you noticed what the above verse is saying? Compare it with what is said about Jesus in verse 6: "… being in very nature God". Those words "in very nature" mean "having the essential characteristics of". In verse 6 we might say that Jesus has all the Godness of God: all that makes God "God", Jesus is. Then in verse 7, Jesus takes the essential characteristics of a bond slave – what a come down! All that makes a bond slave, Jesus became. He had neither rights nor status. Legally he was not so much a person but a thing, someone's possession. Those words "made himself nothing" in some versions are translated as "he emptied himself". What a sharp contrast to our society in which there is a strong tendency not to empty ourselves but to puff ourselves up, like amorous male frogs seeking to impress their ladies – with appearance triumphing over substance.

John 13:3–5 says: "Jesus knew that the Father had put all things under his power… so he… took off his outer clothing, and wrapped a towel round his waist… he poured water into a basin and began to wash his disciples' feet". The verse suggests that it was because of Jesus' power that He chose to do the most demeaning task. Astonishing! In a Jewish household, washing guests' feet was done by a gentile bond slave as it was considered too lowly a task for a Jewish slave.

To what extent is the servant nature of Christ exhibited in me? Do I serve Christ content with an audience of One to please? Am I hurt if what I do does not receive due recognition? Do I resent it if others get preference over me? Do I give money provided I control how it is spent or I can see my name on a metaphorical or literal plaque? Or do I give first and foremost to him?

Lord, make me humble and express through me your servant heart today. Amen!

John 17:15

"My prayer is not that you take them out of the world but that you protect them from the evil one."

INSULATED OR ISOLATED?

Jesus had just eaten his last meal with his disciples, knowing that within twenty-four hours he would be hanging on a cross. We can be sure that what he prayed for them was of the utmost importance to him. What did he ask for them? That they would not be taken out of the world – that is, become isolated from it – but that they would remain in the world, insulated from its corrupting influences, and witness to him. Jesus instructed them (and us) to go into all the world and tell others about him. Often we invite "the world" to leave their comfort zone and come to ours. But that's the opposite of what Jesus did. He wants us to leave the place and environment where we feel at ease and get alongside those who do not yet know him, to be with them where they are geographically, culturally, in their pain, hurt, alienation, and so on.

Jesus has another name – Emmanuel – "God with us", not "God way up there". John wrote of Jesus in 1:14: "The Word became flesh and blood, and moved" – where to? – "into our neighbourhood" (*The Message*). Too often our reaction to the challenge of living in the world is to retreat out of it. We become negative towards the place where God has put us, denying by our attitudes the fact that God is Creator and Sovereign. We are the incarnation of the gospel to our family, neighbours, colleagues, fellow students, and whoever we happen to meet. For many we are possibly the first and only evidence of the reality of the grace of God.

If that is indeed the case – that I am the first, perhaps only, evidence of the truth of the good news of salvation for many, how convincing or compelling am I in what I say and do? Food for thought…

God, use me out there in the world today. Amen!

DIRTY OR CLEAN?

Matthew 8:3

"Jesus reached out his hand and touched the man. 'I am willing,' he said. 'Be clean!'"

In 2005, a sixteen-year-old girl called Katie Davis, left her comfortable middle-class life in Tennessee, to go to an orphanage in Uganda. Three years later she set up her own orphanage and adopted fourteen children. Her life in the USA was comfortable and clean. Although she grew up in a Christian family, she only prayed for her own comfort. Her dad went to visit her in Uganda to persuade her to come home, to leave behind the filth, stench, and sickness. But Katie knew God had called her to live and breathe and minister in that dirt. She left America as a princess but was soon washing off thick layers of dirt and filth from the poorest and most helpless in society.

Jesus knew what it was to leave the throne of heaven and to come and touch the unclean. It's easy to follow the world's view and to look at the outward appearance, at how clean people are. But God looks at the heart (1 Samuel 16:7). He's not bothered by a squeaky clean image, rather he's after a longing heart.

Katie Davis soon realized that she couldn't tell the street children in her orphanage that God loves them, because most were completely unaware of the concept of love. Instead she had to clean and hug and cradle and caress her filthy and smelly children so that they gradually learned that she loved them. Then she told them about their heavenly Father.

Few of us are called to live in slums, but all of us are called to see beyond the dirt of the homeless, the smell of elderly incontinent, and even the masks of the self-sufficient – to see the person made in the image of God, and love them unconditionally. It's about cleaning others by humbling and going beyond ourselves, and getting our hands dirty.

Lord, I choose to get dirty for you today. Amen!

John 15:4

"Remain in me, and I will remain in you."

STRIVING OR ABIDING?

In the 1940s, Eric "Bash" Nash started holiday camps for boys at Britain's top boarding schools. They had a huge influence in due course on the Church of England, raising up future leaders like John Stott, Nicky Gumbel, Archbishop Justin Welby, and many more. Indeed those camps were used to bring me to faith as well.

When he was training as a young ordinand at Ridley Hall, Bash would rarely turn up to the daily morning service in chapel; and those times he did, he'd inevitably arrive late. One morning after chapel his tutor knocked on his door and found Bash still curled up in bed. From beneath the covers Bash muttered, "It's about abiding, man!"

Do you tend more towards striving or abiding? Striving is necessary at times of course, but abiding is no less so, and is invariably sacrificed when we find ourselves under pressure.

As a church community, we can end up striving to do all the ministries possible, such that to the outsider, our church looks busy and successful. We have groups from the cot to the grave, for both genders, meetings every night of the week; we have prayer groups before breakfast and run every conceivable course on evangelism and discipleship. And yet we still seem to plateau and tread water, and despite all the striving, to make little progress.

Sometimes we need to forget how we look, forget what others will think, forget about being accessible to anyone at any time, and instead to take a rest in the green meadows and beside the peaceful streams that David talks about in Psalm 23. It's there that our strength is renewed and restored to then re-enter the fray.

Here's a good question to reflect on today: Is your striving a joyful reflection of God's grace and your abiding a disciplined communion with Christ?

Lord, I choose to remain in you today. Thank you that you will remain in me. Amen!

COMMANDS OR SUGGESTIONS?

Psalm 119:60

"I will hasten and not delay to obey your commands."

If God has spoken, we must not delay, put off, or procrastinate. We must act. Oswald Chambers said, "Never intend to look up a word. *Do it now.*" He knew from experience that intentions – however well-meant – do not necessarily lead to actions. We can all relate to feeling a deep sense of conviction at certain moments and resolving to do something about it, but then drifting along and never actually enacting what the Lord had been leading us to do.

In William Booth's last speech to the Salvation Army, explaining the immediacy and urgency of his actions, he bellowed:

> *While women weep, as they do now, I'll fight. While little children go hungry, as they do now, I'll fight. While men go to prison, in and out, in and out, as they do now, I'll fight. While there is a drunkard left, while there is a poor lost girl upon the streets, while there remains one dark soul without the light of God, I'll fight – I'll fight to the very end!*

What has God been challenging you about this past month? What do you sense he's asking you to do? Do it now! As both student and teacher, I've been told and have taught that unless we put into practice the skills being explained at the time within a week, we will never do them at all. Do you agree? Can you think of an instance in your own life where good intentions have remained just that, with no follow-through at all? Here's the thing: if we wait until we feel ready, until all our ducks are in a row, until we have time, until the circumstances are just right, we will never do anything. The danger is we end up treating his commands as mere suggestions.

Lord, forgive my disobedience, my putting off doing what you've asked of me, my treating your commands as mere suggestions. I choose to obey you today. Amen!

Numbers 13:33

"There we saw the giants, and we were like grasshoppers in our own sight, and so we were in their sight." (NKJV)

GIANT OR GRASSHOPPER?

When the twelve spies went to check out the Promised Land, they all saw the same things. They all saw the huge fruit, the huge walls, and the huge men! The only difference was in their attitudes. Ten were fearful; two were fearless! Caleb's attitude was, "Let's go take them down!" He had faith in his God and himself to get the job done. The trouble was that the rest of the people heard the bad report and were scared. They listened to the fearful ones and not the faith-filled ones. They tested God's patience and ended up in the wilderness for another forty years.

How many opportunities do we miss because we look through eyes of fear and not faith? Like the Israelites when confronted by Goliath, they and David had two options: they chose to look at Goliath through the eyes of man and saw he was too big to beat, while David looked at him through the eyes of God and saw he was too big to miss.

Christopher Reeve, the actor who played Superman, was paralyzed from the neck down in a horse-riding accident in 1995. After his accident, he made this comment: "When the first Superman movie came out I was frequently asked, 'What is a hero?' I remember the glib response I repeated so many times. My answer was that a hero is someone who commits a courageous action without considering the consequences – a soldier who crawls out of a foxhole to drag an injured buddy to safety. Now my definition is completely different. I think a hero is an ordinary individual who finds strength to persevere and endure in spite of overwhelming obstacles."

What are you up against today? Choose to find your strength, perseverance, and endurance from God, so that you likewise will enter your Promised Land.

Lord, help me live by faith today, knowing with you I can do whatever you call me to. Amen!

AFRAID OR UNAFRAID?

Psalm 118:6

"The Lord is with me, I will not be afraid. What can people do to me?"

22

OCTOBER

Many of us experience times of feeling afraid, out of control, in danger, or under threat. Promises like the verse above can help us handle such situations better. If you feed those fears, your faith will starve; but if you feed your faith, your fears will starve instead.

Max Lucado writes insightfully on the effects of living in fear:

> *Fear creates a form of spiritual amnesia. It dulls our miracle memory. It makes us forget what Jesus has done and how good God is. And fear feels dreadful. It sucks the life out of the soul, curls us into an embryonic state, and drains us dry of contentment. We become abandoned barns, rickety and tilting from the winds, a place where humanity used to eat, thrive, and find warmth. No longer. When fear shapes our lives, safety becomes our god. When safety becomes our god, we worship the risk-free life. Can the safety lover do anything great? Can the risk-averse accomplish noble deeds? For God? For others? No. The fear-filled cannot love deeply. Love is risky. They cannot give to the poor. Benevolence has no guarantee of return. The fear-filled cannot dream wildly. What if their dreams sputter and fall from the sky? The worship of safety emasculates greatness. No wonder Jesus wages such a war against fear.*
>
> *His most common command emerges from the "fear not" genre. The Gospels list some 125 Christ-issued imperatives. Of these, 21 urge us to "not be afraid" or "not fear" or "have courage" or "take heart" or "be of good cheer". The second most common command, to love God and neighbour, appears on only eight occasions. If quantity is any indicator, Jesus takes our fears seriously. The one statement he made more than any other was this: don't be afraid.*

Lord, I resolve to feed my faith, not my fears, today. Thank you for all your promises. Thank you that I don't need to live in fear. Help me live full of faith. Amen!

Jeremiah 29:11

"'For I know the plans I have for you,' declares the Lord."

DESTINY OR CHANCE?

Destiny is not a matter of chance, it's a matter of choice. Life is a succession of choices we make – either consulting God in the process or going our own way.

Dallas Willard wrote in *The Divine Conspiracy*:

> *We should not think of ourselves as destined to be celestial bureaucrats, involved eternally in celestial "adminisitrivia". That would be only slightly better than being caught in an everlasting church service. No, we should think of our destiny as being absorbed in a tremendously creative team effort, with unimaginably splendid leadership, on an inconceivably vast plane of activity, with ever more comprehensive cycles of productivity and employment. This is the "eye hath not seen, neither ear heard" that lies before us in the prophetic vision of Isaiah 64:4.*

That's worth re-reading and meditating on!

God has plans for each one of us. We all have a role to play. Sometimes it may not seem very glamorous, but the glamorous roles are usually overrated. As Vaclav Havel wrote, "The real test of a man is not when he plays the role that he wants for himself, but when he plays the role destiny has for him."

St Francis of Assisi wrote in "Letters to the Rulers of the People":

> *Keep a clear eye toward life's end. Do not forget your purpose and destiny as God's creature. What you are in his sight is what you are and nothing more. Remember that when you leave this earth, you can take with you nothing that you have received – fading symbols of honour, trappings of power – but only what you have given: a full heart enriched by honest service, love, sacrifice, and courage.*

Spend some time with God today, asking him if you're on track and headed in the right direction.

Lord, I choose to live faithfully the role you've given me. Amen!

TIPS AND TECHNIQUES OR INTIMATE DESPERATION?

Psalm 42:1

"As the deer pants for streams of water, so my soul pants for you, O God."

The deer's life depends on water – especially when being pursued by hunters, as the psalmist was by his oppressors. Hence the desperation and panting. How desperate are you today?

John Eldredge writes:

> *Either we wake to tackle our "to do" list, get things done, guided by our morals and whatever clarity we may at the moment have. Or we wake in the midst of a dangerous Story, as God's intimate ally, following him into the unknown.*
>
> *If you're not pursuing a dangerous quest with your life, well, then, you don't need a Guide. If you haven't found yourself in the midst of a ferocious war, then you won't need a seasoned Captain. If you've settled in your mind to live as though this is a fairly neutral world and you are simply trying to live your life as best you can, then you can probably get by with the Christianity of tips and techniques. Maybe. I'll give you about a fifty-fifty chance. But if you intend to live in the Story that God is telling ,and if you want the life he offers, then you are going to need more than a handful of principles, however noble they may be. There are too many twists and turns in the road ahead, too many ambushes waiting only God knows where, too much at stake. You cannot possibly prepare yourself for every situation. Narrow is the way, said Jesus, how shall we be sure to find it? We need God intimately, and we need him desperately.*

I have driven along roads on which others have been ambushed and killed. I always drove along such dangerous stretches with a heightened perception of reality. I meant it when I prayed for safety. I was desperate. I was on my guard and alert. May you likewise recognize the potential seriousness of what lies ahead. Tips and techniques won't be enough.

Lord, help me see how desperately I need you today. Amen!

WIN OR LOSE?

Luke 9:25

"What good is it for a man to gain the whole world and yet lose or forfeit his very self?"

What is winning, and what is losing? Back in the fourth century, St Ambrose reflected: "Our whole Roman world had gone dead in its heart because it feared tragedy, took flight from suffering, and abhorred failure. In fear of tragedy, we worshipped power. In fear of suffering, we worshipped security. During the rising splendour of our thousand years, we had grown cruel, practical, and sterile. We did win the whole world, but in the process, we lost our souls."

In contrast, there was a beautiful incident in the Washington Special Olympics in 1976 when a group of special needs children set out to run the 100m. When the starting gun sounded, they all took off down the track. About halfway along, one boy tripped and tumbled a few times before landing in a heap, crying. Another runner, a girl with Downs Syndrome, stopped and gave the boy a kiss to make it better. Another child also turned back and gave the injured boy a hug. The children then walked with their fallen friend to the finish line. While they didn't win the race, they won the hearts of all the spectators, and the event is still talked about to this day.

The Bible compares life to a race. We're told to set our face towards the finish line, to be focused and undistracted as we press on – but if we miss those who are hurting as we run past, we've somehow missed the point of our existence. The children in the race were not interested in the glory or honour of a big finish. They were interested in each other. I wonder if sometimes God is waiting to see if we will lay down our own agenda, prioritize people over our own pursuits, and get down on our knees to hug the hurting of this world. Could you do that today?

Lord, teach me what you consider true winning and losing to be. Amen!

HEAVEN OR HELL?

Deuteronomy 30:19

"I have set before you life and death, blessings and curses. Now choose life!"

One day a successful female executive was knocked down by a bus and killed. She found herself at the Pearly Gates with St Peter. He said to her: "Before we let you in to heaven, we'll let you experience twenty-four hours in both heaven and hell, and then you can choose." The woman said she knew already what she wanted, but he insisted. So she got into the lift and went down to hell.

The door opened and she stepped out into a beautiful country club. Old friends and new ones rushed up and hugged her. She was the centre of the party, and absolutely loved it. The food, the dancing, the jokes – the whole experience surpassed her wildest dreams. Soon enough the day was over. She was blown away.

Her twenty-four hours in heaven were delightful as well, but when she found herself back in front of St Peter and needing to make her decision, she surprised herself by saying: "You know, heaven was wonderful, truly it was. But I have to say hell was simply out of this world. I never thought I'd hear myself saying this, but I think I'm going to choose hell." "Are you sure?" asked St Peter. Down she went in the lift for the second and last time. When it opened, there was no more country club. Her former friends were there, but this time in rags scavenging for food in the filth. She screamed and tried to get back into the lift, but it was shut. The Devil came up to her and put his arm around her. "I don't understand," she stammered. The Devil looked at her and smiled: "Yesterday we were recruiting you, today you're staff…"

If you're looking for sound theology, the above story's somewhat lacking – but it makes a strong point. We're all responsible for our choices. Things are not as they seem. Choose well today.

Lord, I choose life. Help me help others do the same. Amen!

Deuteronomy 33:27

"The eternal God is your refuge, and underneath are the everlasting arms."

FAITH OR COMMITMENT?

One bleak night in Putney there was a fire on a housing estate. All the family members were able to make their way through the smoke-filled rooms and into the courtyard except a five-year-old boy. He found himself cut off in the upper bedroom, and sat crying by the window and rubbing his eyes. His desperate father tried running back in but was beaten back by the flames. He looked up to his son and yelled, "Son, jump! I'll catch you." Through the billowing smoke and in between the sobs, the little boy bleated, "But I can't see you." His father answered with great assurance: "No, Son, you can't, but I can see you!" The boy jumped and landed safely in his father's arms. He had faith in his father, but when he jumped he made a commitment.

Whenever I'm in situations outside of my control, I'm comforted by the thought of the size of God's hands! He's got the whole world in his hands, so they're big enough to catch me when I'm in free-fall. When he says "Jump", I can be confident of the result. He is our refuge, as the verse says, and underneath are his everlasting arms. Sometimes, however, despite the head knowledge or mental assent (faith) to the fact that he will catch us, we refuse to commit to the jump. We want to remain in control even when it's long been wrested from us.

Whatever you're facing today – financial issues, relational problems, health concerns, or whatever – commit them fully to God. Trust him with them. Put yourself in his hands. Be comforted that with him you will get through.

Lord, today, I choose to cast all my anxieties on you, because you care for me. Amen!

DENIAL OR CONFRONTATION?

Ephesians 4:15

"... speaking the truth in love..."

28

OCTOBER

An old story tells of a desert nomad who woke up hungry during the night. He lit a candle and began eating dates from a bowl he'd placed next to his bed. He took his first bite and saw a worm in it, so he threw it out of his tent. He bit into a second date, and to his dismay found another worm, so he threw it away too. Reasoning that he wouldn't have any dates left to eat if he continued, he blew out the candle and quickly ate all the remaining ones!

Many there are who prefer darkness and denial to the light of reality. In another incident, Charles Capewell was with his son on BA flight 009 from Australia to Indonesia a few years ago. Suddenly, above the Indian Ocean, the Boeing 747 encountered problems. They oxygen masks fell down and there were shrieks and gasps throughout the cabin. The captain's voice came on the intercom, "Ladies and gentlemen, this is your captain speaking. We have a small problem. All four engines have stopped. We are doing our best to get them going again. Please remain calm." The son looked out of the window and saw flames coming from the engine. "Dad, the engine's on fire!" Charles responded, "Well you'd better pull the blind down and pretend it's not happening."

Throughout history, people have been in denial. Some deny the holocaust ever took place, others in our day deny the reality of melting polar icecaps – because confronting the facts seems too daunting. But ignoring them doesn't make them disappear, however much Mr Capewell or the desert nomad might wish them to.

We often find it difficult to be emotionally honest. Confrontation might cause total breakdown, ructions, and further damage. It seems easier to minimize or ignore the issues altogether. Are you choosing denial on any level today? Is there a situation where confrontation is called for? Do so wisely, firmly, gently, prayerfully.

Lord, help me face the facts and deal with any tricky situations that need confrontation today. Amen!

Ephesians 4:27

"Do not give the Devil a foothold."

PEG OR PEGLESS?

The context of the above verse is dealing with anger so that we don't give the Devil the chance to make damaging inroads in our lives, but there are many other ways he can use to take us down.

A Haitian pastor illustrated the need for total commitment to Christ with this parable: A certain man wanted to sell his house for $5,000. Another man desperately wanted to buy it, but because he was poor, he couldn't afford the full asking price. After much haggling, the owner agreed to sell the house for half the original price with just one stipulation – he would retain ownership of one small nail protruding from just over the door. Several years later, the original owner wanted the house back, but the new owner quite naturally didn't want to sell. So first the owner went out, found the carcass of a dead dog, and hung it from the nail he still owned. Soon the house became unliveable, and the family was forced to sell the house to the owner of the nail. The Haitian pastor's conclusion was as follows: "If we leave the Devil with even one small peg in our life, he will return to hang his rotting garbage on it, making it unfit for Christ's habitation."

What is your biggest weakness? Is it pornography, low self-esteem, or greed? Is it gossip, jealousy, or resentment? Is it your tongue, your eyes, or your stomach? Is it money, sex, or power? Don't let the enemy stick a rotting carcass over the gateposts of your life.

Sometimes, our biggest strengths can be our greatest weakness, if we succumb to pride and complacency in that area. A famous and gifted pastor once said, "The one area the enemy will never get me is my marriage." Sadly one night after a speaking engagement, he fell in that very area in the loneliness of his hotel.

Lord, I don't want to leave a single peg for Satan to use against me. Help me be totally yours today. Amen!

FLEX OR FLAB?

Proverbs 27:17

"Iron sharpens iron as one man sharpens another."

In the nineteenth century, with the dawn of worldwide travel, rich Californians spent more and more time in Europe. There they developed an insatiable appetite for Atlantic salmon. However, this caused a real problem for them. The Panama Canal hadn't been built yet – it was only finished in 1914 – so in order to get to California from the Atlantic Ocean, ships would have to sail right around the Cape Horn of South America carrying tanks of live salmon. Many salmon died en route and the ones that made it lost muscle tone and didn't taste as good as they did back in Europe. Eventually, an ingenious solution was found. The sailors were instructed to throw a few northern pike into the tank of young salmon. This changed everything. While a few salmon got eaten on the way, the rest arrived toned and healthy as they outswam their natural predator.

This is a true story with a simple moral: conflict can be good for us. It can keep us toned and sharp. As we flex and manoeuvre through the difficulties of life, we become strong and fit for purpose. Hopefully you can look back and think of times when trials came your way, you dealt with them appropriately, and grew through the process. Having a northern pike on your tail sometimes is a good thing!

That incredibly irritating colleague or family member could just be God's instrument to help you work on your impatience. That insurmountable obstacle could be God's offer of partnership in the process of overcoming. That apparent humiliation could be God's invitation to the school of character formation. You might struggle to do this, but how about trying to praise God for the people who get up your nose, or the situation that requires increasing self-control? Choose to redeem their negative influence on your life by seeing them as dumb-bells to your character – then pick them up and get pumping!

Lord, I choose to take each experience today and use it to sharpen me rather than make me blunt and ineffective. Amen!

Ephesians 5:16

"... making the most of every opportunity."

INTERRUPTION OR OPPORTUNITY?

Billy Graham once said, "Life is filled with interruptions – some insignificant, others life-changing."

In 1997, I experienced a life-changing one. I was travelling in Egypt with some friends, and our journey was interrupted for a number of days by red-tape. It was hugely frustrating to have our plans and schedule so thoroughly inconvenienced, but there was nothing we could do but wait. In the meantime we hired some donkeys and saw some sights, along with a few other tourists. As I was talking to one of them, a huge South African, I detected something vaguely familiar in his eyes: "Did you do all your schooling in South Africa?" "Yes, apart from three years at a prep-school in Buckinghamshire." It was only then that it struck me. He was my tennis partner when I was twelve years old!

That God-incident led to him changing his holiday plans, joining us at church in Cairo, then doing an Alpha Course in London, getting converted, leaving merchant banking, and starting a dynamic charity back in South Africa called Starfish, which has changed the lives of tens of thousands of orphans. Thank God for that interruption to our plans, which proved to be such an opportunity for rekindling a friendship and further down the line leading to so many changed lives!

Jesus' three years of ministry were characterized by multiple interruptions on his journeys. In Mark 5, he was on his way to pray for Jairus' dying daughter when he was interrupted by a woman who touched his cloak in the hope of being healed. Rather than sticking rigidly to his fixed schedule, he seized the interruption and transformed it into a teaching opportunity as well as a time to bring healing and restoration.

This week, you will face "interruptions". Try to walk so close to Jesus that you come to see some of them as opportunities in disguise.

Lord, feel free to interrupt me today in any way so that I can be used by you. Amen!

BACA OR BLESSING?

Psalm 84:6

"As they pass through the valley of Baca, they make it a place of springs."

The Atchafalya Swamp in Mississippi is a body of water 9 miles wide and stretching for 120 miles. It's made up of swampland, bayous, and small grass marshes. This makes it a pleasant place for parasites, snakes, and alligators. In the 1800s, slaves who ran away would flee to such a place. You see, it was so awful no tobacco merchant, cotton trader, or hired foreman dared follow.

Mark Buchanan talks of a place called "borderland" where many of us find ourselves. It's not quite the Atchafalya Swamp, nevertheless it sounds pretty grim. He writes:

> *Most Christians I know are stuck. We feel caught in jobs we barely endure and often despise, in relationships that plunder us and baffle us and deepen rather than remove our aloneness, in activities that are soul-wizening in their triviality and yet insatiably addictive. We squander jewels and hoard baubles. We experience harrowing emotions over mere trifles and can barely muster a dull ache over matters of shattering tragedy. We feel we've no time and no energy for the things that we know matter deeply, even eternally, but waste much time in silly and stultifying diversions. We gossip, even though we've made repeated resolves not to. We read* People *magazine, maybe even* Playboy, *and futureshop flyers, but not our Bible much. We feel that everyone else has more money, longer vacations, newer cars, nicer clothes, and fewer things going wrong with their hot water tanks, automobiles, and children than we do.*

In the verse above, we're reminded that "Baca" (or maybe "borderland") doesn't have to be a place of death. God's people, who "dwell in your house... ever praising you... whose strength is in you" (verses 4, 5), can transform it into "a place of springs", of blessing. That is in fact part of our job description. We are where we are for a reason. God wants to use us today, so let's choose a good attitude and be available.

Lord, help me turn my "Baca" into a blessing today. Amen!

PRIORITIZING OR HAPHAZARD?

Isaiah 32:8

"But the noble man makes noble plans and by noble deeds he stands."

Scottish author Ian Banks, aged fifty-nine, on finding out he had terminal cancer, said he was overwhelmed by all the support he received from the public and fellow writers. Ian then proposed to his long-term girlfriend with the words: "Will you do me the honour of becoming my widow?" Like many of those who have been given not much longer to live, Mr Banks kept a sense of humour but also found a sense of urgency and the need to formalize what mattered most to him.

The only certain thing in life is death. That need not be a fearful concept, but rather one that brings focus. One advantage of living in a warzone surrounded by death for many years was an awareness of the fragility of my life. When someone said they were going to kill me, I actually felt very alive at that moment and wanted to continue to do so! It made me prioritize and invest in what mattered. Time became a precious commodity. People were likewise precious, but not a commodity themselves. It made me analyse relationships and get my house in order. Unfinished conversations or damaging situations needed confronting and closure. In contrast, peacetime deceives us into drifting along, devoid of urgency, addressing situations haphazardly.

If you had to do an audit of your personal world today, would you be at peace? Your priorities are what you spend most of your time, money, and energy thinking about and pursuing. Here are some questions to help you sharpen your focus:

- What am I spending most of my time, money, and energy on at this stage of my life, i.e. what are my priorities?
- Do they fit in well and are they consistent with my values and who I want to be?
- If not, what am I going to do about it to rectify the situation?

Don't live out those questions in isolation. Tell someone, so they can hold you accountable.

Lord, help me choose good priorities today. Amen!

John 1:42

"Andrew brought him to Jesus."

UP FRONT OR BEHIND THE SCENES?

We don't hear much about Andrew in the Gospels, apart from the fact that he was always busy behind the scenes bringing people to Jesus (6:8; 12:22), while his brother, Simon Peter, was much more high profile as the upfront leader of the early church. Much as many of us would like to gain kudos and credit, we can't all be Simon Peters, but we can all do what Andrew did – we can bring people to Jesus.

Albert McMakin was a 24-year-old farmer who had become a follower of Jesus. He was so excited by his faith that whenever possible he would fill his truck with people to take them to the latest outreach to hear the gospel. There was one neighbouring farmer's son who was very resistant to his invitations. He was good-looking and was constantly falling in and out of love with the local ladies, who proved a greater draw than evangelistic meetings. Eventually, Albert managed to talk this young man into coming by asking him to drive the truck. They arrived at the church and Albert was thrilled that his reluctant guest decided to go in. The gospel presentation convicted the young man to his core, and he came back night after night before taking the plunge and giving his life to Christ. The year was 1934. The young driver of the truck was Billy Graham. Nobody led more people to the Lord in the twentieth century than him.

Choose to be an Andrew today. You don't have to be confident. You don't have to have all the answers. Just be the authentic you and allow God to use you. I remember being turned down and "wasting" time walking across town to pick up a similarly reluctant young man to take to a meeting who stood me up, but who did eventually respond to a later invitation and is now an active fisher of men. You received an invitation and accepted it – now get offering it to others!

Lord, use me today, this week, this month, to bring someone to Jesus. Amen!

WANTED IT UNWANTED?

Deuteronomy 7:7, 8

"The Lord did not set his affection on you and choose you because you were more numerous than other peoples, for you were the fewest of all peoples. But it was because the Lord loved you..."

4 NOVEMBER

Johnny Lingo was a wealthy young entrepreneur living on the Polynesian island of Nurabi. He was in love with Mahana, who lived on the neighbouring island of Kiriwadi. Objectively speaking, Mahana's looks could at best be described as "plain". So her father was delighted she had found a suitor. The tradition on Kiriwadi stated that a man had to bargain for his future wife with his potential father-in-law by offering cows. The usual price for a bride was four cows. The most beautiful young ladies went for six cows. Sam Korad, Mahana's father, had decided to ask for two cows but would be willing to settle for one. On the day of trading, the two respective families gathered around in anticipation. They were astonished when Johnny Lingo arrived and offered eight cows for Mahana! They wondered why a smart trader would waste so many cows so unnecessarily...

... but six months later, they discovered the reason. Mahana had become the most beautiful woman in all the islands, thriving as she loved and served her husband. She had been given value, and she had blossomed.

We all have the same value in the eyes of Jesus Christ. We're all eight-cow saints! He paid exactly the same great price for you as he paid for me, for the apostle Paul, or for Billy Graham. The great theologian Paul Tillich used to say, "Accept the fact that you are accepted." When you do so, you will thrive, and you will accept other people around you as well, and serve them – and they won't owe you anything, and you won't mind that at all. That's the beautiful fruit and security that comes from knowing you are accepted, valued and wanted.

Lord, I choose to blossom today in the knowledge of how accepted, valued and wanted I am by you. Amen!

Ephesians 2:6

"God raised us up with Christ and seated us with him in the heavenly realms in Christ Jesus."

UNDER OR OVER?

An old widower lived alone in New Jersey. He wanted to plant his annual tomato garden on his allotment, but it was very difficult work for him in his decrepit state because of the hard ground. His only son, Vincent, used to help him but was now incarcerated in New Jersey State Prison in Trenton, NJ. The old man wrote a letter to his son and described his predicament: "Dear Vincent, I'm feeling pretty sad because it looks like I won't be able to plant my tomato garden this year. I'm just getting too old to be digging up a garden plot. I know if you were here my troubles would be over. I know you would be happy to dig the plot for me, like in the old days. Love, Papa." A few days later he received the following note from his son: "Dear Papa, don't dig up that garden! That's where the bodies are buried. Love, Vinnie." At 4.30 a.m. the next day, FBI agents and local police arrived and dug up the entire area without finding any bodies. They apologized to the old man and left. That same day the old man received another note from his son: "Dear Papa, go ahead and plant the tomatoes now. That's the best I could do under the circumstances. Love you, Vinnie."

Vinnie was indeed "under the circumstances"! But it's a false phrase for followers of Christ because he is *over* all circumstances, and as our verse above states clearly, we have also been "raised up with Christ" and "seated with him in the heavenly realms". We may on occasion seem as helpless as that old widower, but our cries for help are heard loud and clear – not by a disempowered prisoner – but by the risen Christ who is *over* all circumstances and eager to intervene and assist us in our crises. Call out to him in confidence today.

Lord, thank you that I'm never "under the circumstances". Help me today with… Amen!

GOLD OR IRON?

Proverbs 27:21

"The crucible for silver and the furnace for gold, but people are tested by their praise."

During his reign, King Frederick William III of Prussia found himself in crippling debt because of the war effort. As he sought to build his nation, finances had simply run out. His loyal long-suffering subjects trusted him to provide for them, but he felt cornered. Capitulation to the enemy was unthinkable, but what else could he do? In the end, he devised a creative plan. He asked all the women of Prussia to bring their gold and silver jewellery to be melted down for king and country. As a replacement for each ornament, they would receive a bronze or iron decoration as a symbol of gratitude. Each insignia had inscribed, "I gave gold for iron. 1813." He could not have anticipated the overwhelming response that followed. Most women prized their gifts from the king much more highly than their former jewellery. The reason why became quickly apparent. The insignias were proof that they had sacrificed for their king. In due course, it actually became unfashionable to wear them as jewellery. Thus was established the Order of the Iron Cross. Members wore no ornaments except a cross of iron for all to see.

When we as followers of Christ come to our King, we're invited likewise to exchange material excesses and adornments for a cross. Of course jewellery is not wrong in itself, but as the women of Prussia discovered with joy when offered the chance to sacrifice for the king, laying down our valued possessions for a greater cause is so much more worthwhile. As John Piper wrote, "God is calling us to be conduits of His grace, not cul-de-sacs. Our great danger today is thinking that the conduit should be lined with gold. It shouldn't. Copper will do. No matter how grateful we are, gold will not make the world think that our God is good; it will make people think that our god is gold."

How will what I have just read affect my choices today?

Lord, I choose to give "gold for iron" today. Amen!

CONDEMN OR UNDERSTAND?

John 8:9–11

"When the accusers heard this, they slipped away one by one,... Then Jesus stood up again and said to the woman, "Where are your accusers? Didn't even one of them condemn you?"

Most people behave in a way that is consistent with how they want to be perceived. Jesus had a gift of being able to see what was really going on with them. The woman in this story must have felt worthless and hopeless. Jesus started with the main issue, which was the hypocrisy of the accusers. He then told her that he did not condemn her, but that she must cease what she was doing wrong. Through love and truth he exposed the darkness of the situation and set her free.

I count some precious prostitutes among my friends. None of them as little girls had dreams and aspirations of growing up to sell their bodies. It was a dangerous, painful, degrading decision of last resort for each of them. Do we condemn or seek to understand such people? In the West, it's difficult to understand how people can kill each other just for being from the wrong tribe – but without Christ's work of grace in your life, wouldn't you want to kill those who'd raped your mother or killed your siblings?

Is that person on welfare because they're inherently lazy parasites, or because the years of serial abuse they suffered at home left them deeply damaged? Are those children so feral because their absentee single mum is lazy or because she's out trying to hold down three jobs to pay the bills? And is she single because she was promiscuous or because she kept the baby despite calls to abort having been raped? There are myriad issues attracting our armchair condemnation...

Indeed, we're often quick to condemn, haughty in our own self-righteousness, entrenched in our own prejudices. How about seeking out someone obviously messed up and "different" today, and trying to understand and engage with them?

Lord, forgive my condemning judgmental attitude. I choose to seek to understand today. Amen!

ALERT OR ASLEEP?

8

NOVEMBER

Matthew 24:38, 39, 42

"For in the days before the flood, people were eating and drinking, marrying and giving in marriage, up to the day Noah entered the ark; and they knew nothing about what would happen until the flood came and took them all away. That is how it will be at the coming of the Son of Man... Therefore keep watch, because you do not know on what day your Lord will come."

The Californian steamer was 1,500 miles from the port in Boston when a crewmember saw light flares a few miles away coming from another ship. Various attempts were made to contact the vessel, which seemed to be heading further off in the other direction – to no avail. At 1.40 a.m., the lights disappeared definitively. Only a few hours later did the captain discover what he had accidentally witnessed. Neither he nor his first officer had taken the lights seriously. They hadn't realized how fortuitous it was that they were in the vicinity. They themselves had hardly moved all day because of the proliferation of icebergs, and their delay had put them in a position – without realizing it – to witness a historic event. The crew didn't think that those lights were in fact distress signals, otherwise they would have taken the nine-mile detour to help out. The sinking ship had sent out numerous SOS signals, but the steamer's radio operator was fast asleep the whole time while on duty. And so, from the bridge, the captain and his right-hand man unwittingly witnessed the sinking of the *Titanic*.

You probably saw the Hollywood blockbuster, which so visibly depicted the disaster. People continued to dance, drink champagne, and stuff their faces, blissfully and tragically unaware that the ship had already begun to sink. Similarly, today, people we love and spend time with are living their lives without realizing how precarious their situation is, if they are ignoring God. What will we do about it today?

Lord, I choose to be alert. Use me today to help waken others to what's going on. Amen!

CHARACTER OR REPUTATION?

Acts 17:11

"Now the Bereans were of more noble character than the Thessalonians, for they received the message with great eagerness and examined the Scriptures every day to see if what Paul said was true."

It seems that the Bereans' reputation of being noble in character was born out as true in their behaviour. Their character was consistent with their reputation. Sadly that is not always the case.

Two sportsmen who dominated their respective fields and were idolized by tens or even hundreds of millions of people worldwide were cyclist Lance Armstrong and golfer Tiger Woods. Armstrong's subsequent confessions of cheating after years of denial negated all the pious pronouncements he had previously made, while Wood's quote below rang somewhat hollow after the revelations of his serial infidelity. He said in one interview: "Life is never all about golf. Golf is what I do. I don't want to be defined as a golfer. I want to be defined by my character as a person."

However, there's no room for us to judge. As celebrities and icons in the world of sport, entertainment, politics, and even the church get caught either metaphorically or literally with their pants down, it simply highlights how critical it is for each one of us to keep our feet on the ground, to be on our guard, to nurture our inner life. Be warned, talent can take you way beyond your character.

Character is so much more important than image or reputation. If we picture character as a tree, then reputation is the tree's shadow; the shadow is what we think of it but the tree is the real thing. While reputation is what people think of us, character is what God knows we are. As with the Bereans, if we can live where our character and reputation are consistent with one another, then we are people of integrity, which is the ring of authenticity in the life of a child of God.

Lord, I choose to nurture character above image or reputation today. Amen!

FED OR FED UP?

Hebrews 5:11–14

"... you are slow to learn... You need milk, not solid food! Anyone who lives on milk, being still an infant, is not acquainted with the teaching about righteousness. But solid food is for the mature, who by constant use have trained themselves to distinguish good from evil."

Many disenchanted people leave the church with the parting shot: "I'm not being fed." Hopefully, most preachers at least aspire to nourishing their flock with a well-balanced nutritious diet of sermons. I certainly want to move people on from milk to solid food. But listen! My three children learned to feed themselves when they were toddlers. You can't blame others if you're not being fed – it's your responsibility, because you – unlike suckling infants – are response-able. So do not abdicate your own responsibility by delegating the task of Bible study to your pastor. Back in the Middle Ages, before the Reformation, you would have an excuse, but the Bible's long since been unchained from the pulpit.

As Mark Batterson writes:

> *If you are relying on a preacher to be fed, I fear for you. Listening to a sermon is second-hand knowledge. It is learning based on someone else's words or experiences. A sermon is no replacement for first-hand knowledge. You've got to see it and hear it and experience it for yourself. It's not enough to hear the truth. You have to own it. Or more accurately, it has to own you. Honestly, I'd rather have people hear one word from the Lord than a thousand of my sermons. And that happens when you open your Bible and start reading.*

I hope and pray these daily readings are helpful in your ongoing journey. But the Holy Spirit wants to take us much deeper through His Word. C.S. Lewis wrote this dialogue between Aslan and Lucy once reunited:

"Welcome child"
"Aslan, you're bigger."
"That is because you are older, little one."
"Oh, not because you are?"
"Oh, I am not. But every year you grow, you will find me bigger."

Lord, I resolve to go deeper and find you bigger today. Amen!

2 Timothy 1:6, 7

"I remind you to fan into flame the gift of God… for God did not give us a spirit of timidity, but a spirit of power, of love, and of self-discipline."

FULFILLED OR FAILED?

There is untapped potential in each one of us. Paul saw something special in his protégé, Timothy, and he didn't want Timothy to settle for less than God's best. He knew there would be setbacks along the way but he wrote to encourage Timothy to press on despite them.

Sometimes events that seemed like a "failure" in our lives keep us from fulfilling our potential. Can you look back over your life and see a time when an apparent failure meant you stopped pursuing a dream in that area?

John Maxwell writes on failure:

> *Vincent Van Gogh failed as an art dealer, flunked his entrance exam to theology school, and was fired by the church after an ill-fated attempt at missionary work. In fact, during his life, he seldom experienced anything other than failure as an artist. Although a single painting by Van Gogh would fetch in excess of $100 million today, in his lifetime Van Gogh sold only one painting, four months prior to his death. Before developing his theory of relativity, Albert Einstein encountered academic failure. One headmaster expelled Einstein from school and another teacher predicted that he would never amount to anything. Einstein even failed his entrance exam into college. Prior to dazzling the world with his athletic skill, Michael Jordan was cut from his sophomore basketball team. Even though he captured six championships, during his professional career, Jordan missed over 12,000 shots, lost nearly 400 games, and failed to make more than 25 would-be game-winning baskets. Failure didn't stop Vincent Van Gogh from painting, Albert Einstein from theorizing, or Michael Jordan from playing basketball, but it has paralysed countless people and prevented them from reaching their potential.*

Lord, by your grace I choose to fulfil my potential for your glory. Amen!

ADMIRE OR FOLLOW?

Luke 9:23

"If anyone would come after me, he must deny himself, take up his cross daily and follow me."

12

NOVEMBER

Kierkegaard wrote, "To want to admire – instead of follow – Christ is not an invention of bad people. No, it is more an invention of those who spinelessly want to keep themselves detached at a safe distance from Jesus." To a certain extent, if I'm truly honest, I identify with that latter category. I resonate with the disciples at Jesus' crucifixion, who maintained a respectable distance so as not to let life get too messy. Yet embracing danger is implicit in our call to follow Jesus.

M. Scott Peck challenges us:

> *What we desperately need to re-understand is that it is dangerous to be a true Christian. Anyone who takes his or her Christianity seriously will realize that crucifixion is not something that happened to one man two thousand years ago, nor was martyrdom just the fate of his early followers. It should be an omnipresent risk for every Christian. Christians should – need – in certain ways to live dangerously if they are to live out their faith. The times have made this apparent. And in combating the entrenched forces, the principalities and powers of this world, that very much includes the risk of martyrdom. It is time for communal, congregational action and corporate risk.*

Such is the life of faith. Does it fill you with a sense of anticipation or dread? E. Stanley Jones elaborates:

> *Faith is an adventure of the Spirit, a going out of the whole inner life in response to something we believe to be supremely worthwhile. It is the wagering of the life, and not merely nodding of the head. It is not discussion, it is decision. It is the launching out on the highest hypothesis I know – with my life. I don't believe a thing unless I act upon it. I don't believe in Christ unless I am prepared to wager all to follow Him. That is faith.*

God, grant me such faith to follow you today. Amen!

DEATH OR GLORY?

Romans 8:18

"I consider that our present sufferings are not worth comparing to the glory that will be revealed in us."

The SAS have a motto: "Who Dares Wins". Actually the first ever mission for these supposedly crack troops was a complete disaster. It would have been easy for them to have retreated to the safety of their barracks and we'd never have heard of them again. But they didn't. They went back to the drawing board, sharpened their trade, and proved the value of daring and winning on numerous subsequent occasions. Another military motto, from the 17th Regiment of Dragoons, reads, "Death or Glory". These soldiers were the ones who led the Charge of the Light Brigade during the Crimean War. Their bravery was unparalleled, and despite serious casualties, their fierce reputation was such that the Russian cavalry refused to confront them for the entire duration of the war.

However, for Christians it's never a case of death or glory – rather it's death *and* glory. Re-read the above verse by Paul. Elsewhere he writes, "For me to live is Christ, to die is gain" (Philippians 1:21).

Many followers of Christ throughout history have similarly echoed those words. Christopher Love was a missionary in India. He was captured, tortured, and put to death. He had already written a note to his wife that stated, "Today they will sever me from my physical head, but they cannot sever me from my spiritual head, Christ." As he walked to his death, his wife applauded while he sang of glory. As his persecutors began to skin him alive, he looked directly at them and said, "I thank you for this. Tear off my old garment, for I will soon put on Christ's garment of righteousness."

Few of us will be called to be martyrs, but may we all be inspired by such stories of total commitment. Our task is more important than any earthly military, so let's embrace the commission whatever the cost.

Lord, I choose to live and die wholly commissioned by and committed to you. Amen!

FACE OR FLEE?

Hebrews 2:14, 15

"… so that by his death, Jesus might destroy him who holds the power of death – that is, the devil – and free those who all their lives were held in slavery by their fear of death."

One in one person dies – it is the ultimate statistic. Many fear death, refuse to talk about it, shrink from facing it, do everything to put it off. But it will come, and it is not something to be feared. As the verse above makes clear, Jesus has destroyed the devil through his own death, and has freed us from any need to be afraid of death.

An old legend tells of a merchant in Baghdad who sent off his servant one day to the market. It wasn't long before the servant returned, white as a sheet, and trembling. In great agitation he said to his master, "Down in the marketplace I bumped into a lady in the crowd, and when I turned around I saw that it was Death that jostled me. She looked me right in the eye and made a threatening gesture. Master, please may I take my leave for a few days? Could you lend me your horse, for I must hasten away to avoid her. I will ride to Samarra and hide there, so that Death can't find me."

The merchant complied and watched as his servant galloped off into the distance. Later that day, the merchant went down to the marketplace and came across Death standing in the crowd. He went over to her and asked, "Why did you make a threatening gesture to my servant?" "That wasn't a threatening gesture," Death said. "He just caught me by surprise. I couldn't believe he was here in Baghdad, because I have an appointment with him tonight in Samarra."

Each of us has an appointment in Samarra. But there's no need to flee – in fact it's futile to flee. So live free from the fear of death today.

Lord, I choose to live free from fear and to share this gift of hope and assurance with those around me today. Amen!

2 Corinthians 5:14

"For Christ's love compels me..."

CONSTRAINED OR RESTRAINED?

We are called to share our hope in Christ with the lost, and as stated above, love is to be the motivating force behind our willingness to step out of our comfort zones. Below is a challenging clarion call to get involved, called "If", by J. Wilbur Chapman:

If today is the day of salvation, if tomorrow may never come and if life is equally uncertain, how can we eat, drink and be merry when those who live with us, work with us, walk with us and love us are unprepared for eternity because they are unprepared for time?

If they who reject Christ are in danger, is it not strange that we, who are so sympathetic when the difficulties are physical or temporal, should apparently be so devoid of interest as to allow our friends and neighbours and kindred to come into our lives and pass out again without a word of invitation to accept Christ, to say nothing of sounding a note of warning because of their peril?

If Jesus called his disciples to be fishers of men, who gave the right to be satisfied with making fishing tackle or pointing the way to the fishing banks instead of going ourselves to cast out the net until it be filled?

If I am to stand at the judgment seat of Christ to render an account for the deeds done in the Body, what shall I say to Him if my children are missing, if my friends are not saved or if my employer or employee should miss the way because I have been faithless?

If I wish to be approved at the last, then let me remember that no intellectual superiority, no eloquence in preaching, no absorption in business, no shrinking temperament, no spirit of timidity can take the place of or be an excuse for my not making an honest, sincere, prayerful effort to win others to Christ.

Lord, I choose to get involved, not out of guilt but out of gratitude. Use me today for your glory. Amen!

CROSS OR COMFORT?

Galatians 6:14

"May I never boast except in the cross of our Lord Jesus Christ, through which the world has been crucified to me, and I to the world."

Only a fool, when given the choice between a cross and comfort, would choose a cross. Or so you would have thought. But as Billy Graham wrote, "Comfort and prosperity have never enriched the world as adversity has done. Out of pain and problems have come the sweetest songs, the most poignant poems, the most gripping stories. Out of suffering and tears have come the greatest spirits and the most blessed lives."

Maybe today you're going through adversity, discouragement, or difficulty. Maybe you feel stale, frustrated, or stagnant. Reaching for comfort is a seductive sedative but it seldom satisfies. I don't think we should go looking for problems in the Christian life, but they inevitably come our way. And much as we'd prefer that they didn't, they can be used to shape us and conform us to his likeness. It's an unpalatable truth, and one which we resist.

Tony Lambert observed the extraordinary growth of the church in China through seasons of intense persecution, and came to the following conclusion:

> *The reason for the growth of the church in China and for the outbreak of genuine spiritual revival in many areas is inextricably linked to the whole theology of the cross… the stark message of the Chinese church is that God used suffering and the preaching of a crucified Christ to pour out revival and build his church. Are we in the West still willing to hear? The Chinese church has walked the way of the cross. The lives and deaths of the martyrs of the 1950s and 1960s have borne rich fruit.*

Those myriad believers embraced a theology of the cross, not of comfort. Paul did likewise, following in his Master's footsteps. It was costly, but it was fruitful. So let's do the same today.

Lord, I choose to shun comfort and embrace an authentic theology of the cross today. Amen!

GUILT OR GRATITUDE?

Romans 12:1

"Therefore… in view of God's mercy… offer your bodies as living sacrifices."

I'm proud to be English but I'm not so proud of our national pastime – moaning. We're World Champion moaners, and yet we're living in the most affluent time in the history of humanity, with access to so many wonderful benefits and blessings.

When I give talks around the world, I often say very explicitly, "Listen people. I don't want to give you a guilt trip. But I do want to give you a gratitude trip." And then I tell them about the time someone was trying to kill me and in one of his unpleasant letters to me he said he was going to cut out my eyes! You know, for the first time in my life, I thanked God for the gift of eyesight. And it is a gift, isn't it? It's by no means a right – just ask a blind person.

That experience was an epiphany for me. Most of us have grown up in an entitlement culture. It's all about our rights. That's why most of us are grumpy. If you recognize everything you have is a gift, you'll live a life of gratitude to the Giver – and grateful people make happy people.

In Paul's words above, the original Greek word for "mercy" is plural. He's saying in effect, "in view of all the grace gifts (mercies) of God in your life, live and die for him." When I'm tempted to moan, I often go through all the gifts I have: sight, food, peace, education, family, clean water, and more. What an amazing list! How blessed am I!

Listen, Jesus says, "To those who have been given much, much will be required" (Luke 12:48). With privilege comes responsibility. Don't feel guilty about how blessed you are, but do feel grateful, and then think about how you can use what you've got to make a difference in Jesus' name.

Lord, forgive my times of grumpy ingratitude. Help me choose to live a life of gratitude today. Amen!

DISTRACTED TO DEATH OR ALERT AND ALIVE?

John 10:10

"The enemy comes to steal, kill and destroy."

18

NOVEMBER

George Orwell once observed:

> *I thought of a rather cruel trick I played on one occasion on a wasp. He was sucking jam on my plate, and I cut him in half. He paid no attention, merely went on with his meal, while a tiny stream of jam trickled out of his severed oesophagus. Only when he tried to fly away did he grasp the dreadful thing that had happened to him. It is the same with modern man. The thing that has been cut away is his soul.*

How perceptive he is, and yet how insidious is the danger! How is your soul doing today – cut away or well preserved? Satan is described in the Bible as "the father of lies", who "was a murderer from the beginning", and when "he lies, he speaks his native language, for he is a liar" (John 8:44). It is so easy for us to get distracted to death by the endless array of possibilities offered to us in our consumer society.

In another vivid instance of distraction, a swarm of gulls were feasting on the carcasses of dead fish embedded in a number of blocks of ice floating down the river towards Niagara Falls. As they came to the brink, they would rise up effortlessly on their wings and escape from the falls. But one particular gull was deeply engrossed in the carcass of a fish, and when it finally came to the brink of the falls, out went its powerful wings. It flapped and flapped and even lifted the ice out of the water, but it had delayed too long and its feet had frozen into the ice. The weight of the ice was too great, and the gull plunged to its death in the thundering water below.

Are you distracted or alert today? Peter warns us: "Be self-controlled and alert. Your enemy the devil prowls around like a roaring lion looking for someone to devour. Resist him" (1 Peter 5:8).

Lord, I choose be to alert today. Amen!

ENOUGH OR MORE?

Isaiah 55:2

"Why spend money on what is not bread, and your labour on what does not satisfy?"

When is enough? John Bogle wrote on contentment, "At a party given by a billionaire on Shelter Island, Kurt Vonnegut informs his pal, Joseph Heller, that their host, a hedge fund manager, had made more money in a single day than Heller had earned from his wildly popular novel *Catch-22* over its whole history. Heller responds, 'Yes, but I have something he will never have… enough.'"

Material things simply cannot fill our aching void, rather they leave us wanting more. Nicky Gumbel elaborates:

> *Elvis Presley in his heyday grossed $100 million in 2 years of stardom. He had three jets, two Cadillacs, a Rolls Royce, a Lincoln Continental, Buick and Chrysler station wagons, a jeep, a dune buggy, a converted bus and 3 motor cycles. His favourite car was his 1960 Cadillac limousine. The top was covered with pearl-white naugahyde. The body was sprayed in 40 coats of specially prepared paint which included crushed diamonds and fish scales. Nearly all the metal trim was plated with 18 carat gold. Inside the car were 2 gold plated telephones, a gold vanity case containing a gold electric razor and gold hair clippers, an electric show buffer, a gold-plated TV, a record player, an amplifier, air-conditioning and a refrigerator. He had everything. Yet he was unfulfilled.*

God offers an alternative to us through the prophet Isaiah. Instead of spending money "on what is not bread, and your labour on what does not satisfy", "come to me" (verse 3). Then our "soul will delight in the richest of fare" (verse 2). The average Westerner is bombarded by 3,000 adverts every day. Each one is screaming that you don't have enough, that you are inadequate without what they are offering you, that you are lacking just one more piece to complete the puzzle. Most of them are lies from the pit of hell. Choose instead to live content in Jesus. He satisfies. That in itself will challenge others around you.

Thank you, Lord, that in you I have enough. Amen!

BITTER OR BETTER?

Colossians 3:13

"Forgive as the Lord forgave you."

It was unfair. You, or perhaps someone who means a lot to you, were treated unfairly. But what are you going to do about it? You can choose to hold on to the hurt, or you can forgive. If you choose to nurse that grievance, it will fester into unforgiveness, grow into resentment, and bear fruits of bitterness. You may even become a person defined by bitterness.

Gordon Wilson held the hand of his daughter Marie as they lay trapped under a pile of rubble. It was 1987, and they had been standing watching a peaceful Remembrance Day service in Enniskillen, Northern Ireland, when a terrorist bomb went off. Marie died. A few hours after the bombing, when interviewed by the BBC, Gordon Wilson made his choice: he forgave the terrorists and begged that no one take revenge for Marie's death. The loss of Marie shattered Gordon Wilson and his wife Joan, but his willingness to forgive not only released him but astounded the public and contributed in a small but significant way to achieving peace in Northern Ireland.

Faced with a disaster, any given person can either get bitter or better through it.

In Malaysia, monkeys were perpetually invading a farmer's land and destroying his crops. The damage jeopardized his very livelihood so he needed to act fast. The ingenious solution he devised was to put peanuts in hollowed-out coconuts. He then hid and waited. The monkeys came, scaled the walls, and smelled the peanuts. When they found them in the coconuts, they grabbed them, but now their clenched fists couldn't pull them out – they couldn't fit through the narrow apertures if they remained clenched. Neither could the monkeys now scale the walls again without releasing the peanuts, but they didn't want to, so they were stuck. The farmer then reappeared and shot them one by one. Their freedom was so easily attainable. All they had to do was let go, but they chose to hold on.

Are you holding on to anything still? Let go!

Lord, I choose to forgive… today, to let go and move on. Amen!

CONSOLATION OR INSPIRATION?

Psalm 121:1, 2

"I lift my eyes up to the mountains – where does my help come from? My help comes from the Lord, the Maker of heaven and earth."

As the American Civil War continued unabated, a discouraged Abraham Lincoln used to seek refuge in a Presbyterian church in Washington. The war was tearing both the nation and his soul apart. Furthermore, he had just lost his own precious eleven-year-old son, who had succumbed to fever. He was at rock bottom, and needed both consolation and inspiration. After one such midweek service, the congregation slowly dispersed and Lincoln stood up. His aide asked him, "What did you think of the sermon, Mr President?" Lincoln replied, "I thought the sermon was carefully thought through, eloquently delivered." The aide said, "You thought it was a great sermon?" "No," replied Lincoln, "I thought he failed." "He failed?" said the surprised aide, "Well, how? Why?" "Because he did not ask of us something great," said the President.

Our job as the church, the body of Christ, is both to console and to inspire. I was once smuggled into a squalid refugee camp, where an average of ten people were dying each day. It was horrific. I preached on the verses above. God had not forgotten them, even if the international community had. God was there if they lifted their eyes upwards, bigger even than the mountains. The "something great" I asked of them, was simply to hold on to hope, to not give up.

That could be the same for you today.

I felt the sense of urgency in my appeal because these people were dying so fast. Our commission is indeed urgent. At Bristol Cathedral after one service, an angry man from the congregation accosted Canon Samuel Barnett and berated him about his sermon, "I come to church to be comforted, but you sounded like a fire alarm!"

Lord, I choose to hold on to hope today, to be both consoled and inspired, and to seek to both console and inspire others to something great. Amen!

WELL LIVED OR WELL SPOKEN?

1 John 3:18

"Dear children, let us not love with words or speech but with actions and in truth."

Mother Teresa was eight-five years old when she was invited to address the Presidential Prayer Breakfast in Washington, DC. This frail old lady, dressed as ever in her simple cheap clothing, passionately and eloquently called on the powerful luminaries gathered around her to enshrine the protection of unborn babies in law. She pleaded for compassion on behalf of the "little ones": "How can we speak out against violence, when we are the most brutal with the most defenseless?"

It was obviously a controversial and sensitive subject, and many of the media elite spoke of that awkward moment for President Clinton, Vice-President Gore, and their wives as this humble diminutive lady spoke with such conviction. As she stood down, the audience gave a roaring standing ovation. However, a number of people, who were seated on the stage, very ostentatiously chose not to stand up, in obvious disagreement with what she'd said.

Afterwards, President Clinton was asked in an interview what he thought of Mother Teresa's pointed message. He paused and said only this, "It is very difficult to argue against a life so beautifully lived." He was wise to keep his words to a minimum, because he recognized that all the arguments supporting his opinion about her words were irrelevant at that time. Anything he said would only reflect his attitude toward Mother Teresa the person; and in the presence of a life well lived, he was no longer responding to an issue at hand, but to a person in front of him.

Will we speak well, or live well? People *look* as they *listen*, and what they *see* must be one with what they *hear.* Dorothy Day's life in many ways followed a similar trajectory to Mother Teresa's. It was said of Dorothy Day that "she loved the truth enough to live it." Will we?

Lord, I choose to live in such a way that it will be said of me that I loved the truth enough to live it. Amen!

DECLINE OR ACCEPT?

Revelation 3:20

"Here I am! I stand at the door and knock. If anyone hears my voice and opens the door, I will come in and eat with him, and he with me."

The verse above contains the most glorious invitation to each one of us. Will we decline or accept it?

Jean-Francis Gaudet (1824–97) was one of the greatest tightrope walkers of all time. Probably his most famous feat came at the Niagara Falls, where a huge crowd gathered to watch his daring escapades. He began by simply walking across, making it look so easy despite the foam, the winds, and the sound of roaring water ringing in his ears. He proceeded to repeat the journey several times, while cooking an omelette, carrying a pole, and even taking a wheelbarrow across. Arriving back to rapturous applause, he asked the Duke of Newcastle in the royal party, "Do you believe I could take a human across?" "Yes," said the Duke confidently. "Well get in!" came the invitation. The Duke declined, so Gaudet opened it up to anyone. There was a long pause before an old lady came forward. The crowd sat entranced as he wheeled her across both ways, to huge cheers. It turned out the old woman was his mother!

Our heavenly Father is inviting us to get on board today and embark with him on a journey fraught with danger, except that he is the one leading us and so we are completely safe. Faith is not merely intellectual. It involves an active step of putting our trust in Jesus Christ. John Paton was a missionary to the New Hebrides Islands. He was struggling to translate the word "faith" into the local language, and in the end the best he could come up with was to "lean heavily on". Charles Kingsley wrote in a similar vein, "I do not want merely to possess a faith. I want a faith that possesses me."

Lord, help me choose to accept your invitation, lean heavily on you, and not just possess a faith but have a faith that possesses me. Amen!

GOT IT, WANT IT, OR HAPPY WITHOUT IT?

Acts 1:8

"You will receive power when the Holy Spirit comes..."

A.W. Tozer observed:

> *Satan has fought the doctrine of the Spirit-filled life about as bitterly as any doctrine there is. He has confused it, opposed it, and surrounded it with false notions and fears. The Church has tragically neglected this great liberating truth that there is now, for the child of God, a full and wonderful and completely satisfying anointing with the Holy Spirit. The Spirit-filled life is not a special deluxe edition of Christianity. It is part and parcel of the total plan of God for his people.*

Moody was the most effective evangelist of the nineteenth century. After one service early in his ministry, two old ladies approached him and told him, "You are good, but you haven't got it... we have been praying for you... you need power!" Moody, an already well-respected minister, was shocked, "I need power? Why, I thought I had power!" The ladies poured out their hearts in intercession for him to receive the anointing of the Holy Spirit, and soon he became desperate for more of God. He wrote, "I felt I did not want to live any longer if I had not this power for service." Six months of pleading with God ensued. Then God visited him in power as he walked down Wall Street in New York, and he was never the same again. Although his sermons were verbatim the same, those same words saw many dozens come to faith each time where before it had been a mere handful.

John Stott wrote, "What we need is not more learning, not more eloquence, not more persuasion, not more organisation, but more power from the Holy Spirit." Now this remains a hotly contested doctrine, but the bottom line is, whatever work we're involved in, surely we want more of him in our lives? I know I need more power. How about you? Seek him today!

Lord, I know there's got to be more. I'm desperate for more. Take me deeper and fill me afresh with your Holy Spirit today, for your glory. Amen!

ENEMY OR FRIEND?

Matthew 5:44, 46

"But I tell you: love your enemies and pray for those who persecute you... If you love those who love you, what reward will you get? Are not even the tax-collectors doing that?"

During the American Revolutionary War, a Baptist pastor called Peter Miller was good friends with General Washington. Miller lived in Ephrata, Pennsylvania, and found himself hounded and abused by an aggressive and antagonistic man called Michael Wittman. Wittman found himself arrested on suspicion of treason and sentenced to death. The old preacher set out on foot and trudged the whole seventy miles to Philadelphia to plead for this man's life. Washington welcomed him in and heard him beg for the traitor's life to be spared. He then addressed Miller, "I'm sorry, Peter, I cannot grant you the life of your friend." The preacher exclaimed, "My friend? He is the bitterest enemy I have!" Washington cried, "What? You've walked seventy miles to save the life of an enemy? That puts the matter in a different light. I *will* grant the pardon." And he did. The next day, Peter Miller took Michael Wittman from his cell on death row back to their home in Ephrata – no longer as an enemy, but as a friend.

We all have enemies, or at least people who rub us up the wrong way. Think of them right now. God loves them, died for them, and wants them to know him. However hard it might be, could you do something positive for them? However undeserved, could you take the first step in building or rebuilding a bridge towards them? Abraham Lincoln was once rebuked by his advisors for being so kind to his enemies. He replied, "Do I not destroy my enemies by turning them into my friends?" A friend of mine in Burundi called Jack has destroyed his enemy by going back to the spot where the latter murdered Jack's father, and preaching love and forgiveness arm in arm with him. What could you do today?

Lord, in your strength I choose to love my enemies. Amen!

ENCOURAGED OR DISCOURAGED?

26

NOVEMBER

2 Thessalonians 2:16, 17

"May our Lord Jesus Christ himself and God our Father, who loved us and by his grace gave us eternal encouragement and good hope, encourage your hearts and strengthen you in every good deed and word."

An old legend tells how a man was once lost for days in a dark forest and stumbled across an imposing barn. He sought shelter inside it because of the howling winds. His eyes grew quickly accustomed to the dark and he was amazed to discover that this barn was where the devil kept his storehouse of seeds. These were the seeds that were sown in the hearts of humans. He lit a match and looked at all the different types of seeds. Most of them, surprisingly, were labelled "Seeds of Discouragement". Just then one of the devil's helpers arrived to pick up a new load of seeds. The man asked him, "Why so many discouragement seeds?" The helper laughed and replied, "Because they're so effective and they take root so quickly." "Do they grow everywhere?" the man asked, to which the helper suddenly grimaced back at him and said in disgust, "No. They never seem to grow in the heart of a grateful person."

It's simplistic to put down all our discouragements to a lack of gratitude, but gratitude has an undeniably powerful and positive effect on us when we're going through tricky times. The sages said that ingratitude was our most besetting sin, so they developed a good motto: "Nothing taken for granted; everything received with gratitude; everything passed on with grace."

Are you discouraged today? Is anything sapping your joy or dragging you down? Re-read the above verse, which encourages us to keep things in perspective. List all the positives in your life, the blessings you have, and be renewed in your spirit.

Lord, I choose today to take nothing for granted, to receive everything with gratitude, and to pass on everything with grace. Amen!

Matthew 22:29

"Jesus replied, 'You are in error because you do not know the Scriptures or the power of God.'"

PERSONAL OR ABSTRACT?

Jesus was replying to a question from the Sadducees (who did not believe in the resurrection – which is why they were sad-you-see!). He accused them of not knowing the Scriptures. What could he mean? They had studied the Scriptures since childhood and could recite whole chunks off by heart. Many had their equivalent of masters degrees in biblical studies – apparently though, even if they were masters of the word, they weren't mastered by the word. They were over the word, not under it. It's all too easy to be eighteen inches from salvation: to have the word in the head, but not in the heart.

What about power? After all, we often hear that knowledge is power. But that type of power exploits ignorance and takes advantage of others; it's a power that is lost once others get the same knowledge; it's not a knowledge that is content to serve; it's a knowledge to score points and cause sparks in debates without bringing light.

What was the knowledge of which Jesus spoke? Jesus meant knowledge that is rooted in and springs from a personal relationship with God; knowledge that becomes part of our practical life and experience. Paul wrote, "Let the word of Christ dwell in you richly" (Colossians 3:16). Internalized truth then leads to externalized action – or at least it should do. As James warns, "Do not merely listen to the word, and so deceive yourselves. Do what it says" (1:22).

Do I hear but not do? It's not enough to be biblically literate – we must be biblically *obedient* too. Telling my wife I love her is no substitute for living out that love with acts of kindness and service. She knows my love by experiencing the outworking of it. It's personal, not abstract. So get personal with Jesus today, which will mean getting practical too.

Lord, I choose to be both biblically literate and biblically obedient today. May my personal knowledge lead to practical action. Amen!

ACCEPTING OR EXCLUSIVE?

Luke 14:21

"Go out quickly into the streets and alleys of the town and bring in the poor, the crippled, the blind and the lame."

A jetlagged Tony Campolo was preaching in Hawaii but couldn't sleep so went to a café at 3 a.m. In walked a dozen prostitutes at the end of their night's work. He overheard one of them, Agnes, say it was her birthday the following day. "What do you want from me? A birthday cake?" was the sarcastic reply. "Why be so mean?" she replied, "I was just telling you. I don't expect anything. I've never had a birthday party." When they left, Campolo asked the owner, Harry, to make a cake and prepare a party. The following night, at 3 a.m. Campolo had brought decorations and Harry had baked a cake, and word had got out so the café was packed with almost every prostitute in Honolulu. When Agnes entered, she nearly fainted. She was overwhelmed. She nipped out for a moment and there was a stunned silence. So Campolo piped up, "What do you say we pray?" And they did. Campolo led a group of prostitutes in prayer at 3.30 a.m. When they were done, Harry said, "Hey! You never told me you were some kind of preacher. What kind of church do you belong to?" In a flash of inspiration, Campolo answered, "I belong to a church that throws birthday parties for prostitutes at 3.30 a.m." Harry thought for a moment and then sneered, "No you don't. There's no church like that. If there was, I'd join it. I'd join a church like that."

Wouldn't we all? Wouldn't we all love to join a church that throws birthday parties for prostitutes at 3.30 a.m.?! Jesus loved spending time with society's outcasts: the tax-collectors, prostitutes, "sinners". Pious people couldn't relate to him but those lonely folk who didn't usually get party invites were drawn to him.

Could you or your church do something crazy like that? Go for it!

Lord, help me invite and include everyone in your party. Amen!

TIME WASTED OR WELL SPENT?

Ephesians 5:16

"... making the most of every opportunity, because the days are evil."

In the *Effective Father*, Gordon MacDonald writes:

> *It is said of Boswell, the famous biographer of Samuel Johnson, that he often referred to a special day in his childhood when his father took him fishing. The day was fixed in his mind, and he often reflected upon many things his father had taught him in the course of their fishing experience together. After having heard of that particular excursion so often, it occurred to someone much later to check the journal that Boswell's father kept and determine what had been said about the fishing trip from the parental perspective. Turning to that date, the reader only found one sentence entered:*
>
> *"Gone fishing today with my son – a day wasted."*

Spending time investing in meaningful relationships is never a waste. On the other hand, it is a total waste of time to indulge in shallow living, petty thinking, trivial talking, faithless worrying, thoughtless doing, useless regretting, or hurtful resenting. Spending endless hours on Facebook, Twitter, YouTube, shopping, or playing video games is a waste of time.

Back in the nineteenth century, Robert Murray McCheyne was mightily used in Scotland. His small rural church grew to 1,200 people. He sent out missionaries, mobilized others to help with the local poor, and wrote a daily Bible-reading plan. His impact was huge, and all accomplished by the time he was twenty-nine, when he died of typhus. When he was twenty years old, having wasted an evening, he penned these words in his journal, "My heart must break off from these things. What right have I to steal and abuse my Master's time? '*Redeem it*', He is crying to me."

All people who live well use their time well. Will you choose to be one of them?

Lord God Almighty, with the limited time I have before me today, I choose to spend it well, for your glory. Amen!

STAY OR GO?

Psalm 23:4

"Even though I walk through the valley of the shadow of death, I will fear no evil, for you are with me; your rod and your staff, they comfort me."

The film *Of Gods and Men* was based on events in Algeria in the 1990s. Eight Cistercian monks were faced with the ultimatum of leaving their monastery and calling or getting killed by Islamic militants. Violence escalated, a group of Croatian aid workers were murdered, but the monks refused all army protection. Each one had to decide for himself whether to stay or go. The film as a whole is a powerful witness to the monks' love for their Muslim neighbours, and their belief in the possibility of community between the two religions. The audience is left to battle with what decision they might have taken, and whether the monks' collective decision to stay (and die) was the right one.

I resonate with so much that the monks went through. I admit to living with fear in the immediate aftermath of my own death threats in Burundi, but once processed, those fearful emotions were replaced by deep peace. As one of the monks said, "I'm not scared of terrorists, even less of the army. And I'm not scared of death. I'm a free man." Free because death is an emasculated enemy for the child of God. As D.L. Moody said, "The valley of the shadow of death holds no darkness for the child of God. There must be light, else there could be no shadow. Jesus is the light. He has overcome death."

How does that apply to those of us who aren't living in dangerous places? It comes down to living and taking decisions based out of fear, or of faith. Your decisions to stay or go, to speak or to remain silent, to give or to withhold, will be flawed if they are made out of fear. Trust God. "Perfect love drives out all fear" (1 John 4:18).

Lord, guide me in my decision-making. May I choose to make them from a place of faith rather than fear. Amen!

SLUMBER OR WONDER?

Romans 13:11

"The hour has come for you to wake up from your slumber, because our salvation is nearer now than when we first believed."

1
DECEMBER

As children, I'm guessing we all sang "Twinkle, twinkle little star" hundreds of times, but did we ever really wonder "what they are"? At any rate, the sheer fascination, curiosity, and wonder we began life with became quickly eroded as we grew up. According to the research of Rolf Smith, children ask 125 probing questions per day while adults ask only 6; somewhere along the line we lose 119 questions per day. As Christians, we've sought to prove that God is factual, which he is, but facts don't awe us. We've sought a God of logic and thereby missed out on worshipping the God of wonders. Approaching him deductively as an object of knowledge is dangerous as we miss experiencing him inductively as the cause of wonder.

Advent helps us address this issue. Historically, the church sets aside Advent as a four-week pre-Christmas season in which to prepare spiritually for Christ's coming. It's a time of quiet joyous anticipation and wonder. It's an invitation to awaken from our slumber. As Alfred McBride wrote:

> *Each year, God asks us to shed one more coat of awareness, one more dream state and come alive to the vision of God's plan for each of us and the world-at-large. The older we get, the harder this is to do. As children we had a sense of wonder. Our eyes were wide open and drinking in the fascinating gifts we beheld… Then, somehow, we grew too old to dream. We tired of the abundance of the world, or at least grew weary and stepped away from the banquet of life. The natural gift of wonder God gave us as children was meant to be kept alive… Instead we let wonder go to sleep. We entered the typical dream state of most humans. Advent says, "Wake up and realize the gifts of love you have received".*

Lord, I choose to use this Advent season to live wide awake with wonder and gratitude and anticipation. Amen!

THROW AWAY OR HOLD ON?

Hebrews 10:35, 36

"So do not throw away your confidence; it will be richly rewarded. You need to persevere so that when you have done the will of God, you will receive what he has promised."

A ship sank several hundred miles west of Indonesia, and one man floated for days before being washed up on a remote uninhabited island. He felt initially euphoric that he hadn't died, but that soon gave way to anger, and then loneliness and despair. He managed to stay alive eating certain roots, collecting bugs, and trapping animals. As days became weeks, he built a makeshift home and searched the horizon repeatedly for any sign of a ship. He asked God to save him, but felt totally forgotten. One day while out hunting, he saw smoke rising in the sky from near the beach. He rushed there to discover to his horror that his shack had caught fire and burned down. He railed at God, "Why? I'm trying to trust you. I want to keep hold of my faith in you, but now you let this happen!" Hours later, he looked into the distance and couldn't believe what he saw: a fishing vessel was coming towards him! When it arrived, he asked them, "How on earth did you know I was on this island desperately waiting for help?" The captain answered, "We didn't, but we saw your smoke signals."

Often we're tempted to throw away our confidence in God. When I was called to Burundi, it was so clear that I had to go. Yet that clarity soon dissipated amidst confusion as to what I would end up doing, having my money stolen, being robbed by street kids, being isolated, misunderstood, and more. But God's ways are not our ways. Sometimes it's only later that we can look back with gratitude at the messiness of what we had to go through which taught and grew and shaped us to become more like him.

Lord, I choose to hold on rather than throw away my confidence in you. Help me persevere with you today. Amen!

Psalm 139:13, 14

"You knit me together in my mother's womb. I praise you because I am fearfully and wonderfully made."

COMPARE OR ACCEPT?

Gladys Aylward was born in 1904. She was from a poor background. She was short, had black hair, and by all accounts was not outwardly very beautiful. In fact, as she grew up she railed at God for having made her the way she was, and was deeply jealous of the taller blonde girls in her class. However, God laid hold of her and called her to China. She didn't know anything about China, had never seen a Chinese person, and didn't know where it was. But in obedience she applied to be a missionary at the China Inland Mission. She was rejected. In 1930, she pooled her money and bought a one-way boat ticket to China. When she arrived in China, she suddenly realized why God had made her the way he had. All around her were short people with black hair, just like her! Her tiny frame and dark hair meant that she was far more quickly accepted by the Chinese community, perceived as less different by them than the other Western missionaries. This remarkable little lady evangelized across China until evicted by the communist authorities in the late 1940s, and was known as the "Virtuous One".

How easy it is to compare ourselves to others, and in our jealousy wish we were more beautiful, intelligent, wealthy, popular, or whatever! Comparison is often the enemy of joy and contentment. God in his infinite wisdom has made each one of us just the way we are. There's no point railing at him as Gladys did. Far better to accept the raw material that we are, and trust him to use us as he sees fit. That might not be clear to you right now, but in his time it will become so. In the meantime, accept yourself, and walk in trust with him day by day.

Lord, I choose to thank you for making me me. Use me as you see fit today. Amen!

ACCEPT OR REJECT?

Romans 5:3–5

"We rejoice in our sufferings, because we know that suffering produces perseverance; perseverance, character; and character, hope. And hope does not disappoint us..."

Bill Porter accepted who he was, but rejected the world's verdict on his life. Because of his cerebral palsy, which made it difficult for him to speak clearly, to walk, and to use his right arm, the social services labelled him "unemployable". But Bill refused to accept the option of being on government disability for the rest of his life. And, as shown in the heart-warming film *Door to Door*, his sheer stubbornness and force of will meant that eventually he was given a job by a firm with a range of household products. He hobbled from house to house for ten miles a day, battling his constant pain and weakness, and somehow overcame his speech impediment to communicate and sell his wares. When he made a sale, he couldn't even hold a pen so the customer had to fill out the form. Somehow, he became the company's top salesman – first in that city, then in the region, and finally in the entire country. This "unemployable" broken man who could hardly walk or talk made a career for himself as a door-to-door salesman for forty years!

We all face situations where the deck seems to be stacked against us. Bill Porter's life encourages us to reject the temptation to give up, to be discouraged, or to lose hope. And no matter how insurmountable the obstacles may appear, we have something far greater than Bill's courageous example on which to base our confidence – we have the promises of God to rely on and his presence and his power at work in our lives.

Note the progression in the above verse: "suffering produces perseverance; perseverance, character; and character, hope. And hope does not disappoint us." Stand tall today, even if you're limping, confident that God's "power is made perfect in weakness" (2 Corinthians 12:9).

Lord, the only verdict I choose to accept on my life today is the one you give. Use me for your glory. Amen!

CRIPPLED OR EQUIPPED?

Genesis 32:25–31

"When the man saw that he could not overpower [Jacob], he touched the socket of Jacob's hip so that his hip was wrenched… Then the man said, 'Let me go… Your name will no longer be Jacob, but Israel, because you have struggled with God and with men and have overcome.'… and [Jacob] was limping because of his hip."

Jacob (meaning "he deceives") had his name changed to Israel (meaning "he struggles with God"). Up to that point in his life, he had lived up to his first name repeatedly, as he cheated his brother Esau out of both his birthright and their father's deathbed blessing, and then had to flee for his life. But this encounter with an angel was a pivotal moment. After it, he limped for the rest of his life; but his crippling was in fact his equipping. His crippling brought greater humility, teachability, and wisdom to deal with all that lay ahead.

A tourist in Israel came across a sheepfold located high on a hilltop. She noticed a poor sheep lying by the side of the road bleating in pain. Looking more closely, she saw that its leg was injured. She asked the shepherd how it had happened. "I had to break it myself," he answered sadly. "It was the only way I could keep that wayward creature from straying into unsafe places. From past experience I have found that a sheep will follow me once I have nursed it back to health. Because of the loving relationship that will be established as I care for her, in the future she will come instantly at my beck and call."

Do we ever need some firm handling by Jesus, the supremely good shepherd? I can look back and be grateful for the time he punctured my pride with a public failure – it felt humiliating and crippling at the time, but it became a moment of equipping for God's glory. Trusting he is indeed good, submit to him today.

Lord, equip me by whatever means to make me your obedient faithful servant. Amen!

IMMUNE OR INFECTED?

Galatians 5:22, 23

"The fruit of the Spirit is love, joy, peace, patience, kindness, goodness, faithfulness, gentleness and self-control. Against such things there is no law."

There are lots of bugs floating around and infecting countless people at this time of year, some of which are truly debilitating. May you avoid all the nasty ones, but I hope you're not immune to the following bug. Be warned, it's powerful. It's the Advent Virus. Signs to look out for include contagious hope, love, joy, and peace. The hearts of many have been exposed to it. If it spread to epidemic levels, it could pose a serious threat to the fairly stable and consistent level of conflict in the world. The impact could be truly earth-shaking. Other major symptoms include the following:

Frequent attacks of smiling, contented feelings of connectedness with others and nature, an increasing tendency to let things happen rather than make them happen, an increased susceptibility to the love extended by others as well as the uncontrollable urge to extend it, frequent and overwhelming episodes of appreciation, a tendency to think and act spontaneously rather than on fears based on past experiences, an unmistakable ability to enjoy each moment, a loss of interest in judging other people, a loss of interest in interpreting the actions of others, a loss of interest in conflict, and a loss of the ability to worry.

If infected, what might be the outworking for you? It could lead to mending a quarrel, telling someone "I love you", forgiving someone who's treated you wrongly, giving something away anonymously, visiting an old or lonely person, being especially kind to a colleague, lending a listening ear to someone in obvious distress, turning away wrath with a soft answer, paying for a struggling couple to go out on a date, caring for someone infected with a nasty virus… the potential is endless.

We're in Advent. Joy to the world! May you catch the bug and be truly infectious as a carrier of the good news!

Lord, I choose to be chronically infected with the Advent Virus today. Amen!

TRASH OR TREASURE?

Matthew 6:19, 20

"Do not store up for yourselves treasures on earth, where moths and rust destroy, and where thieves break in and steal. But store up for yourselves treasures in heaven."

Twenty-four hours after the iPhone 5S went on sale around the world, Apple had sold out. Apple's press release announced it had sold nine million iPhones in the three days since the launch. According to one survey, 95 per cent of those who queued outside the New York store were there for the iPhone 5S in gold.

Contrast this with the following statistics:

- About 21,000 people die every day of hunger or hunger-related causes.
- AIDS kills approximately one person every 20 seconds.
- Pneumonia and other forms of acute respiratory infection kill over one million children each year.
- About half a million people die from malaria each year and many millions are seriously weakened by it.

When Jesus came to earth as God incarnate, he "became poor so that [we] through his poverty might become rich" (2 Corinthians 8:9), he became nothing so that we could become something (Philippians 2:7). He chose to enter into our broken world so that we could access the richness of his kingdom on earth. Salvation, restoration, peace, and joy are ours because of his death on the cross. So what do we do with these resources? Do we hoard them? Do we huddle in our churches, never looking beyond our own walls? How can we be generous with the things we have been given? We need to care, turn to prayer, and share, which will involve both going and giving.

Steve Jobs, co-founder of Apple Inc., was by most accounts a brilliant man with a flawed personality. He died from cancer at fifty-six, and one thing he said that resonates with me is this: "Being the richest man in the cemetery doesn't matter to me. Going to bed at night saying we've done something wonderful, that's what matters to me."

Father, help me do something wonderful today with the gifts you've blessed me with. Amen!

RETIREMENT OR GRADUATION?

Deuteronomy 33:25

"As your days, so shall your strength be."

Evelyn "Granny" Brand was widowed in India aged fifty. She and her husband Jessie had targeted five mountain tribes that were fiercely resistant to the gospel and remained unreached. They had laboured for many years with no apparent fruit until a dying Hindu priest whom they loved and nursed converted and entrusted his children to them. Granny Brand was expected to return to England as a widow but carried on the work by herself until she turned seventy. Her mission board then refused to allow her to stay on – at her age she was surely a liability – but at her farewell party, she revealed she had higher orders to follow! She'd built a shack in preparation and had a horse she rode on as she travelled from village to village telling people about Jesus. After five years she fell off and broke her hip. Her son Paul, by now world-renowned as a surgeon, said, "Surely it's time to call it a day." She refused, and continued another eighteen years! By the age of ninety-three, she could no longer ride horseback so some men in the villages who loved her deeply carried her on a stretcher to help the poorest of the poor. She lasted another two years before she eventually breathed her last. All five unreached groups and a further couple had by this stage come to know Jesus. Paul said of his mother, "This is how to grow old. Allow everything else to fall away until those around you see only love." She died, but she never retired. She just graduated.

Doesn't that inspire you? No matter what stage of life we're at, looking ahead, what will our attitude be? We may "retire" from our jobs but not from our calling. Many think of coasting in self-indulgence from retirement to the grave, but what a waste that would be! Or as John Piper says, "If you don't believe in heaven, it makes sense that retirement should be as heaven-like as possible."

Lord, I choose to graduate, not retire. Amen!

SERVICE OR STATUS?

Acts 6:1–4

"The Hellenistic Jews… complained… because their widows were being overlooked in the daily distribution [diakonia] *of food. So the Twelve gathered all the disciples together and said, '… choose seven men from among you who are known to be full of the Spirit and wisdom. We will turn this responsibility over to them and will give our attention to prayer and the ministry* [diakonia] *of the word.'"*

We're all naturally status-conscious. We readily assign rank to roles. Indeed we need structures and chains of accountability and responsibility, but Acts 6 establishes an important principle which is often missed. Luke is saying that all service has great value because it is service to Jesus. He uses the same word (*diakonia*) and the same qualifications (those "who are known to be full of the Spirit and wisdom") to describe both food distribution and preaching, thus emphasizing that both are equally service. The functions are clearly different but the value and motivation are the same: service to the Master. Indeed if the ministry of food had not been given to others, the ministry of the Word may have been eclipsed or rendered ineffective by division.

Jesus is our role model for service. He was humble (unconcerned about his status) and meek (unconcerned about his rights, see Matthew 11:29). He became in very nature a bond slave (Philippians 2:7), making himself of no reputation and being obedient even to a horrific death on a shameful cross.

What is more important to me: recognition and reputation or obedient service to the King? Someone once quipped: "Many people want to serve God… but only as advisors!" Sadly we're often more interested in "serve us" than "service". However, we're blessed to be a blessing and we're saved to serve.

In Paul's metaphor in 1 Corinthians 12, we're all members of the body of Christ. Every part has value, a key role to play, and significance as part of the whole. Be content today in your God-given role, serving him with pure motivations, and seeking his glory above all things.

Lord, I humbly choose service over status today. Amen!

BOOT CAMP OR HOLIDAY CAMP?

2 Timothy 3:12

"In fact, everyone who wants to live a godly life in Christ Jesus will be persecuted."

I came to faith through Scripture Union's youth camps. We used to have a twelve-minute Bible talk in the morning, and a seventeen-minute talk in the evening, and lots of fun and games in between. Then the Lord called me to work for SU in war-torn Burundi and I expected our youth camps to work the same way – but I found the spiritual hunger was so great that the students wanted to start at 6.30 a.m. and finish at 9 p.m., every day! The limited precious opportunity to learn and share together had to be maximized. Then I read Brother Yun's *The Heavenly Man*, which tells his own story of dogged perseverance and faith amidst repeated torture and imprisonment. He is part of the "Back to Jerusalem" missionary movement, and their methodology is much more boot camp than holiday camp. In their training, they major on three areas:

- How to suffer and die for the Lord;
- How to witness for the Lord; and
- How to escape for the Lord.

He writes:

> *We know that sometimes it is the Lord who sends us to prison to witness for him, but we also believe the devil sometimes wants us to go to prison to stop the ministry God has called us to do. We teach the missionaries special skills such as how to free themselves from handcuffs, and how to jump from second-storey windows without injuring themselves… If you ever visit one of our camps, you will see how serious we are to fulfill our destiny in God. You may see people with their hands handcuffed behind their backs, leaping from second-storey windows!*

It strikes me how the ease of our circumstances tends to dictate the intensity of our spiritual hunger and commitment. Thank God we don't have to experience what our Chinese brethren do, but may we still aspire to their deep hunger and commitment.

Lord, fill me with greater hunger and commitment for you today. Amen!

John 16:13

"When he, the Spirit of truth comes, he will guide you into all truth."

PERSON OR INFLUENCE?

The Holy Spirit is a Person, not an abstract force. If we simply think of him as an influence, we'll be keen to have more of "it"; but if we rightfully recognize him as a Person, we'll desire that he has more of us. Back in the first and second centuries, a group of believers experienced great blessings through the Holy Spirit. They became known as the Montanists. Sadly things unravelled when they began claiming to be the embodiment of the Holy Spirit, to reject all other Christians, and to refuse to have their teachings submitted to the Scriptures. What started as a clear move of the Spirit ended with everyone losing, as both the mainstream church and the Montanists wrote one another off.

Within a few months of Jesus saying the words above, they were fulfilled. He died, was resurrected, ascended, and then the Holy Spirit came in power at Pentecost. And He, not "it", as the Spirit of truth, guided the disciples into all truth. J.B. Phillips, after months of painstaking research and immersion in study, wrote upon completing his translation of the book of Acts:

> *These men did not make acts of faith, they believed; they did not say their prayers, they really prayed; they did not hold conferences on psychosomatic medicine, they simply healed the sick... The Spirit of God found what he must always be seeking – a fellowship of men and women so united in love and faith that he can work in and through them with the minimum of hindrance.*

From the time of the Montanists until now, Christians have argued and debated and often created more friction than light in this area, but let's agree on one thing: we want to be a part of that "fellowship of men and women so united in love and faith that he can work in and through them with the minimum of hindrance". Agreed?

Spirit of truth, guide me into all truth today, for your glory. Amen!

CLUMSY OR SOPHISTICATED?

Song of Songs 1:2

"Let him kiss me with the kisses of his mouth."

12

DECEMBER

A few years ago, I wrote the following in a prayer letter to supporters:

Zac is ten months old, and growing fast. As of last week, he started to consciously wave goodbye to people. The latest development which has brought such joy to Lizzie and I is when I say to him: "Zac, give me a kiss!" and he lurches forward clumsily and head-butts me on the lips! This morning he joined me in worshipping the Lord with the guitar. He's definitely a budding charismatic, waving both hands in the air with ecstatic squeals!

*As we worshipped together, it made me think of the Greek word for worship. It's "*proskuneo*", and means literally "to lean forward and kiss". Such is the intimacy our Heavenly Father desires with us. I'll be honest and tell you there are times – plenty of them – when I look at the problems around me and get totally discouraged, almost sinking in despair. I've felt like that in the last few weeks. I can talk a good game most of the time, but it hurts to deliver the goods. We get wounded and bruised and tired and disillusioned and broken and discouraged. Intimacy with God? I want to be in that place, but it's frequently elusive – and in any case, feelings are often deceptive – the best proof of our love for God is obedience…*

… Sometimes I know I'm lazy and disobedient, and I need a kick up the backside. Other times I know I gave it my best shot, even if it wasn't great. I obeyed. When Zac leans forward and headbutts me on the lips, I respond by kissing and cuddling and squeezing him closely. The love I feel is quite overwhelming. And I sense my Heavenly Father receiving my worship in the same way, even if my best efforts resemble a clumsy badly-aimed head-butt!

God sees your heart, he knows you completely, and he loves you. Lean in and head-butt him today!

Lord, receive my clumsy heartfelt adoration. Amen!

WWJD OR WDJD?

John 14:12

"I tell you the truth, anyone who has faith in me will do what I have been doing."

What Did Jesus Do? We read about it in the Gospels. What Would Jesus Do today? The same as he did back then.

So what should we do today? Surely the same as his followers did then! What is holding us back? I guess if we're honest, it's largely fear. I know I care more for my reputation than God's. What if I step out in faith and end up looking a fool…?

Last year, we sent out 762 evangelists for two weeks in teams around Burundi, and – wait for it – they led over 18,000 people to Jesus! No doubt Burundi is more ripe than where you are, but it's staggering nonetheless. And they didn't just preach the gospel, they also demonstrated the power of the gospel by healing the sick and casting out demons, just as in the book of Acts.

For example, one notorious witchdoctor, Joselyne, gave her life to Christ. Her sister refused to believe, but brought over the demon-possessed neighbour, and challenged the believers, "If you heal this girl, I'll know that you are serving the one true God." God healed the girl, and twenty-one people (including the sister) promptly gave their lives to Christ. Beautiful!

Why not more such stories in the West, Lord? Honestly, I wrestle with that one. But our guys are bold practitioners, willing to suffer, and full of faith, so that would be part of a difficult and incomplete answer.

Don't give in to the temptation to feel hopelessly inadequate and discouraged. Rather simply cry out to God for his kingdom to come, on earth as it is in heaven. "What Did Jesus Do?" is straightforward enough to verify. Whereas my concern with "WWJD" is that it might allow me to justify by conjecture a more tame response to his dangerous call on my life.

Lord, I choose to do what you would do and plead that you'd let me do what you did. For your glory. Amen!

COMMITTED OR CASUAL?

Psalm 139:23, 24

"Search me, O God, and know my heart. Test me, and know my anxious thoughts. See if there is any offensive way in me, and lead me in the way everlasting."

Most of us, in our work lives, operate at our best when we're committed to giving it our best. Sadly we're often much more casual with our spiritual lives. Below are twenty-two questions which the members of John Wesley's Holy Club asked themselves *every day* in their private devotions over 200 years ago:

1. *Am I consciously or unconsciously creating the impression that I am better than I really am? In other words, am I a hypocrite?*
2. *Am I honest in all my acts and words, or do I exaggerate?*
3. *Do I confidentially pass on to another what was told to me in confidence?*
4. *Can I be trusted?*
5. *Am I a slave to dress, friends, work, or habits?*
6. *Am I self-conscious, self-pitying, or self-justifying?*
7. *Did the Bible live in me today?*
8. *Do I give it time to speak to me every day?*
9. *Am I enjoying prayer?*
10. *When did I last speak to someone else about my faith?*
11. *Do I pray about the money I spend?*
12. *Do I get to bed on time and get up on time?*
13. *Do I disobey God in anything?*
14. *Do I insist upon doing something about which my conscience is uneasy?*
15. *Am I defeated in any part of my life?*
16. *Am I jealous, impure, critical, irritable, touchy, or distrustful?*
17. *How do I spend my spare time?*
18. *Am I proud?*
19. *Do I thank God that I am not as other people, especially as the Pharisees who despised the publican?*
20. *Is there anyone whom I fear, dislike, disown, criticize, hold a resentment toward or disregard? If so, what I am doing about it?*
21. *Do I grumble or complain constantly?*
22. *Is Christ real to me?*

Ouch! How about writing those out and spending some time taking a reality check.

Lord, I choose to take action today based on the above. Help me. Amen!

SINK IN IT OR SHAKE IT OFF?

Psalm 40:2

"He lifted me out of the slimy pit, out of the mud and mire; he set my feet on a rock and gave me a firm place to stand."

Due to God's faithfulness, constancy, and promises, King David knew he could always bounce back from the grimmest of circumstances – even when they were of his own doing. Similarly, our lives are usually not so much determined by what happens to us but by how we react to what happens to us, by the attitude we bring to life. A positive attitude can often cause a chain reaction of positive thoughts, events, and outcomes.

Comedian Jerry Clower tells a story about Uncle Versie Ledbetter who had a mule named Della. One day Della fell into a cistern that Uncle Versie had accidentally left uncovered:

> *Uncle Versie had a problem. There was his best mule down at the bottom of that cistern and no way he could get the mule out of there. He didn't want her to stay down there and starve to death, so he decided he would get a shovel and cover her up. It would be cruel, but it wouldn't be as cruel and inhumane as to let Della starve to death in the bottom of that deep cistern. Uncle Versie took a shovelful of dirt and threw it down into the cistern and every time a shovelful of dirt hit old Della, she'd shake the dirt off and stomp on it... shake it off and stomp on it... and it wasn't long before Della had shaken off enough dirt and stomped on it so that she was high enough to jump out of the cistern.*

Hopefully as you review some of the darker experiences you've been through in your life, you will be able to see that you unknowingly adopted Della's attitude. If not, then choose to adopt that attitude from hereon in when clumps of dirt land on you!

Lord, help me use the dirt to grow. Thanks that ultimately you lift me out of the slimy pit. Amen!

WEARY OR STILL TRUSTING?

Isaiah 40:28

"He will not grow tired or weary, and his understanding no one can fathom. He gives strength to the weary and increases the power of the weak."

16

DECEMBER

In John Wesley's last letter, addressed to the abolitionist William Wilberforce, he wrote, "Unless God has raised you up for this very thing, you will be worn out by the opposition of men and devils. But if God be for you, who can be against you? Are all of them together stronger than God? O be not weary of well doing!" Hudson Taylor reflected, "All God's giants have been weak men who did great things for God because they reckoned on his being with them. They counted on God's faithfulness."

God is faithful. He is trustworthy, even when we are weary and weak. His understanding, strength, and power are available to us today. If we are becoming weary, he is the solution. Whenever you get weary, try to remember and avoid the "Seven Steps to Failure":

1. *When a thought becomes a worry or concern, do not pray, or if you pray, make sure you do not actually trust him with it.*
2. *Take the burden on yourself; load yourself up so you do not have to depend on him.*
3. *Experience the weariness that sets in over time; we were never meant to carry the burden.*
4. *Continue steps 1–3 and feel the discouragement grow; it will actually bleed over to other areas that used to be fine.*
5. *Linger in the discouraged state so that you can become disillusioned.*
6. *Now disengage from people so they will not discover you are disillusioned and offer you help, so you will be isolated.*
7. *Make an absolutely terrible decision in an act of desperation.*

If that rings true, choose to act on it today. God is faithful, and calls you to live by faith. The beginning of fear is the end of faith; the beginning of real faith is the end fear. Fear or anxiety never strengthens you for tomorrow – it just makes you weary today.

Lord, I choose to trust you. Be my strength today. Amen!

2 Corinthians 9:15

"Thanks be to God for his indescribable gift!"

WHAT OR WHO?

Some missionaries were visiting an orphanage and shared the Christmas story with the children for their first time ever. They sat enthralled, and were then given materials to re-create the manger scene. All was going to plan until one of the visitors spotted six-year-old Abu's efforts – he had put two babies in the manger. He was asked to repeat the story, and he did so perfectly until the end when he made up his own version.

He went on: "And when Mary laid the baby in the manger, Jesus looked at me and asked me if I had anywhere to stay. I told him both my mamma and my papa are dead, so I didn't have any place to stay. Then Jesus told me I could stay with him. But I told him that wasn't possible, because I didn't have a present to give him like everybody else did… But I so wanted to stay with Jesus that I wondered if there was anything at all of mine I could offer him as a gift. I thought maybe if I kept him warm, that would be a good gift. So I asked Jesus: 'If I keep you warm, will that be a good enough gift?' And Jesus told me: 'If you keep me warm, that will be the best gift anybody ever gave me.' So I got into the manger, and then Jesus looked at me and he told me I could stay with him – for always."

As little Abu finished his story, his eyes filled up with tears. He then slumped down on the table and began sobbing deeply. This precious little orphan had found someone at last who would never abandon him or let him down, someone who would stay with him – as he put it – for always.

Amidst all the excess of this Christmas season, may you know deeply that it's not *what* you have in your life, but *who* you have in your life that really counts.

Lord, I choose you over stuff today. Amen!

DISTANT OR INCARNATE?

John 1:12

"The Word became flesh and made his dwelling among us."

18 DECEMBER

A devout Hindu from India was visiting America and exploring the Christian faith. His deep reverence for life meant he would never kill an animal, fearing it might be one of his reincarnated relatives. He couldn't accept Christianity's claim that God actually visited this planet in the flesh in the person of Jesus Christ. How could the Great Creator God of the Universe become a man, and why would he do it? One day as he meditated in a field he came across an anthill. He observed in wonder the thousands of industrious ants. But then he heard an approaching tractor ploughing the field. It would shortly reach the anthill and flatten it. He became frantic, desperate to warn them of their impending destruction. He thought to himself, "How can I warn them? If I wrote in the sand, they wouldn't be able to read it. If I shouted to them, they wouldn't understand me. The only possible way I could communicate with them would be by becoming an ant, if I had that ability." And then it dawned on him as the Spirit of God revealed to him the reason for the incarnation – the God of the Universe becoming one of us in the person of the God-man, Jesus of Nazareth. He understood for the first time Paul's words in Philippians 2:6, 7:

> *He did not consider equality with God something to be grasped, but made himself nothing, taking the very nature of a servant, being made in human likeness.*

That is the message of Christmas! The Son of God became man so we could become sons of God (Galatians 3:26). He incarnated the message and calls us to do the same today – to live out his message of costly love, to bring life and meaning and purpose to others. And remember, the stakes are high, so let's get out there and reason, explain, urge, and beg the people we interact with to beware of the approaching tractor.

Lord, help me incarnate your message faithfully and urgently today. Amen!

Acts 20:35

"It is more blessed to give than to receive."

GIVE OR RECEIVE?

Many of us – although by no means all us – have just about everything we need. I thank God I do. Whatever the case, may you not be deceived by the endless barrage of adverts this Christmas season sowing seeds of dissatisfaction and false hopes that only with their product will you be truly happy and whole.

To enjoy the reality of Jesus' above pronouncement this year, I have a proposition for you:

Any day now, I will receive an email (as I have for the last several years) from Tharcisse, our Scripture Union Treasurer, with a plea as follows to intervene on the staff's behalf: "Simon, will you remember us this Christmas and help us to be able to give our wives and children at least *something* on Christmas Day? We never eat meat as it's too expensive, but at least once a year please can you help make that possible?"

That email rips my heart out. Why? Because it's wrong! And because I know my children will receive stacks of presents next week from family members, while my hardworking colleagues who slog their guts out all year for Jesus will not give a single present to their kids – literally – or eat a remotely special Christmas meal, unless I intervene. Such is their poverty. And so, each year, I forward Tharcisse's email to our supporters, and they generously respond so that Great Lakes Outreach (GLO) can then give about 250 families an extra month's wages, so that they can spend Christmas Day differently from every other backbreaking day of the year. Let me tell you, as I am enjoying Christmas Day with my family, I love thinking of maybe 1,500 people – proud dads, with their wives and children – having a great time because people have chosen to be blessed by giving rather than receiving.

How about it? It doesn't have to be through GLO. You probably know someone working with deprived people, abroad or locally. Act on it now, and bless their socks off!

Lord, I choose to be generous and bless others less fortunate out of my relative abundance today. Amen!

PATHETIC OR PROPHETIC?

Psalm 105:15

"Do not touch my anointed ones; do my prophets no harm."

In this little phrase from the Psalms, God makes the point that there is a sense in which all his children are prophets. Obviously not every one of us is an Elijah or a Jeremiah (praise the Lord!), but Scripture makes it clear that God's purpose is for us to be a *prophetic* people. As the body of Christ, we are God's clear incarnate word to this twenty-first century confused world. But what does it mean?

One aspect is that we, as the community of God's redeemed people, by our very existence and lifestyle, bear witness to what God is doing today in the world. Our witness to Jesus by the way we live and by telling others of him is the work of "the Spirit of prophecy who bears testimony to Jesus" (Revelation 19:10). For many people, we are the only evidence they may see that the gospel is true and is good news – indeed great news because it tells of God's intervention in history to rescue and redeem us for this world and the next. Eternal life for us starts now, and is not merely a matter of length, but supremely of quality; it is the life of the kingdom of God, demonstrating the ever-increasing fullness of the Spirit of God.

Sadly, many of us who claim to be Christians simply talk the talk without being willing to walk the walk. We're still the number one in our lives. Our priorities for life are not aligned with those of the kingdom. And therefore our credibility as witnesses is in danger of being pathetic rather than prophetic.

Is my life compelling evidence that Jesus Christ is Lord and risen from the dead? Is there anything that compromises or blurs my testimony to Jesus? Is there one thing I can do today to improve the quality of the prophetic witness of my life?

Lord, forgive me for where I've been more pathetic than prophetic. I choose to be the latter today, for your glory. Amen!

SINNER OR SAINT?

Romans 7:24, 25

"What a wretched man I am! Who will rescue me from this body of death? Thanks be to God – through Jesus Christ our Lord!"

What is your identity? Are you a filthy, unworthy sinner, or a saint clothed in righteousness? In the verse above, Paul knew he was wretched, but also fully redeemed through Jesus. Peter wrote that we are "a chosen people, a royal priesthood, a holy nation, that [we] may declare the praises of him who called [us] out of darkness into his wonderful light" (1 Peter 2:9). Knowing our true identity in Christ is critical to being able to live out our purpose in him.

Do you believe you've got what it takes to be who God has called you to be? He does! Yet for many of us, we struggle to grasp the potential God sees in us. Mark Aldridge writes:

> *Purpose can only be redefined when we have first redefined identity. If I am a worm squirming in the mud of my sin then my purpose is minuscule. If I am a saint clothed in the holiness given by Christ I might just do more collateral damage to the kingdom of darkness than I once imagined… Now with identity and purpose fixed in my renewed mind I can at last set out on my adventure. I am done with vicarious heroes; I want to be one myself. Someone once said that "if your life's work can be accomplished in your lifetime then you're not thinking big enough". I like that. It tells me that it is not just about my adventure but ours. As the people of God we are in something together.*

We're all sinners, but beyond that we're all redeemed saints. As martyred missionary Jim Elliot once said, "The saint who advances on his knees, never retreats." We've work to do. There are battles to be fought and adventures to be lived – and by his grace, we've got what it takes.

Father, thank you that by your grace I'm a saint. Use me to accomplish your purposes today. Amen!

CONFUSED OR CLEAR?

22
DECEMBER

Luke 2:11

"Today in the town of David a Saviour has been born to you; he is Christ the Lord."

A little boy and girl were singing their favourite Christmas carol in church the Sunday before Christmas. The boy concluded "Silent Night" with the words, "Sleep in heavenly beans". "No," his sister corrected, "not beans, peas." On another occasion, Brenda Roberts was reading the story of Jesus' birth to her day-care children. As usual, she stopped to see if they understood. "What do we call the three wise men?" she asked. "The three maggots!" replied a bright five-year-old. "What gift did the *Magi* bring baby Jesus?" she corrected. "Gold, Frankensteins and Smurfs!" the same five-year-old replied.

So much confusion!

So what or when is Christmas? Mother Teresa said: "It's Christmas every time you let God love others through you… yes, it's Christmas every time you smile at your brother and offer him your hand." May we do that today!

What is it not? Calvin Coolidge wrote, "Christmas is not a time nor a season, but a state of mind. To cherish peace and goodwill, to be plenteous in mercy, is to have the real spirit of Christmas." William Parks added, "Christmas is not just a day, an event to be observed and speedily forgotten. It is a spirit which should permeate every part of our lives."

I'm a foodie, and I love my family, so naturally I'm going to love Christmas! But I have to say that all the best Christmases I've ever had – the ones I most remember – were the ones spent serving with others, be it at a homeless shelter, or with street kids. How might we embody the Spirit of Christmas this year?

Let's close with a prayer by Wilda English:

"God grant me the light of Christmas, which is faith; the warmth of Christmas, which is love; the radiance of Christmas, which is purity; the righteousness of Christmas, which is justice; the belief in Christmas, which is truth; the all of Christmas which is Christ. Amen!"

CHRISTMAS LIGHTS OR THE LIGHT OF THE WORLD?

John 8:12

"I am the light of the world. Whoever follows me will never walk in darkness, but will have the light of life."

When Pope Julius I authorized 25th December to be celebrated as the birthday of Jesus in AD 353, nobody could have foreseen what it would become in our day. And then when Professor Charles Follen lit candles on the first Christmas tree in America in 1832, nobody in their wildest dreams could have imagined how elaborate the decorations would become in our day. It is a long time since 1832, longer still since 353, and even longer still since that dark night was brightened by a guiding star that led the wise men to King Jesus' humble birthplace. Yet as we approach 25th December again, amidst all the excitement, decorations, and commercialization, let's be very intentional in keeping Christ at the centre. Let's pause to reflect and worship God as we consider afresh the outlandish Christmas story of His rescue plan for humanity by actually taking on flesh and blood.

In December 1903, after many failed attempts to get their "flying machine" off the ground and into the air, Orville and Wilbur Wright were successful for the first time at Kitty Hawk. Elated at their accomplishment, they telegraphed the following message to their sister Katherine: "We have actually flown 120 feet. Will be home for Christmas." Katherine hurried to the editor of the local newspaper and showed him the message. He glanced at it and said, "How nice! The boys will be home for Christmas." He totally *missed the big news* – that for the first time in human history, man had flown!

How many of our loved ones, colleagues, and friends are completely missing the big news! Jesus' words above provide comfort for us but also a warning for those who remain in darkness. How desperate it will be if they ignorantly remain in darkness! Choose today to overcome your fear, pride, or self-consciousness and share with them the "reason for the season".

Lord, give me the boldness to make and take opportunities to share your story today. Amen!

RECOGNIZE OR MISS?

Isaiah 53:2

"He had no beauty or majesty to attract us to him, nothing in his appearance that we should desire him."

24

DECEMBER

An old shoe cobbler once dreamed on Christmas Eve that Jesus would come to visit him the next day. The dream was so real that he was convinced it would come true. So he awoke and anxiously awaited Jesus' arrival. An old man was his first visitor, seeking shelter from the winter cold. As the cobbler talked with him he noticed the holes in the old man's shoes, so he reached up on the shelf and got him a new pair of shoes, before sending him on his way. Then a hungry old woman came in, and when he discovered she hadn't eaten in days, he gave her a meal before sending her on her way. Still Jesus hadn't come. Then he heard a little boy crying out in front of his shop. He went out, discovered the boy was lost, so put on his coat and led the boy home to his parents. As dusk came and it was time to lock up, he cried out, "Oh Lord Jesus, why didn't you come?" And then in a moment of silence he seemed to hear a voice saying: "Oh shoe cobbler, lift up your heart! I kept my word. Three times I knocked at your friendly door. Three times you welcomed me beautifully. I was the man with the bruised feet. I was the woman you gave something to eat. I was the lost boy out on the street."

Jesus had come. The cobbler simply hadn't realized it.

All we know about Jesus' appearance is from Isaiah 53:2. He looked nothing special. Mother Teresa identified her best gift as an ability "to see the face of Jesus in its most distressing disguise". May God help us to do the same, because Jesus warned us in Matthew 25: "Whatever you did (or did not do) for one of the least of these, you did (or did not do) for me" (verses 40, 45).

Lord, help me recognize and respond to you today. Amen!

Luke 1:47

"My spirit rejoices in God my Saviour."

DISMAY OR DELIGHT?

25

DECEMBER

Merry Christmas! May you have a precious time today with loved ones. Be grateful for all God's richest blessings in your life. Rejoice and be glad in him.

Not everybody enjoys this time of year. "What has the world come to?" and "What has Christmas come to?" are repeated refrains we hear with the onslaught of its commercialization. However, E. Stanley Jones gave us a much more positive take on things in his 1942 devotional *Abundant Living*:

> *The early Christians did not say in dismay: "Look what the world has come to!" but in delight, "Look what has come to the world!" They saw not merely the ruin, but the Resource for the reconstruction of that ruin. They saw not merely that sin did abound, but that grace did much more abound. On that assurance, the pivot of history swung from blank despair, loss of moral nerve, and fatalism, to faith and confidence that at last sin had met its match.*

Amidst all of today's festivities, the copious quantities of food and the discarded wrapping paper, may we choose to delight in God's supreme gift of his Son. If our greatest need had been information, God would have given us an educator; if our greatest need had been technology, God would have given us a scientist; if our greatest need had been money, God would have given us an economist; if our greatest need had been pleasure, God would have given us an entertainer; however, our greatest need was forgiveness, so God gave us a Saviour.

Lord, thank you so much for giving us a Saviour. I choose to delight myself today in this indescribable gift. However much dismay I may feel at the state of the world or at the apparent triumph of Santa over Christ in the hearts of many, I declare your Lordship and seek to live it out, for your glory. Amen!

TIME OR MONEY?

Ecclesiastes 3:13

"That everyone may eat and drink, and find satisfaction in all his toil – this is the gift of God."

A boat docked in a tiny Thai village. An American tourist complimented the Thai fisherman on the quality of his fish and asked how long it took him to catch them. "Not very long," answered the Thai. "But then, why didn't you stay out longer and catch more?" asked the American. The Thai explained that his small catch was enough to meet his needs and those of his family. The American asked, "But what do you do with the rest of your time?" "I sleep late, fish a little, play with my children, and take a siesta with my wife. In the evenings, I go into the village to see my friends, play the guitar, and sing a few songs. I have a full life." The American interrupted, "I have an MBA from Harvard and I can help you! You should start by fishing longer every day. You can then sell the extra fish you catch. With the extra revenue, you can buy a bigger boat." "And after that?" asked the Thai. "With the extra money the larger boat will bring, you can expand your fleet of trawlers. Instead of selling your fish to a middle man, you can then negotiate directly with the processing plants. You can then leave this little village and move to the capital! From there you can direct your huge new enterprise." "How long would that take?" asked the Thai. "Twenty, perhaps twenty-five years," replied the American. "And after that?" "Afterwards? Well, then you can start buying and selling stocks and make millions!" "Millions? Really? And after that?" asked the Thai. "After that you'll be able to retire, live in a tiny village near the coast, sleep late, play with your children, catch a few fish, take a siesta with your wife and spend your evenings enjoying your friends."

The above is not an endorsement of laziness but a lesson in values and priorities. Have you learned it?

Lord, help me live by godly values and priorities today. Amen!

Ephesians 5:15, 16

"Be very careful, then, how you live... making the most of every opportunity."

MAXIMIZE OR WASTE?

Someone I care about died today. Two days ago he was fine. Yesterday he slipped into a coma and now he's gone. Another friend is right on the edge after multiple surgeries. I hope he makes it, but only time will tell. For the former, it was very sudden; for the latter, he has been able to "get his house in order". He's experienced the truth of what Samuel Johnson wrote in 1777, "When a man knows he is to be hanged in a fortnight, it concentrates his mind wonderfully."

Orville Kelly received the dreaded news one day that he had a very aggressive cancer. He was given two years to live at best. He returned home from the hospital with his wife and they cried their eyes out. They prayed about whether to tell people or not, and then felt that they should have a party. They invited all the people they cared most about, and had a huge celebration. The guests didn't know the reason for the party until Orville stood up to make a speech during the festivities. He said, "You may have wondered why I called you all together. Well, this is a cancer party! I have been told I have terminal cancer. Then my wife and I realized we are all terminal. So we've decided to start a new organization. It's called MTC – Make Today Count. You are all charter members." MTC as an organization grew dramatically, and Orville, with a whole new appreciation for each day of the rest of his life, sped around the country telling people to make the most of what limited time they had.

How will we make today count? Is there any unfinished business, anything that needs saying to someone, a relationship that needs addressing, forgiveness that needs to be offered or received, a risk that needs to be taken? Go for it!

Lord, I choose to make today count, for your glory. Amen!

PASS OR FAIL?

John 19:30

Jesus said: "It is finished!"

Tullian Tchividjian tells the story of his friend's daughter, Robin, who desperately wanted to avoid an English literature class for fear of failure. She cried before her seasoned teacher, who looked at her and said, "Robin, I know how you feel. What if I promised you an 'A' no matter what you did in the class? If I gave you an 'A' before you even started, would you be willing to take the class?" Robin replied through her tears, "Well, I think I could do that." The teacher said, "I'm going to give you an 'A' in the class. You already have an 'A', so you can go to class." Later the teacher explained what she had done. She explained how she took away the threat of a bad grade so that Robin could learn English literature. Robin ended up making straight 'A's *on her own* in that class.

Tchividjian concludes:

> *That's how God deals with us. Because of Christ's finished work, Christians already have an "A". The threat of failure, judgment, and condemnation has been removed. We're in – forever! Nothing we do will make our grade better, and nothing we do will make our grade worse. In his life, by his death, and with his resurrection, Christ our substitute secured for us the everything, the "A", that we come into this world longing for and yet are incapable of securing for ourselves. All the pardon, the approval, the purpose, the freedom, the rescue, the meaning, the righteousness, the cleansing, the significance, the worth, and the affection we crave and need are already ours in Christ. We don't need to add anything to it. The operative power that makes you a Christian is the same operative power that keeps you a Christian: the unconditional, unqualified, undeserved, unrestrained grace of God in the completed work of Christ. As I said, the banner under which Christians live reads, "It is finished." So relax, and rejoice. Jesus plus nothing equals everything; everything minus Jesus equals nothing. You're free!"*

Reflect on the above – just beautiful!

Lord, I choose to live free today. Amen!

JOYFUL TRIALS OR PAINFUL SHORTCUTS?

James 1:2–4

"Consider it pure joy, my brothers, whenever you face trials of many kinds, because you know that the testing of your faith develops perseverance. Perseverance must finish its work so that you may be mature and complete, not lacking anything."

Has it been a tough year? It has for me. When going through difficult or challenging seasons of life, I take comfort from Oswald Chambers words: "Trials are God's vote of confidence in us!" He's rooting for us, and believes we can get through them, so we need to believe it too. In any case, would life really be better if everything always went according to plan and we never faced any battles?

One day, a man sat observing a cocoon slowly opening as the butterfly inside struggled to force its body through the little hole. After several hours, progress came to a halt. Apparently, it would get no further. So the man decided to intervene and help the butterfly by making a shortcut – literally – as he snipped the end of the cocoon with a pair of scissors. The butterfly emerged without any further struggle, but its body was swollen and its wings were shrivelled. The man expected the butterfly to expand and fly away, little realizing that his "kindness" had signed the butterfly's death warrant. The restricting cocoon and the struggle required for the butterfly to get through the tiny opening were nature's way of forcing fluid from the body of the butterfly into its wings so that it would be ready for flight once it achieved its freedom from the cocoon.

Sometimes struggles are exactly what we need in our life. In the verses above, James makes clear that life's trials develop perseverance in us, which leads ultimately to maturity. If God allowed us to go through our lives without any obstacles or trials, it would cripple us. We would not be as strong as we could have been. We could never fly.

Lord, I choose to embrace the tough times, knowing you're with me in them. Help me fly with and for you. Amen!

30

DECEMBER

UPS OR DOWNS?

Philippians 3:12–14

"Not that I have already obtained all this, or have already been made perfect, but I press on to take hold of that for which Christ Jesus took hold of me. Brothers, I do not consider myself yet to have taken hold of it. But one thing I do: forgetting what is behind and straining towards what is ahead, I press on towards the goal to win the prize for which God has called me heavenwards in Christ Jesus."

The end of the year provides a natural opportunity for reflection; reviewing the past twelve months, and in anticipation, planning the next twelve. No doubt this last year threw up a few unplanned and unwelcome experiences, as well as hopefully some surprise unexpected joys. I believe an authentic life in Christ, like Paul's who wrote the above, will naturally include any number of ups and downs, highs and lows – or as Gregg Levoy humorously wrote: "Jesus promised those who would follow him only three things: that they would be absurdly happy, entirely fearless, and always in trouble!"

Whatever state of heart and mind you're in, how about embracing Shoedel's list of 7-Ups for the coming year:

1. *Wake-up – Begin the day with the Lord. It is His day. Rejoice in it.*
2. *Dress-up – Put on a smile. It improves your looks. It says something about your attitude.*
3. *Shut-up – Watch your tongue. Don't gossip. Say nice things. Learn to listen.*
4. *Stand-up – Take a stand for what you believe. Resist evil. Do good.*
5. *Look-up – Open your eyes to the Lord. After all, He is your only Saviour.*
6. *Reach-up – Spend time in prayer with your adorations, confessions, thanksgivings and supplications to the Lord.*
7. *Lift-up – Be available to help those in need – serving, supporting, and sharing.*

Lord, I choose to end this year with fresh resolve to live for you with all I've got through whatever ups and downs. Amen!

2 Timothy 4:7

"I have fought the good fight, I have run the race, I have kept the faith."

BACKWARDS OR FORWARDS?

So it's New Year's Eve and the end of another calendar year. How would you evaluate the last 365 days? In verse 7 above, Paul was looking backwards on his whole life and doing a positive evaluation, sensing he was soon to die. In verse 8, he then looked forward in anticipation to receiving his "crown of righteousness, which the Lord will award to me on that day". May we in due course be able to look back on our lives and similarly say that we fought the good fight, ran the race, and kept the faith! If we're honest in our evaluation of this last year, maybe the verdict might be more along the lines of fighting a scrappy fight, running a chequered race, and barely clinging on to our faith through some difficult times. Certainly that's been some of my story as I wrote this. So today's a chance to look backwards, with a view to better moving forwards.

Louise Haskins penned the following words: "I said to the man who stood at the gate of the year, 'Give me a light, that I may tread safely into the unknown', and he replied, 'Go out into the darkness and put your hand into the hand of God. That shall be to you better than light and safer than a known way'." King George VI used them in his 1939 Christmas message to the British Empire as the Second World War embroiled more and more nations and caused such untold suffering and grief. They describe the type of faith we need to cope with adversity and uncertainty.

Similarly, as we look both backwards and forwards, we can rest assured that, whatever the darkness, putting our hand into the hand of God is "better than light and safer than a known way". Hold on tight! God bless you richly. Here's to a year of good choices!

Lord, help me continue to make good daily choices through the coming year. Amen!

GREAT LAKES OUTREACH

Back in 2003, I set up Great Lakes Outreach (GLO), which works in partnership with a number of organizations in the Great Lakes region of Central Africa, notably in Burundi. Its purpose is to respond to the area's massive needs and the huge potential impact of strategic involvement in cooperation with key Burundian partners.

The main areas of GLO's involvement include:

- Evangelism and discipleship through schools and churches
- Mentoring and leadership development of key individuals
- Printing of teaching materials
- Theological education
- An indigenous missionary movement
- Fighting the AIDS pandemic
- Helping to sustain two orphanages, two medical clinics, and four schools
- Equipping and encouraging informed dialogue between Christians and Muslims
- Training university students in outreach
- Agricultural project support
- Business development opportunities to enable income-generation and self-sustainability

All proceeds from the sale of this book will go to the work of GLO. *I would love you to get involved in what the Lord is doing out in Burundi*, so do get in touch by contacting info@greatlakesoutreach.org.

There are opportunities to come out on short-term teams, to contribute financially, to become a regional representative, and to subscribe for more detailed and personal prayer information. I look forward to hearing from you.

Connect further with the work by visiting www.greatlakesoutreach.org

My blog is www.simonguillebaud.com

Twitter: @SimonGuillebaud

Also by Simon Guillebaud

MORE THAN CONQUERORS

Life is not a dress rehearsal.
We only get one shot at it.
Most people are just trying to arrive safely at death,
but Jesus offers a better way.

ISBN 978 1 85424 973 9

More Than Conquerors is a book and DVD series (13 chapters with 13 accompanying films, all on one DVD) which calls us to radical discipleship in the twenty-first century. Although it describes the life of faith as an exciting adventure, it also warns us that to be an authentic follower of Jesus involves rejecting the comfortable cross of contemporary Western Christianity. This is the only way to experience life to the full, which is the reason we were created.

To find out more, and see previews to the films, visit:
www.more-than-conquerors.com

ACKNOWLEDGMENTS

I love the power of words encapsulated in juicy quotes. Contained in this book are numerous quotes from multiple writers. I've acknowledged them where I could, but some might have slipped through the net. I'm grateful for the friendship, support, and constructive criticism of Mark and Charlotte Hutchinson in making this book a little tighter than it might otherwise have been.

Thanks too for those who contributed their ideas, thoughts, and potential entries for this devotional, which I reworked to fit in with the rest of the material: to Ron White, Arthur Goode, Ruth Tong, Chris Pix, Gordon Smith, Ellie Carman, Jen Eckersall, Hugh Griffiths, Bettina Wearn, Tessa Bees, Pete Askew, and Emma Tanner.

I'm always deeply grateful to the thousands of people who pray for us, support us financially, who fly the flag for us around the world, and who thus enable God's beautiful work through Great Lakes Outreach to continue in Burundi.

Finally, I want to thank my gorgeous Lizzie for holding the fort wonderfully through a challenging year when I haven't been able to pull my weight as much as I'd have liked to as husband and father because of being laid low.

TEXT ACKNOWLEDGMENTS

Every effort has been made to trace the original copyright holders where required. In some cases this has proved impossible. We shall be happy to correct any such omissions in future editions.

Scripture quotations taken from the Holy Bible, New International Version, copyright © 1973, 1978, 1984 International Bible Society. Used by permission of Hodder & Stoughton, a member of the Hodder Headline Group. All rights reserved. 'NIV' is a trademark of International Bible Society. UK trademark number 1448790.

Scripture quotations marked ESV are from The Holy Bible, English Standard Version® (ESV®) copyright © 2001 by Crossway, a publishing ministry of Good News Publishers. All rights reserved.

Scripture quotations marked LB are from The Holy Bible, Living Bible Edition, copyright © Tyndale House Publishers 1971. All rights reserved.

Scripture taken from The Message. Copyright © by Eugene H. Peterson 1993, 1994, 1995, 1996, 2000, 2001, 2002. Used by permission of NavPress Publishing Group.

Scripture quotations marked NASB taken from the New American Standard Bible®, Copyright © 1960, 1962, 1963, 1968, 1971, 1972, 1973, 1975, 1977, 1995 by The Lockman Foundation. Used by permission.

Scripture quotations marked NKJV taken from the New King James Version. Copyright © 1982 by Thomas Nelson, Inc. Used by permission. All rights reserved.

Scripture quotations marked NRSV are from The New Revised Standard Version of the Bible copyright © 1989 by the Division of Christian Education of the National Council of Churches in the USA. Used by permission. All rights reserved.

6 Jan, 7 Apr: Quotes from pp. 346-47 [300 words] from *God's Politics: Why the Right Gets it Wrong and the Left Doesn't Get it* by Jim Wallis. Copyright © 2004 by Jim Wallis. Reprinted by permission of HarperCollins Publishers.

5 Feb, 27 Feb, 27 Jun, 21 Sep: Excerpt from *If You Want to Walk on Water* by John Ortberg, copyright © 2001 by John Ortberg. Used by permission of Zondervan www.zondervan.com

2 Mar: Quote from pp. 52-53 [121 words] from *Teaching a Stone to Talk: Expeditions and Encounters* by Annie Dillard. Copyright © 1982 by Annie Dillard. Reprinted by permission of HarperCollins Publishers.

21 Mar, 17 Apr, 14 Jul: Excerpt from *In the Name of Jesus* by Henri Nouwen, copyright © 1992, Henri Nouwen. Reprinted by permission of Crossroad Publishing.

21 Mar, 8 Sep, 6 Oct, 24 Oct: Reprinted by permission. *Waking the Dead*, John Eldredge, 2007, Thomas Nelson Inc. Nashville, Tennessee. All right reserved.

2 May, 27 May, 15 Jul, 28 Dec: Excerpt from *Jesus + Nothing = Everything* by Tullian Tchividjian, copyright © 2011, Tullian Tchividjian. Reprinted by permission of Crossway.

3 May, 1 Nov: Excerpt from *Your God is Too Safe* by Mark Buchanan, copyright © 2001 by Mark Buchanan. Used by permission of WaterBrook Multnomah, an imprint of the Crown Publishing Group, a division of Random House LLC. All rights reserved.

10 May, 5 July, 23 Oct: Brief quotes from pp. 112-13, 399 [218 words] from *The Divine Conspiracy* by Dallas Willard. Copyright © 1998 by Dallas Willard. Reprinted by permission of HarperCollins Publishers.

4 Aug: Excerpt from *Treasure of the Snow* by Patricia St. John, copyright © 2001 by Patricia St. John. Used with permission of Moody Publishers.

22 Oct: Reprinted by permission. *Fearless*, Max Lucado, 2009,Thomas Nelson Inc. Nashville, Tennessee. All right reserved.

11 Nov: Reprinted by permission. *Failing Forward*, John Maxwell, 2007, Thomas Nelson Inc. Nashville, Tennessee. All right reserved.

12 Nov: Reprinted with the permission of Simon & Schuster Publishing Group from *The Different Drum* by M. Scott Peck, M.D. Copyright © 1987 M. Scott Peck, M.D., P.C.